BY JACK McCALLUM

NONFICTION

Golden Days

The Prostate Monologues

Bleeding Orange with Jim Boeheim

Dream Team

Seven Seconds or Less

Unfinished Business

FICTION

Foul Lines with Jon Wertheim

GOLDEN DAYS

GOLDEN DAYS

West's Lakers, Steph's Warriors, and the California

Dreamers Who Reinvented Basketball

JACK McCALLUM

BALLANTINE BOOKS

NEW YORK

Published in the United States by Ballantine Books, an imprint of Random House, a division of Penguin Random House LLC, New York.

BALLANTINE and the HOUSE colophon are registered trademarks of Penguin Random House LLC.

Poem on pages 260–261 courtesy of Tom Meschery

LIBRARY OF CONGRESS CATALOGING-IN-PUBLICATION DATA
Names: McCallum, Jack, author.
Title: Golden days : West's Lakers, Steph's Warriors, and the California dreamers who reinvented basketball / Jack McCallum.
Description: First edition. | New York : Ballantine Books, 2017.
Identifiers: LCCN 2017038872 | ISBN 9780399179075 (hardback : alk. paper) | ISBN 9780399179082 (ebook)
Subjects: LCSH: Golden State Warriors (Basketball team)—History. | Los Angeles Lakers (Baseketball team)—History. | West, Jerry, 1938- | Basketball—California—History. | BISAC: SPORTS & RECREATION / Basketball. | SPORTS & RECREATION / History. | SOCIAL SCIENCE / Popular Culture.
Classification: LCC GV885.52.G64 M35 2017 | DDC 796.323/6409794—dc23
LC record available at https://lccn.loc.gov/2017038872

Printed in the United States of America on acid-free paper

randomhousebooks.com

9 8 7 6 5 4 3 2 1

First Edition

Book design by Caroline Cunningham

To *Sports Illustrated* editors Jerry Tax (RIP 1999), Bob Creamer (RIP 2012), Peter Carry, and Mark Mulvoy. One read clips from an unknown, one opened the door, one edited my stories, and one trusted me with the pro hoops beat.

"These are the days of miracle and wonder."

—Paul Simon

"The Lakers back then had a pretty good thing going. One night Elgin Baylor would kick the shit out of your team, and the next night Jerry West would kick the shit out of your team."

—Phil Jackson

"When the Warriors play at their highest level they look like they're playing a different sport."

—Miami Heat coach Erik Spoelstra

CONTENTS

PROLOGUE

West Agonistes

The room is dark at sunset, though no darker than the mood. Jerry West, his wife, Karen, and a visitor are watching the Game 4 broadcast of the 2017 NBA Finals from Quicken Loans Arena in Cleveland on a large TV in the large living room of their large home in the Bel Air section of Los Angeles. So are five yapping dogs, a couple of which are in as bad a mood as Jerry. A long time ago when he was on a road trip with the Los Angeles Lakers, West was kept up all night by the incessant barking of dogs in his New York City hotel room. When he complained to the front desk he was told, "We're sorry, Mr. West, but the dogs are our guests, too. They're competing at the Westminster Dog Show." Such was life in the NBA back then.

"The dog who nips belongs to Ryan," says Karen West. (The man who nips belongs to Karen.) The Wests' oldest son dropped off his two dogs so he could take a yapless birthday trip to the desert.

When Ryan, now the assistant general manager for the Lakers, turned six years old in 1985, thirty-two years ago to this day, his father was watching another Finals on TV. As Ryan's birthday party went on, Jerry kept his eyes on his Lakers. To be accurate, he had been keeping his ears on them since his cable had gone out during the party. West preferred listening to Lakers announcer Chick Hearn anyway, so it was Hearn who brought him the joyful play-by-play during which L.A. beat the Celtics at Boston Garden in Game 6 to win the NBA championship. It remains among West's top memories, perhaps *the* best memory, for it partially erased (emphasis on *partially*) the specter of so many defeats on that cursed parquet floor, defeats that scar his soul and, to his mind, define his career.

During this 2017 broadcast, ABC flashes a graphic of Celtics immortal Bill Russell's record in the Finals. It is 11-1, six of those victories having come in the sixties at the expense of West's Lakers.

"Jesus, what a record," says West's visitor impulsively. Wrong thing to say, the Celtics being West's personal bête noire. West says nothing.

The 1985 win was so singularly satisfying that one wonders if West regrets, even decades later, not being there to celebrate with the team he had assembled as general manager. For that matter, why isn't he in Cleveland *right now*? He is just one day back from a quickie fishing trip to Alaska where rough conditions left the anglers salmon-less. So why didn't West fly directly to Cleveland for Game 4? The Warriors, for whom at the moment he is a consultant, part owner, and member of the executive board, came into the game with a 3–0 series lead, the opportunity to become the first team to go through the playoffs undefeated and capture their second championship in three seasons. Why not be there to share the love, take a bow for a job well done, and spray some champagne?

"Oh, hell, I never wanted to go on the road," says West, squirming in his well-worn spot on the couch. "You feel like you're a distraction when you're around. There's enough going on there that they don't need me. The other thing is, when you're in crowds you get so many people . . . look, some are very nice. I understand they want a picture, and I don't like to say no. But my Gawd! So many. I enjoy being around people. But not that much."

"Dammit, Zaza, why would you foul him?" (Warriors center

Zaza Pachulia commits a foul on LeBron James, who then finishes a three-point play.)

When he's out in public, a steady stream of cellphone-holding supplicants does indeed seek out the quite recognizable visage of West, who turned seventy-nine a few days before the Finals began. He's one of those carved-in-granite legends, wide eyes, nine-times-broken nose, his sharp features settled in on themselves, a handsome man, his overall look less haunted than it once was. West does not go anywhere without being recognized, and he invariably complies for a photo, duct-taping a smile to his face as he hunches over to get his still-erect 6'3" frame into the shot. His hips and knees are fine even if his nose is not. "People think I'm a drug addict, I do so much sniffling," says West. For the record, he is not.

Over the years West did attend a few postseason games when he was a general manager, but not many and *never* during a championship series. "I went a few times," says Karen, "even when he didn't." Pat Riley, a former teammate and fellow Lakers immortal with whom West shares so much NBA history, says there is another reason that he stays home. "Jerry thinks he brings his teams bad luck," says Riley, president of the Miami Heat. "It's from all those painful losses in the sixties."

"Steph, you gotta get up on him!" (Warriors guard Stephen Curry goes under, instead of fighting his way over, a screen, and J. R. Smith gets loose for a three-pointer.)

As West watches at home, he is almost positive that he is a de facto ex-Warrior. There could be a saving phone call over the weekend, but it doesn't look good. He is apparently heading for the Los Angeles Clippers, who are in the process of applying a full-court press on West. The Clips, who despite much promise over recent years have never made it to even a conference final, need West in the same way the Warriors needed him a half dozen years ago; in fact, his position as consultant would be almost identical to the one he holds at Golden State.

But . . . West a *Clipper*? Over a decade ago he went to the Memphis Grizzlies, and, while he did a solid job, we kind of forgot that he was there. Then it took a couple of years to come to grips with the fact that West was a Warrior, which we came to understand only when Golden State got good; West is almost always associated with good.

The Clippers obviously aren't the joke they used to be under the ownership of Donald Sterling, but to have West back in Los Angeles and associated with any team besides the Lakers seems, at its mildest, strange. For forty years, beginning with his selection in the 1960 draft, West seemed like the eternal Mr. Laker. He played until early in the 1973–74 season, coached for three years, served as a scout, returned to the bench (under much confusion) as Pat Riley's "offensive coach," and finally found his way upstairs as the team's general manager, where he became the greatest combination of player/general manager that has ever existed in sport. (Denver Broncos general manager John Elway is second.)

West's impact as a GM is felt even today. He is the bar, the paradigm, the (purple and) gold standard, the man who picked up major stars and bit pieces that provided the raw material for two distinct eras of Lakers brilliance: the piloted-by-Magic Showtime and the Shaq and Kobe Show. We still wonder how West did it, for talent scouting is one of the sports world's dark arts. Do the best evaluators possess some unique powers of divination? Can they train their eagle eye on a player for five minutes, watch him zig when he should've zagged, and make a measured judgment? Can they stare into the beating heart of a player and conclude which one is a killer competitor, as West did with Kobe Bryant? Hard to say what makes one a seer and another a sucker, but over the years West has proven to be the former.

All that history notwithstanding—L.A. made eleven Finals and won seven championships with teams that West assembled—it has been a wrenching ordeal to drift apart from Golden State, an organization that signed him in 2011 when it was looking for the kind of credibility that only West could provide. No one around the NBA believes it was mere coincidence that West was part of the management team when the Warriors rose from the ashes of an undistinguished past. He had been a major part of the Golden State decision-making apparatus as the Warriors added pieces, both by the draft and free agency, to build a team that has become a model in pro sports.

And that success, in effect, speaks largely to why West might be gone. Bob Myers was a general-manager-in-training when West came aboard, Curry was the only major piece then on the roster, and there was no sign that the Warriors would be anything but a fair-to-middling club. But by 2017 Myers had become a two-time NBA Executive of the Year, Curry had become a superstar, and the Warriors had become a smooth-running machine with its major parts (Curry, Kevin Durant, Draymond Green, Klay Thompson, and Andre Iguodala) all signed at least through the 2018–19 season. The Warriors seemed to be on automatic pilot and West's handiwork would not be needed nearly as much as it had been.

In light of that, primary owner Joe Lacob thought it justified to adjust his compensation downward. Exact figures are hard to come by because West's salary was partly dictated by franchise evaluation and some monies were deferred to enable him to buy a small stake in the team—remember that "small" in this business means as much as $1 million—but the best estimate is that West was asked to take what one source called a "material" pay cut to about $1 million. The best guess on *material* is about 50 percent, meaning that West was making about $2 million. (Neither West nor Lacob would comment directly on dollar figures.)

The apparent separation, however, has done nothing to diminish West's feeling for the Warriors players, with whom he remains close. And it is killing him that they're getting beaten so badly.

"We just have no energy. Look at our body language. It's whor-a-bull." (The Warriors are behind 29–13 and slump off the court after a time-out.)

This is the twenty-second championship series in which West has been personally invested, either as a player, team executive, or consultant. Thousands of NBA players, coaches, and front-office folk have come and gone without ever knowing the feel of Finals pressure, yet West's heart, the prisoner of an arrhythmia, by the way, has been racing in twenty-two. Twenty-two! Red Auerbach, as coach and general overseer of the Celtics, was involved in eighteen championship series, and Phil Jackson was involved in fourteen as a player and a coach. No one else comes close to West. Were he not the official logo of the league, the NBA would've had to make him the official logo of the Finals.

"This is a whor-a-bull spot for JaVale McGee! I guarantee you they put him in a pick-and-roll with Richard Jefferson and LeBron." (A couple of seconds later James and Jefferson do indeed get the Warriors backup center caught between doubling and covering. McGee does neither and has to foul Jefferson near the basket. Jefferson converts both.)

Ah, but what would that logo look like if it were to truly capture the West essence? Could it show pain as well as joy, agony as well as ecstasy? Could it be ambivalent? Could West be shown as a kind of Janus, looking both forward and backward with downcast expression, past and present mutually unsatisfying? For though West almost always performed brilliantly under championship pressure as a competitor—he remains the only player from a losing team to win a Finals MVP award, which happened in 1969—he lost his first seven Finals appearances in a row and triumphed in only one of nine overall, the season of 1971–72, the magical campaign that comprises a generous part of this book. As a player, West was a cross between Job and Sisyphus, heartache upon heartache, disappointment upon disappointment, his championship rock always rolling back down the hill, a storied career woven into what he considered a tapestry of failure, his lone championship notwithstanding.

"The pain of losing," he has said over and over, "is so much stronger than the joy of winning."

"You know why he got that rebound, Kevin? Because you didn't block him out." (Kevin Durant, West's favorite player on the Warriors and one of his favorite players in the league along with LeBron James and San Antonio's Kawhi Leonard, has indeed allowed Jefferson to secure an offensive rebound.)

Nobody gets away unscathed when West watches a game. Nobody.

This is a tale of yesterday's Lakers—a historically significant team led by West and Wilt Chamberlain—and today's Warriors, a team that is rapidly building its own legend. The teams share not only statehood but also shared, for six eventful years, an uncommon man. In their respective eras they were distinct for the way they played the game, fast yet fundamental, spontaneous yet studied, entertaining yet educated. But both flourished only when a steady hand seized the controls, someone who corralled that abundant talent into a cohesive whole. For the old Lakers, it was, oddly enough, a former Celtic named Bill Sharman; for the new Warriors it is Steve Kerr, an alumnus of two Schools of Hard Knocks—he was a teammate of the demanding Michael Jordan and a player under the equally demanding Gregg Popovich. Sharman and Kerr are aligned in another way, too: both battled significant health issues, Sharman a voice that went away, never returned, and diminished his legacy, Kerr a back damaged by surgery that, at this writing, puts his coaching future in doubt. But what each of them turned out was a product of near-perfection. If there is such a thing as a California basketball ecosystem, the old Lakers and the new Warriors, separated by decades, embody it—cool and collected with a self-awareness bordering on arrogance.

The teams hold a place near each other in the record book for extraordinary displays of sustained excellence in a sport defined by attrition. During the 1971–72 season, the Lakers—considered by many to be too old, too contentious, and too scarred by past failures—won thirty-three games in a row, more than any pro team in any of the four major pro sports, a record that stands today. West, near the end of a storied career that would've been empty without a championship, was that team's haunted essence.

The Warriors are the ultimate modern streak team. In the 2014–15 season they won fifteen in a row early and twelve more consecutively later en route to the NBA championship, only the second in franchise history. They began the 2015–16 season with twenty-four straight victories, which, added to the three straight they had won in the 2015 Finals, gave them twenty-seven wins in a row, a mark that ties them with the LeBron–Dwyane Wade–Chris Bosh–Ray Allen 2012–13 Miami Heat and is second only to the Lakers. In the

2016–17 season Golden State won fourteen in a row, from March 14 through April 8 (all but one with an injured Durant out of the lineup), then ripped off fifteen wins in a row in the postseason, before falling on this Friday night in Cleveland, as West and his wife and the yapping dogs look on, darkness descending on their home near fabled Sunset Boulevard, where they have lived for the past thirty-eight years.

Sad to see such a record blemished by a single loss, but, on the other hand, observing West during a loss is best. That's when all his pessimism, his darkness, and his critical nature come to the surface, and we see the man in his completeness, still raging against the unprepared and the lazy, still refusing to go gently into that good night, still so *involved* at an age when most have taken to the Barcalounger.

"If Shaun would get off LeBron a little bit, he just might fall down. He can't guard LeBron anyway." (James posts up strong against Livingston and draws a foul.)

It's interesting that yesterday's Lakers and today's Warriors intersect across time, because there has rarely been a connection between the franchises in actual time. They've coexisted almost since the league began in 1946—the Warriors started in Philadelphia, the Lakers in Minneapolis—but they never resonated as a rivalry, not even after both of them moved to the West Coast, the Lakers in 1960, the Warriors in 1962. There is a simple reason for that. Over the past half century the Lakers have been dominant and the Warriors, aside from one magical season in the mid-seventies, have been somewhere between abysmal and mediocre. Until recently no one battled for the "bragging rights of California pro basketball"; equally disdainful of the Warriors to the north and the Clippers across town—let's not even get into the Sacramento Kings—the Lakers owned both of them lock, stock, and barrel.

But not now. Oh, not now.

"I look at Steph Curry and what he's done and the popularity of the Warriors, and I'm envious. Not jealous. Jealous is, *I don't want you to have it or anyone else to have it.* Envy is, *I want what they have.*"

Those words were spoken in 2017 by Jeanie Buss, the controlling owner and president of the Lakers, who even five years ago would never have dreamed about a time when the no-account NoCal Warriors were more glitzy, more admired, more flavor-of-the-day than her so-cool SoCal Lakers.

"You know what I might do now? It sounds crazy. But put Steph on Kyrie. Sometimes when you're going bad offensively, you can wake a guy up that way. Maybe he gets his ass torched but at least you're trying something."

This is also a story about very different times. The Lakers played in what now seems to be a shadowy Mesozoic era, arenas lit by candle, cave drawings on the locker-room walls. Teams flew commercial and scrounged for even local TV exposure. In the process of winning every game from November 5, 1971, until January 9, 1972, the Lakers crossed the continent four times, with train rides to Boston and Washington thrown in for good measure. On four occasions during the streak they played three nights in a row, and during one hellacious stretch in November they played five times in six nights. For per diem, they received a cool nine bucks a day.

The owner of the Lakers for much of West's career was a Canadian named Jack Kent Cooke, who emerged from central casting as the pretentious, gaseous millionaire, complete with ascot in the pocket. Cooke, who gave his two sons and one daughter the middle name Kent, cranked out orders like a pompous organ-grinder, arrogance his default mode. He had undeniable imagination and a nose for hiring talent, but he was a notorious penny-pincher who, among other things, refused to okay funds for a new projector that was needed for game preparation. Bill Bertka, a Lakers scout who is still with the team, used a pencil to hold the spool of the old projector in place.

Race was a recurring leitmotif in West's era, as the nation's white fans struggled with the reality that African-American athletes were starting to dominate in the major sports, particularly basketball, and black athletes were trying to figure out how many indignities to endure without speaking up. Two of the central figures in that struggle, Elgin Baylor and Wilt Chamberlain, played with West.

Debate over the war in Vietnam, scaled down but still raging—2,414 American soldiers died in 1971 and another 759 the following year—continued to divide the country. Los Angeles itself was still reeling from both the 1965 Watts riots and the 1969 Charles Manson murders. A parade of Manson-related trials, bloody narrative always at the center, served as a grim backdrop to the Lakers' streak season.

"It all just kind of washed over us," says Riley. "The music, the racial issues, the war, the politics, Marvin Gaye, Richard Pryor. All of it."

Indeed, the outside world seemed to touch West's Lakers only tangentially, as when a would-be hijacker allowed the airline crew to pipe in a Lakers-Knicks playoff game (hijackings were so *quaint* back then), or when Chamberlain stuck a big toe into the political waters by endorsing Richard Nixon. "We were in a bubble," says Riley. "We felt a lot of the things going on around us. But we didn't talk about them much around each other."

How times have changed. Today's Warriors are owned by a deep-pocketed conglomerate headed by venture capitalist Joe Lacob, who in 2010 brought in several of his fellow Silicon Valley heavyweights to steal the franchise away from Larry Ellison, then the CEO of Oracle and the sixth-richest man in the world. The Warriors tilt another way, too, toward Hollywood, through the influence of legendary producer and studio head Peter Guber, who is second-in-command to Lacob. There is no Jack Kent Cooke–style vertical management on a Lacob-Guber team. (No ascots either.) The contemporary Golden State franchise operates nimbly and democratically, a fusion of Silicon Valley and Hollywood.

Then, too, the current Warriors hurl themselves into the social and political issues of the day like divers from a dock. Nothing washes over them; it washes *through* them. After the 2016 election Kerr emerged as a fervent critic of Donald Trump, part of a vocal NBA pack that took the lead in speaking out, pushing back against the code that sports figures should just play the game. Curry, for his part, weighs in on anything and everything—bullying in schools, violence against women, the policies of Trump. If something bad happens anywhere in his neighborhood, Curry is on it, functioning as a kind of Bay Area Mr. Robinson. A young cancer fan needs cheering up? Curry plays him one-on-one. Beloved TNT announcer Craig Sager, who died in 2016 from leukemia, asks Curry about fatigue? Curry interrupts to say that he, Sager, is an inspiration. A tragic warehouse fire in Oakland that kills thirty-six? Curry raises $45,000 by auctioning off sneakers. He even pushed back against a compliment that the CEO of Under Armour, his number one corporate benefactor, made about Trump.

West seemed to feel the tug of the Warriors' sociopolitical bent. He wants to get out the message that many things away from basketball are important to him, to convey the idea that he is something beyond "a basketball guy," something beyond a dribbling silhouette. West speaks of race and social responsibility and pledges fealty to the notion that an athlete shouldn't surrender his voice just because he plays ball. When he is asked to speak these days, his audience expects stories of Wilt and Oscar and Elgin and the good old days, and, while they get some of those, they're just as likely to get a West who talks about race and personal responsibility and maybe even a little politics. The men with whom he plays golf and gin rummy at Bel-Air Country Club weren't too happy, after all, when he supported Barack Obama. He made a speech during a "Legend's Night" at the club, concentrating on things like values and racial acceptance, that he feels very proud of. "I had two guys tell me they had tears in their eyes," West related during a 2016 interview. "That made me feel good, like I had made a difference in their lives for that night."

West's desire to speak out seems tied to a minor regret that he remained relatively quiet when he was a player. Chamberlain, for one, held West's anodyne nature against him. But it was a different time, and voicing opinions wasn't West's way back then.

In 2011 he published an autobiography called *West by West: My Charmed, Tormented Life,* co-authored with Jonathan Coleman, a book that was extraordinary in its honesty, revealing a man who has struggled with depression and been raked with inner turmoil and rage against an unloving father and the emotional deprivations of his boyhood in West Virginia. He is still trying to work out those demons.

"I'm a lot deeper thinker than most people think I am," says West. "I mean, a *lot*. I wouldn't hold my tongue so much if I was still playing now."

"Kevin Durant has twenty-two damn points, and you didn't even know he was out there. Been that kind of game." (West loves efficient scorers, which is what he was. He sees Durant in that light.)

This is also a tale that speaks to the ebb and flow of franchises, and of the league itself. In the years between the Lakers of 1972 and the Warriors of 2017, the NBA added free agency, won a war with the ABA, endured an epidemic of white fan flight, welcomed two saviors named Magic and Bird, canonized a saint named Michael, expanded from seventeen teams to thirty, maximized then minimized the role of the Chamberlain-esque big man, planted its commercial flag in every continent except Antarctica, embraced hip-hop culture, and—lo and behold—discovered the three-point shot, and an even longer version of it, hiding right in front of its eyes.

One man was there for all of it, a subject for history both modern and ancient.

And right now he's not happy. ABC's referee analyst, Steve Javie, has just opined that Kevin Love did not commit a flagrant foul against the Warriors.

Jerry West begs to differ.

"Javie, shut the hell up, for God's sake."

The phone call doesn't come that weekend, and West is gone from the Warriors by the beginning of Game 5, three nights later, though not everyone in the organization knows it.

Some consider the breakup to have been inevitable. Perhaps West had done all he could with this golden franchise in Golden State, which has made W the coolest letter in the alphabet, the Warriors known league-wide as the "Dubs." And won't working for the Clippers be easier for West? Every time he went to the Bay Area he had to hop on a plane—well, a nice private model belonging to one of the plane-rich Warriors owners—whereas the Clippers' offices in Playa Vista and games at the Staples Center are only a drive away for a man who loves to outwit the L.A. traffic and find the quickest surface route. The Clippers need some fixing, and, even at his age, West is considered a Mr. Fix-it.

In the days that followed the news that West had left, the parties remained civil. Lacob called West "an incredible asset to our organization over the last six years" and insisted that he had wanted West to remain with the franchise, albeit at the lower figure. West called Golden State "the best-run organization I've ever been around." There is no reason to disbelieve either of those sentiments.

But undeniably, West's feelings were hurt, more so because the Warriors are an organization swimming in cash, the franchise value having increased at least sixfold since Lacob and Guber bought it in 2010. If Lacob saw West's relationship with the Warriors as transactional, West saw it as more like a marriage. And now someone was telling him he wasn't wanted, or at least wasn't wanted as much as he once was. Don't tell Jerry West that something is not personal; it's almost *always* personal.

Down the road, when the endless game of chance that is professional sports starts to turn against the Warriors, when injuries and intrigue build and wholesale changes have to be made, will they miss the man who always seemed to have an answer? Will they ever wonder: *Now, why exactly did we let Jerry West get away?*

GOLDEN DAYS

CHAPTER 1

Uncertain Start to the Revolution

Three nights after the depressing loss in Cleveland, the Warriors back in the protective bosom of Oracle Arena in Oakland for Game 5, it's a different story. West is in a corporate suite watching what he knows is his last game as a Warriors consultant. With about fifty seconds left, here is Curry speed-dribbling away the seconds, the blue and gold confetti about to fall like snow, the Oracle set to explode, Warriors fans eating it up, Cavaliers fans pissed off at the Curry dribbling show.

With the shot clock running down, Curry suddenly straightens and fires, going from handle to shot in a split second, his trademark, something he does better than anyone in the history of the game, and let's hear no back talk. The shot goes in—of course it does—from an official distance of twenty-six feet, an emphatic exclamation point on the season, and, in a way, the Warriors rise from laughingstock to the top of the heap.

The shot was audacious, arrogant, and altogether fitting from a player and a team that have carved a new path over the past half dozen years. Others have played fast and others have fired up three-balls, but no team has ever been as effective at doing both as the Warriors, largely because they have hung a "No Limits" sign on their offense.

"Steph has taken things to a crazy, new place," says Steve Nash, a Warriors consultant and a guy who himself shot some long three-pointers. "Steph is not just stepping back, he's stepping back from three-point distance into never-never land. We've never seen that before, and we've certainly never seen anyone do it with that ac-curacy. What we're seeing is a revolution."

But how did we get here, to a revolutionary place, to that place where the Warriors have come to define basketball greatness and innovation (albeit with some pushback from LeBron) over the past three years, to a place where, going into the 2017–18 season, Golden State seems practically unbeatable? Superlative seasons, such as the ones the Warriors enjoyed over the past three years—and the one that the West-and-Wilt Lakers enjoyed forty-five years ago—do not happen in a vacuum. They result from an endless re-invention process. Coaches get fired, replacements are hired, they get fired, somebody else gets a chance. Rosters turn over, transform, improve, regress, show promise. Ownership strategies get modified, rationalized, modified again, abandoned, and a "For Sale" sign appears on the franchise, come and see if you can turn it around. The hopes of fans rise, wane, rise again, eternal until they are not.

One could close one's eyes, run a finger across virtually any season in the history of the Golden State Warriors, open them up, gaze at the record book, and think, *Wait,* this *is a team that became a champion?* The Warriors won an NBA title in 1975 behind the play of another revolutionary, Rick Barry, a determined iconoclast who aimed a middle finger at everyone while at the same time launching his free throws from between his legs, like some stubborn black-socks-wearing holdout at the YMCA. Then they won no more until the pair that came along in the past three years. In many of those forty seasons from 1975 to 2015, the Warriors were a laughing-stock, the anti-paradigm, the ghost on the Left Coast, the franchise that plays in *Croak*land.

What did it? What turned it around? New owners? New blood in the front office? Old blood (West's) in the front office? Luck?

Playing style? Coaching? Maybe a little bit of all of them. To see how far the Warriors have come one could choose many points in their history. I choose this one:

The date is June 26, 2009. The Warriors are coming off a 29-53 season. Curry, the son of an NBA player known for his marksmanship but more of a sixth man than an all-star, sits uncomfortably on a podium, tentative smile airbrushed on his boyish, twenty-one-year-old face. He is surrounded by Warriors owners, executives, and coaches, none of whom are still around today. His mien is somewhere between bewildered and resigned. He didn't want to be drafted by Golden State in the first place, but then he heard he was being traded to the Phoenix Suns. Is there hope of avoiding Golden State? But, no, apparently that deal didn't go through, and here he is in the Land of Losers with a Team That Time Forgot.

With a few exceptions, this was a feeling-is-mutual situation. Curry wasn't wanted by the Warriors players any more than he wanted them. When incumbent point guard Monta Ellis was asked soon after the draft if he and Curry could coexist in the same backcourt, he doubled down on his doubts. "We can't. We just can't," he said.

Move ahead several months, to their first season together, a game against the lowly Minnesota Timberwolves at Oracle Arena on November 9, five months after the draft. The Warriors score 146 points, but Curry, demonstrably frozen out, gets off only eight shots and scores only eight points. Ellis, Stephen Jackson, Kelenna Azubuike, Acie Law, Anthony Morrow, and C. J. Watson—guards to one degree or another—all score more points than does Curry, who seems to be on an island of his own.

Why, oh why, Curry thought for the thousandth time after that game, *couldn't I have gone somewhere else?*

That's quite a journey from there to that moment in the 2017 Finals when his audacious three-pointer goes through the hoop and the noise goes through the roof.

Some consider the Warriors' rise as rather a cautionary tale and view the franchise as a kind of Icarus in sneakers, daring to add too-weighty pieces and tamper with ancient formulas. The basketball world seemed a lot more logical when the Dubs were a cult attraction, the noir film playing at the Capri off the main drag, defined by the resolutely eccentric Don Nelson, who wore his spectacularly awful fish ties and walked his potbellied pet pig through his Alameda neighborhood.

Golden State's transformation to overdog started a couple of years ago, perhaps during the 2014–15 season, after which Curry won his first of two straight MVP awards. Everybody loved the Warriors, it seemed, when they were underdogs clawing their way to the top with this smiling, skinny kid beating the odds. But when Curry morphed (almost magically it seemed) from question mark to superstar, the Warriors became something different. No matter how many Silicon Valley "Moneyball" references were attached to the Warriors, they had in fact grown into a team no longer fueled by low-salaried, high-performing scrappy B-listers, the kind that Billy Beane wanted for his Oakland A's. They were a superpower with a superstar.

And when they added Durant in the summer of 2016? Why, something must be rotten at the very core of an organization that wants *too much* talent, it was said. Durant had always been a popular player but was pilloried for leaving Oklahoma City and daring to join a better and more glamorous team. Even NBA commissioner Adam Silver expressed his skepticism about "super teams" being good for the league. Somehow the Warriors became the first franchise that ever wanted to get better, and Durant became the first player who ever changed teams.

And what else would a thoroughly modern team like Golden State be expected to do but flee its ancestral home for that biblical Shining City upon a Hill? That's what the Warriors will do in 2019 when they leave Oakland's ancient Oracle, where they've played since 1971, for a bright and shiny, self-financed (at somewhere around $1.4 billion), decked-out, teched-out arena in the Mission Bay area of San Francisco near AT&T Park, home of the baseball Giants.

Lacob and Guber claim that a new arena wasn't on their agenda on day one. But it's hard to believe that those two weren't from the beginning thinking about setting up shop in the lovely "Baghdad by the Bay," as columnist Herb Caen labeled San Francisco back when that was a compliment. The owners' introductory press conference, after all, was held at the tony Epic steakhouse on the Embarcadero, where, incidentally, one can pay forty-three bucks for a martini made with Hangar 1 Fog Point vodka, a splash of vermouth, a twist of lemon, and water "harvested" from the San Francisco fog. Apparently nothing was available in Oakland that day. "For a guy like Peter Guber," observes veteran *San Francisco Chronicle* columnist Bruce Jenkins, "Oakland just doesn't resonate."

The Chase Center—whose groundbreaking ceremony in January 2017 was a Guber extravaganza, with acrobats, a choir, and synchronized, dancing backhoes—is the symbol of a franchise that, in some respects, is searching for its soul or, at the very least, trying to keep it. The Warriors were born as the league's counterculture team, moved around the Bay Area (Memorial Gym, Civic Auditorium, Cow Palace) like an unsettled grad student, landed in hardscrabble Oakland, and finally established what seemed to be a comfortably symbiotic relationship with the place: The club drew its oxygen from a fan base that remained fiercely loyal despite years of underperforming, and the Bay Area fans got a (sometimes) entertaining underdog that satisfied their basketball cravings going way back to pioneering offensive player Hank Luisetti and pioneering defensive player Bill Russell. Sure, the swells from across the bay were welcome—the Warriors have always drawn equally from each side—but the essence of the franchise, its *soul*, was gritty Oakland. And beginning in 2019 the Warriors will be gone.

*"People would say, 'How did you do that?' and I'd say,
'I don't know. What did I do?'"*
—ELGIN BAYLOR

CHAPTER 2

The Terrific Tandem of West and Baylor

Jerry West could never accurately be described as happy-go-lucky, but there was a certain joie de vivre about him when he came to Los Angeles after the Lakers made him the second pick of the 1960 draft, right behind Oscar Robertson, with whom he had co-captained the '60 Olympic team to the gold medal in Rome. A photo in the *Los Angeles Times* from September 20, 1960, shows a crew-cutted West, wearing a sport coat and tie for the signing ceremony, posing over a contract with Fred Schaus, his college coach, who—no coincidence—was taking over the reins of the Lakers. That first story about West hangs half a nickname on him that he grew to despise—"the Kid from Cabin Creek." It was Elgin Baylor, the Lakers' designated nickname-giver, who later replaced "the Kid" with "Zeke," illustrating what Baylor saw as West's rubedom. Anyway, as West always tried to explain, he was not from Cabin Creek but from a nearby burg called Chelyan; Cabin Creek was only where the West family picked up its mail.

The Olympic triumph dovetailed nicely with the Lakers' move from Minneapolis. Young West heads west, his basketball bildungsroman continuing far, far away from the West Virginia hills where he was born. In Hollywood, story line is all. He and his wife, the former Martha Jane Kane, his college sweetheart whom he had married in April 1960, settled into a small apartment on Century Boulevard, hard by the noise of the airport, and West reveled in the energy of the city.

"When I first came out to Los Angeles it was kind of an amazing transition," West told me in 2017. "To be coming from something that small, like Morgantown, to something that vast. I wasn't familiar with anything, and one thing that served me well was that I knew my north, south, east, and west from hunting and being in the woods back home. I navigated that way a lot. I doubt many people were getting around Los Angeles by hunting knowledge from West Virginia. One of the things I liked about L.A. from the beginning was that it was a melting pot. I heard somewhere we speak over a hundred languages."

A delicious Disneyesque newness permeated Los Angeles as the sixties dawned. The place could still feel comfortably small in the cocoon where athletes live part of their lives. West became a regular at Westwood Drugs, a hangout run by a sports fan named Hollis Johnson, who invited Lakers and UCLA players to munch on burgers and slurp down shakes at a discount or sometimes for nothing. (Johnson later became a fishing buddy of West's.) It was like a little club, a bunch of millionaires and soon-to-be millionaires sitting on milk crates as they chewed burgers and the fat.

But L.A. was also getting big. What Horace Greeley had urged in 1871 was happening on a large scale. People were going west. By 1962, West's second year in the league, California had supplanted New York as the most populous state in the union. The aerospace industry—less celebrated than the movie industry but just as robust—had put L.A. on firm economic footing. Music was exploding on Sunset Strip—the Byrds, the Doors, Buffalo Springfield—and L.A.-based producer Lou Adler, later known as the bearded guy who sits by Jack Nicholson at Lakers games and has more money, was turning the Mamas and the Papas into a raging success. A talented group of studio musicians, as yet unnamed, were backing up everybody from Sinatra to Ike and Tina Turner and in 1966 worked with Brian Wilson in the release of the Beach Boys' immortal *Pet Sounds*. Later the musicians would get a name—the Wrecking Crew. That's what they could've called Baylor and West.

Moreover, L.A. had gathered under its sprawling wings both a basketball and a baseball transplant. L.A., ocean to the west, mountains to the north and south, desert to the east, glamour everywhere, was warm, exciting, and identity-stripping. Almost from the moment they arrived, the Lakers were no longer "Minneapolis," just as the Dodgers were no longer "Brooklyn."

More instant acceptance was afforded the Dodgers, who were already a nationally known commodity, their minor-league affiliates sprinkled around the country like so much salt in a sport that was still very much our national pastime. It remained for a fast-talking, Illinois-born announcer named Francis Dayle "Chick" Hearn and two franchise players named Baylor and West to bring fans into the pro-hoops fold. Though the Lakers' arrival predated John Wooden's string of NCAA championships at UCLA—Wooden's first was in 1964, West's fourth season—L.A. basketball in the early sixties meant college basketball. Even Southern Cal hoops resonated more than Lakers hoops.

In an effort to attract a fan base, the Lakers adopted primitive marketing schemes. West remembers standing in the back of a pickup truck and driving through countless neighborhoods in an effort to sell tickets. *"Come see the Lakers play!"* West says, imitating a carnival barker. "Can you imagine asking players to do that today? And I was painfully shy. I couldn't even bring myself to wave from a truck. My Gawd! I felt like I was on display."

A video taken early in his career shows West, wearing long pants and a sport coat—to this day, even when he goes to the drugstore, West rarely goes casual—mingling awkwardly with a bunch of kids at a West L.A. playground.

"Getting in an extra workout?" the setup announcer asks him.

"Well, I guess," says West, who looks like he'd rather be slathered in honey and strapped down near a giant beehive.

"We were a sideshow to the Dodgers and the Rams," West says now. "When I went to a Dodgers game shortly after I came, I was amazed at how many fans they had and how small the smattering of applause a Laker got. There was a huge number of transplanted New Yorkers who had followed the Dodgers." But not nearly as many Minnesotans who had followed the Lakers.

(That pattern was duplicated in the Bay Area. The arrival of the baseball Giants was heralded with one of the biggest parades in San Francisco history, while the 1962 welcoming parade for the Warriors was labeled a bust by the papers even though NBA sensation Wilt Chamberlain was on the team. A photo in the *San Francisco Chronicle* shows Wilt waving from a convertible to a nearly empty street. Wilt had more people at a housewarming party, as we shall see.)

The Baylor-West tandem act—and it was clearly that from the beginning of their pairing, right up until the arrival of Chamberlain in 1968—did not catch on right away at the Lakers' first home, the Los Angeles Memorial Sports Arena. Owner Bob Short put up a large board that clicked off the count of paying customers as they entered, but it served only to reinforce the reality that the Lakers were a B movie.

"I remember seeing the number 4,790," West says. "The next night, a second straight game against the Knicks [his recollection jibes with *Basketball Reference*], the number was about 4,200. My Gawd! It was very strange for me because I had played before large crowds in college. It's hard to imagine how primitive and unimportant we were as a basketball team in those early years."

Still, West's rep grew and grew. He was not the game's first white superstar, an honor that belonged to the Minneapolis Lakers' bespectacled, robotic center George Mikan and the Celtics' clever playmaker Bob Cousy. But they had played when the game was largely the domain of white players. West came along when the NBA was starting to be dominated by African-Americans, and West became the touchstone reference for the Alpha Caucasian, even for blacks. Comedian Richard Pryor, who lived in L.A. and did a lot of his performing there, had a bit about West. "You brothers better get serious," Pryor would say from the stage, "because this white guy is kicking your ass."

That gave the Lakers star even more cultural currency.

Tougher than a Cossack and blessed with natural talent, West was hip. West was cool. West was even, in a strange way, Hollywood. His size, a legit 6'3" with a massive wingspan, surprised people when they met him. He had a kind of countrified, rawboned strength about him. He didn't have movie-star good looks but, rather, the face of a hard extra, someone who tumbled down stairs, dusted himself off, and went back looking for more. West's penchant for getting his nose rearranged only added to his allure.

He was also a perpetual-motion machine that never seemed to get tired. "We'd play in L.A., get on a plane, play the second game of a doubleheader in New York the next night right from the airport, then take a Sunday afternoon train to play in Boston," West says. "You were so tired inside that you were shaking, but I never got outwardly tired. Maybe it's genetics. Maybe it's the way I grew up. We had no car so I ran everywhere, up and down the mountains."

In 1969 West was immortalized in another way. The NBA commissioned a branding consultant named Alan Siegel to design a logo for the league. During his research Siegel happened upon a *Sport* magazine photo that showed West in mid-dribble going to his left. Ironically, West was known for going mostly to his right. Siegel didn't know that and didn't care anyway; he just loved the photo.

"It had a nice flavor to it," Siegel told the *Los Angeles Times* in 2010, "so I took that picture and we traced it. It was perfect. It was vertical and it had a sense of movement. It was just one of those things that clicked." In a theme that echoes again and again, and would be repeated years later by Massachusetts-born Warriors owners Lacob and Guber, Siegel was a Knicks fan but put rival West on a pedestal. ("There have been so many times I've been around him when someone will come up and say, 'I was a Celtics fan but I loved your dad,'" says Jonnie West, Jerry's youngest child and the director of player programs for the Warriors. "That's not supposed to happen. That's when I realized how popular my father really is.")

The NBA accepted the Siegel design with no fanfare, preferring that the image be looked upon as generic, not specific. After all, why wouldn't Russell or Chamberlain, two figurative and literal giants of the game, have been picked? Or if a Laker were to be chosen, why wouldn't it have been West's teammate Baylor? Even today the league won't officially admit that the Logo is West, and West played it coy until he finally conceded in the summer of 2016 that he was the model, but even then he said it quietly, almost like he didn't want it to get out. Jerry, it's been out for forty years.

Elgin Baylor is wearing a sweater when he answers the door to his home in the Hollywood Hills. In the years when he worked as general manager for the Los Angeles Clippers and the abhorrent Donald Sterling, Baylor was known for his sweaters, most of them dreadful. He was also known for ending up on the sad side of the L.A. story, imprisoned in the Clip Joint and alienated from the Lake Show, the one he had helped create. Could anyone—could Jerry West for God's sake?—have saved the Clippers from Sterling's mismanagement? We'll never have the answer.

One other misfortune Baylor is known for: leaving the game on the day—the *day*!—that the Lakers began their thirty-three-game winning streak. He played for fourteen seasons, gritted his teeth through various gruesome injuries, scored 23,149 points, grabbed 11,463 rebounds, lifted the Lakers on his back hundreds of times, left thousands of defenders scrambling for balance ("Elgin was so tricky it was almost like he had an inborn disability," says Phil Jackson), and never once got to pop a locker-room cork.

"If you can keep a secret," Baylor says during a 2016 interview, "I used to sneak some helium in my sneakers." He had just been asked about his leaping ability and also his seemingly magical knack for hanging in the air.

The answer was typical of Baylor. He always had a jokey aspect about him. Ask any of his former teammates about Baylor, and the first thing they will likely mention is his broad sense of humor, particularly his fondness for dispensing nicknames. Besides being responsible for "Zeke from Cabin Creek," Baylor also hung "Tweety Bird" on West because of the West Virginia twang. Later, Baylor stuck him with an even worse moniker, as West writes in his autobiography—"Louella Parsons." She was a famous gossip columnist at the time, and Baylor claimed that West was always gossiping.

From Baylor's inventive mind also came "Stumpy" for Gail Goodrich (who had a stocky build), "Biggie Rat" for Tommy Hawkins (who resembled the gangster character in *King Leonardo and His Short Subjects,* an animated cartoon series from the sixties), "General Custer" for Keith Erickson (who had a droopy mustache and long hair), "Billy Barty" for Johnny Egan (who stood 5'11" which, to be fair, was much taller than the famous dwarf actor), and "Chopper" and "Beaverteeth" for Coach Butch van Breda Kolff (who deserved both monikers for obvious reasons). When Chamberlain arrived in 1968, late in Baylor's career, Elgin showed slightly more deference, waiting awhile before deciding on "Big Musty." None of the Lakers disagreed: Wilt was notorious for reeking like a fishing trawler, rarely showering, and shoving his sweaty clothes, as well as old snacks, into a putrid gym bag. Oddly, the nickname that Baylor himself had in college, "Rabbit," never stuck in the pros. He was pretty much Elgin.

Baylor went through all the championship-series angst endured by West but always seemed to emerge emotionally unscathed. The Lakers lost and West retreated into the darkness of West World. But Baylor shrugged and said, "Did you ever hear the one about . . ." No one took Baylor as seriously as they took West because he didn't seem to be taking himself seriously.

But at age eighty-three the man feels his pain. Don't think he doesn't. He should hold a monumental place in the history of the NBA, but he has been monumentally marginalized, and marginalized in a way different from, say, the unpopular Rick Barry. Nobody dislikes Baylor. They just don't remember him the way they should. Russell has his eleven championship rings, Chamberlain his prodigious stats, West his Logo, and Barry his underhand free throw. But Baylor, called "Elegant Elgin" by Cousy, seems to slip through the cracks, forgotten as the first link on the evolutionary chain that produced Julius Erving, Connie Hawkins, and Michael Jordan, forgotten for being rather the George Washington of modern basketball. "Baylor was the guy who changed the game as far as athleticism went," says Barry, who played against Baylor. "Jump, do all kinds of things in the air. It was Baylor. No one else."

Baylor had no contemporary comparison. Russell had Wilt and West had Oscar, but Baylor was sui generis, different from the other skilled but more mechanical forwards of his time, white players such as Dolph Schayes, Bob Pettit, Jack Twyman, Tommy Heinsohn, and Jerry Lucas. The game, even as it was played by the skillful Celtics and the phenomenal Russell, was subject to gravitational pull, but Baylor, who at 6'5" wasn't big for a forward, not even back then, seemed relatively immune to the laws of gravity. The phrase "hang time" was popularized by Erving in the seventies and mainstreamed by Jordan in the eighties, but it could've been used for Baylor in the fifties. "Baylor was the first player I ever saw who risked a twenty-four-second violation by hanging in the air so long," said Red Holzman, who coached the Knicks to two championships. It could be argued that Baylor was the one who brought into the sport the poetic hyperbole that remains a part of the game today.

Baylor is asked about being overlooked. "It's okay," he says with a wave of his hand. "I know what I did." And on a winter night in 1959 he did something really important . . . by not playing in a basketball game.

On the afternoon of January 16, 1959, Baylor's rookie season with the Minneapolis Lakers, the team arrived at a hotel in Charleston, West Virginia, at four p.m., having played the Nationals in Syracuse the night before. Tip-off against the Cincinnati Royals was only four hours away.

What in God's name were they doing in West Virginia in the middle of the season? They were there because Lakers guard Hot Rod Hundley, known for his hotdogging play and his facility with a quip, had been born in Charleston and had gone on to star at West Virginia University, predating West. In those days NBA teams desperate to find an audience would often play a home game in a different city with a connection to a player (and to some degree the practice lives on, though generally during the exhibition season). A few days earlier the Lakers had played a "Baylor game" in Seattle, where Elgin had gone to college.

The team's travel schedule had been merciless. The Lakers had left Minneapolis on January 3 and over the next twelve days played in Philadelphia, Boston, New York, Houston, Dallas, San Francisco, Seattle, St. Louis, and Syracuse. Plus, they had won only one of their previous eight games. So no one was in a very good mood, including the easygoing Baylor, who was on his way to becoming Rookie of the Year.

"The team can stay here, but *they* can't," the front desk clerk told Vern Mikkelsen, the team captain, when he came forward to collect the keys. By "they" he meant Baylor, Boo Ellis, and Ed Fleming, the team's three African-American players. (With that number, the Lakers were at or around the Quota, an unspoken though widely practiced edict that changed, glacially, as the years went on: You can start only one black player at home, two on the road, and three if you need to win. Ex-commissioner David Stern said in 2016, "When I got into the league I was told that teams always have to keep at least one white guy, usually more." And he was talking about the early seventies, never mind the late fifties, when Baylor broke in.)

Baylor, angry but not entirely surprised, confronted the clerk.

"'Pardon me,' I said to the man," Baylor remembered in 2016. "'What did you just say?' But he ignored me. Just turned his back. You know what that feels like?" (No.)

Someone got team owner Bob Short on the phone, and he talked to the clerk. It didn't make a difference. "You all" can stay but "they" can't. That was final.

"Bob was a liberal guy," Baylor remembers, "and he certainly didn't like this. But, look, all he wanted to do was make money, not take stands. So he told us, 'I don't care where you go but you all stay together.'"

So the Lakers moved en masse to a different hotel in the black section of town. It was called Edna's Retirement Hotel, and was, according to what Hundley later told author Terry Pluto in *Tall Tales,* a whorehouse. "I know some of the guys weren't happy about staying there," Baylor said. "But I told them, 'Now you see what it's like on the other side.'"

Baylor, only twenty-four at the time, decided that he was not going to play that evening. He was still feeling his way in the league, but he had begun to realize how good he was. Teams were repeatedly trying to get the cash-strapped Short to trade him, but the owner, tempted though he might've been, had the good sense not to trade away a future immortal. Author Bijan Bayne makes a compelling point in his 2015 biography, *Elgin Baylor: The Man Who Changed Basketball,* that Baylor, drafted one year before Chamberlain, was the first African-American basketball player selected with the specific thought that he would be a star. Russell was seen as a defensive specialist and a complementary player.

Because their status as players was far less certain than that of burgeoning superstar Baylor, Ellis and Fleming said that they would suit up. Baylor gave them his blessing. But, dammit, he was going to sit and, despite entreaties from Hundley, he remained in street clothes on the bench as the Lakers lost 95–91.

Believe this: What Baylor did took cojones in the year 1959.

Incredibly—or perhaps not—a follow-up story the next day detailed the distress felt by the American Business Club of Charleston, which formally protested Baylor's sit-out to the NBA and urged the league to take disciplinary action against him. "His absence from the lineup was most embarrassing to us and damaged our chances of promoting future games here," said a Business Club spokesman, who estimated losses on the game to be "at least $800."

We were in the right, went the club's reasoning, because the Lakers had been informed that "segregation would be enforced at hotels." As Hundley told Pluto later: "It's a white dollar."

Appearing next to that story was another headlined "Baylor Won't Be Disciplined for Sitdown." The league office took a restrained stance and almost apologized for not bringing down the hammer on Baylor.

That's what we must mean when we refer to the good old days.

As Baylor and West rampaged through the NBA in the decade of the sixties, skidding to a halt only when they got to the Celtics' doorstep, they emerged as the first great tandem in the league. Baylor was the more dominant part in their early years together. In a game against the Knicks on November 15, 1960, as rookie West was scoring ten points in a 123–108 Lakers win, Baylor scored seventy-one points. The record to that point was sixty-four by Chamberlain. Asked in a postgame interview if a player might ever score a hundred in a single game, Baylor said that it probably would be Wilt, a prediction that proved to be correct.

The following season Baylor turned in one of the most astonishing single-game performances in NBA history when, in Game 5 of the 1962 Finals against the Celtics, he scored sixty-one points. In Boston Garden. With an in-the-prime-of-his-career Russell guarding the basket.

By the mid-sixties, though, West had started to become the dominant part of the duo. "I don't want this to sound braggadocios," West told me in 2016, "but from my second year in the league on I just honestly felt that no one could guard me. I was going by them or I was going to get a good shot. I felt I had a big physical edge on them. And I know Elgin felt the same way I did."

One more thing—West had a knack for getting to the free-throw line. If you take away five seasons of Chamberlain, who was *always* getting fouled both because he demanded attention and because he couldn't make free throws, the 977 free throws West attempted in the 1965–66 season is the most ever by a player.

Then, too, West became dominant because Baylor had lost a step or two from a devastating knee injury he suffered in the 1965 playoffs against the Baltimore Bullets. Baylor went up for a jump shot and heard what he described as a "pop" when he came down. He had suffered a dislocated patella, which required surgeons to remove part of his kneecap, tendons, and ligaments and scrape out some calcium. Knee surgery being much more primitive in the sixties, Baylor was unable to recapture the old magic and get back to those days when he played defenders like a yard-sale lute. And though Baylor retained his primacy as Head Heckler and Dispenser of Nicknames, it gradually became West's team.

Even today Baylor and West remain on an all-time NBA tandem list that has to include Kareem Abdul-Jabbar and Robertson, Jordan and Scottie Pippen, John Stockton and Karl Malone, Kobe Bryant and Shaquille O'Neal, and LeBron and Wade.

(We must be rigorous about delineating great tandems. Other duos—such as Russell and Cousy, Larry Bird and Kevin McHale, and Magic Johnson and Abdul-Jabbar—don't quite fit because too many other outstanding teammates figured in the mix. Curry and Durant? Too early. Only one season together. Anyway, any offense that also includes Klay Thompson and Draymond Green might be too high-powered to speak only of a tandem.)

The West-Baylor tandem continues to resonate. After LeBron and Cleveland Cavaliers teammate Kevin Love scored thirty-eight and thirty-two points respectively in Game 1 of the 2017 Eastern Conference finals against the Celtics, research showed that no duo had scored more than thirty points each in a Boston Garden playoff game since Baylor and West pulled it off in 1966. "Which one am I?" Love yelled joyously to James, who allowed that Love could be the Logo. (In a predictable postscript, that '66 championship series was one of the most painful to West, whose Lakers lost a 95–93 Game 7 in Boston Garden. West [game-high thirty-six points] and Russell [twenty-five points and thirty-two rebounds] each played forty-eight minutes. Two weeks after that championship series, the Beach Boys released *Pet Sounds,* on which Kevin Love's Beach Boys uncle, Mike Love, sang.)

As far as style goes, the Baylor-West tandem comes closest to LeBron-Wade—both combos featured big-time scorers who could also pass, rebound, play out on the floor, do a lot of everything. But there were distinctions between Baylor and West, who were together for eleven years, longer than any of the duos save Stockton-Malone, who coexisted with the Utah Jazz for eighteen seasons.

Baylor was free-form jazz, improvisational. You couldn't exactly label him as "spontaneous," because he held the ball for long periods of time. But nobody knew what Baylor was going to do until he started doing it, least of all himself. Baylor had this take on his style: "People would say, 'How did you do that?' and I'd say, 'I don't know. What did I do?'"

West was more straight-up rock 'n' roll, predictable yet explosive. If a documentarian had ten seconds to capsulize West's game, he would show this: West dribbles to his right, quick but under control, takes a hard, high dribble as he stops suddenly, and leaps straight up in the air to release a jump shot. That was West's move. He was the ultimate pull-up shooter. One video team that put together a compilation of West's jump shots says it was unable to find even one example of West shooting off the pass. The dribble was his way of getting open, and he used that final hard bounce as a way to propel himself into the air. "I used to hit myself in the face with that dribble," he told this interviewer in 2016. "I had a scar there for a long time. I am not exaggerating." It was the kind of fundamental move that fathers told sons to use. It's there in the NBA 2K16 videogame that shows West breaking Curry's ankles on a spin move and going up for a jumper. It wasn't spectacular, but it got him in precisely the position he wanted to be to release his shot. "Elgin had an It Factor to his game," West says. "I was boring to watch but pretty efficient."

Baylor was insouciant, West was intense. Baylor was the amiable assassin, West the agonized aesthete. Baylor missed thirty-two games because of Army Reserve commitments during the 1961–62 season but thought little of it. "Tell you the truth, I kind of enjoyed that season," Baylor says. West, ever the predaceous competitor, burned from a fire within and would barely have endured time away from the game.

"There are two or three pictures of me that I've seen when my eyes, I swear to God, are *that big*," West says, holding his hands apart. "Even as I talk about it now, it sends chills through my body because I can remember what I felt like. I had so much adrenaline. Winning was *so* important. It made me half crazy. I'm sure there were other players like that, but I doubt if it was to that heightened degree."

In a filmed bio about West, his son David, the oldest child from his first marriage, says that he and his brothers fought to be the one selected to ride home with Dad after games in his one-passenger sports car . . . provided the Lakers had won. After losses? "Nobody wanted to ride with him," says David.

Then, too, there was a little more outlaw to Baylor, both the man and the player. While West was the kid who sat ramrod straight in the middle of the classroom, rarely asking questions but rarely letting his mind wander, Baylor had a semi-subversive streak and a weapons-grade charm that enabled him to cut a few corners. Baylor was regal, West was the battling knight. West didn't touch tobacco; Baylor snuck a smoke now and then. Biographer Bayne unearthed an anecdote from *Sports Illustrated* writer Frank Deford reporting that Baylor bummed a cigarette off him during a halftime of one game. Baylor also conceded, during the interview in 2016, that he didn't have the best work ethic, which puts him a full one hundred and eighty degrees from West.

"I hate to say it, but I could've been better," Baylor said. "I didn't love practicing, and there were things I should've been working on. My ballhandling, for example. It was okay but it could've been better. And maybe I should've gotten a drop step and a couple other things to help my offensive game.

"There were guys who could go out and shoot and shoot and shoot [West and, later, Steph Curry being two of them], but to me that was boring. I just couldn't do it. Tell you the truth, I'm a little lazy. I never exercised in my life. But I loved to compete and I never missed practices. Practice was competition. I played that like a game. And nobody ever got on me for being lazy for the simple reason that I gave it all I had during the game."

Rarely is there equality in the tandem relationship. On-court compromises invariably have to be made—someone gets fewer touches, fewer points, more defensive responsibility, whatever—and someone gets more credit or attention, perceived or otherwise. Fissures begin to appear, which was certainly the case with Jordan-Pippen and Kobe-Shaq. (It's not the sole province of basketball. See Martin/Lewis, Lennon/McCartney, Simon/Garfunkel, Robertson/Helm, Jobs/Wozniak, et al.)

After Chamberlain arrived to play with Baylor and West in 1968, he gradually began to complain, privately and occasionally publicly, about what he considered the favored treatment that West received from almost everyone and Chick Hearn in particular. Though Chick certainly loved him some Jerry, no one ever heard such complaints from Baylor. And when Baylor was asked in 2016 whether he sensed any favored treatment of West, he replied, "I never thought much about it."

Indeed, one could undertake extensive journalistic excavation and uncover precious few public cracks in the Baylor-West relationship. True, they played in the pre–social media age when daily petty aggravations were not let loose in one hundred and forty hasty characters or impolitic Instagrams. But they were also major personalities in a big city on a big stage, and there seemed to be an honest respect between them that continues today. Almost sixty years after Baylor and his black teammates were turned away in West Virginia, it still nags at West that the incident happened in his home state. "I just can't forget that," he says. When in 2016 West was asked what each player had to give up to accommodate the other, he reacted as if he'd never considered the question. "I'd like to think neither one of us compromised," West said. "I was a jump shooter, a quick driver, explosive. Elgin was a little more deliberate but so, so effective. We each had our role, and we knew what it was. We couldn't have worked together any better."

Baylor and West seamlessly blended their talents, racking up statistics, love, and respect even from enemy fans, digits from women, All-Star and playoff appearances—racking up everything, in short, except championships. "Elgin and I were like two kids staring at a Christmas present we wanted and all that separated us was a window pane," said West. "But we couldn't get into the store. That's how close it was yet how far away. Those are the things that really take their toll as an athlete. We went through that together."

But they both understand that Jerry was the lucky one—the white savior, Gentleman Jerry, a champion and the one who later built champions as a general manager. Elgin was the unlucky one—the supremely talented black player who was not entirely appreciated, the one who never won a ring, the one eternally on the outside looking in. For all of West's self-flagellation, Baylor toiled along a more difficult path in Los Angeles. He arrived in the city just as the race-baiting Sam Yorty became mayor, and one William H. Parker, who can be described, at best, as racially insensitive, became police chief. Baylor was in mid-career in 1965 when the Watts riots broke out, five days of mayhem that resulted in thirty-four deaths and $40 million in property damage, and had an impact on the city that lasted through, and probably beyond, the O. J. Simpson trial in 1995.

"All black athletes felt it to varying degrees," Kareem Abdul-Jabbar told me in 2017. "I got to L.A. [to begin his freshman year at UCLA] about ten days after the riots. My mother told me, 'You sure you want to go there?' But as athletes we're protected a little by the games. And as pro athletes we're protected *a lot* by the money."

Baylor was nothing if not a loyal soldier in the Lakers army. He climbed aboard all of Short's flatbed trucks and attended all of Cooke's tedious soirees ("Cooke said you had to be there, so you had to be there," says Baylor), but sometimes he still felt like a second-class citizen, never mind what happened later when he labored in the lair of Sterling, who in 2014 was banished from the league after being caught on tape making racist remarks. Baylor got good press both because he was a great player and he wasn't *difficult,* as were Abdul-Jabbar and Robertson. Two years after the incident in Charleston, Baylor was invited back and stayed at the same hotel where he had been barred. But even some of the glowing stories about Baylor, as was the case with most black athletes, carried racial overtones, as in this piece from Jim Murray, a celebrated columnist with the *Los Angeles Times:*

> But if all this gives the impression that Elgin Baylor is the latest product of the well-worn American stereotype—the happy-go-lucky, levee-singing Negro—it is the biggest con of all. . . . A Negro is supposed to love flashy clothes and be born singing. Elgin's wardrobe runs to white-on-white shirts.

The column speaks to what many white fans thought about blacks back then. (In fairness to Murray, a couple of years later he skewered Vero Beach, home of Historic Dodgertown, for the racism, overt and subtle, that it showed toward black ballplayers. And taking the sum of his career, Murray was a progressive thinker, not to mention an incredibly agile writer.) It's hard to know exactly what was going on in Baylor's mind during those days—and he's not the kind to ruminate much on it now—but at the end of the column he said this to Murray: "A Negro, to make it, has to be just a little bit better. If a White and a Negro have equal ability—and play up to it—they keep the White."

In 2009 Baylor made his feelings clear about racism, at least about his twenty-two years with Sterling, when he filed a wrongful-termination suit against the Clippers and the NBA alleging that he was "discriminated against and unceremoniously released from his position with the team on account of his age and his race." The suit also contended that he was "grossly underpaid during his tenure with the Clippers, never earning more than $350,000 per year, when compared with the compensation scheme for general managers employed by every other team in the NBA."

In 2011, all counts of the Baylor suit were dismissed. He got nothing from Sterling, who had underpaid him for two decades. And it did Elgin Baylor precious little good when Sterling was thrown out of the league.

So on and on Baylor and West went through the 1960s, L.A.'s Terrific Tandem, Mr. Inside and Mr. Outside, trading off starring roles like Newman and Redford. Or a more apt comparison might be Drysdale and Koufax, the Dodgers' peerless pitching combo. Baylor was Don Drysdale, easy and affable, the Dodgers' first bright star. West was Sandy Koufax, quieter and more socially awkward, and whose supplanting of the older player was made easier by the grace of the veteran.

And like the Dodgers pitchers, Baylor and West have a conjoined role in the labor history of sports. After the 1965 season Koufax and Drysdale announced a united holdout—they would report to spring training in '66 only if both pitchers were satisfied with their deals. It was a major story that went beyond the sports page, both because baseball commanded so much attention and because pro athletes were expected to shut up and accept what was given them. But it worked. Koufax got a raise to $125,000 and Drysdale to $110,000, eye-popping sums for that time.

A year earlier, with far less publicity and far less to gain, Baylor and West, along with a couple of dozen other players, had taken their stand. It happened about six months after Martin Luther King's March on Washington and about five months before Congress passed the Civil Rights Act. The spirit of revolution was in the air, even in sports, but it would still be another five years before St. Louis Cardinals outfielder Curt Flood wrote a letter challenging the reserve clause that essentially bound players (in all sports) in perpetuity to their teams.

The action that pro basketball players took at the NBA All-Star Game in Boston in 1964, though, is an often-overlooked early chapter in sports labor history. The players had countless grievances—salaries, travel, dearth of sound medical treatment—but under the leadership of Robertson (then with the Cincinnati Royals) and Boston's Heinsohn they decided to boil their demands down to one: The owners had to immediately begin funding a pension plan. If they didn't agree to that demand, the players would boycott the first All-Star Game scheduled for national television. In the words of Bob Dylan, it was mutiny from stern to bow.

Predictably, there was little sympathy from the owners, and one of the most threatening voices belonged to Short. Bayne writes in his Baylor bio that Short stood in a training room adjacent to the locker room where the players were meeting and shouted: "If any of my players are in on this, they're through!"

West didn't remember his owner's exact words but says the message came down as *You'll never play another basketball game in Los Angeles.* "So I'd pretty much take that as a threat," West said in 2016. "All Short needed was a gun strapped to his hip. So I said, very quietly, 'Well, I guess I'll never play in L.A., maybe never play again.' Then I gulped. Elgin was quiet, but he made it clear that he wasn't going out there either." (This moment was, in some ways, the closest West ever got to his father. The one thing he seemed to admire about Howard West was his passion "for all things political," as he writes in *West by West,* something that led the elder West to engage in union activity where he worked as a machine operator at Pure Oil.)

Another author, John Taylor, in his book *The Rivalry: Bill Rus-*

sell, Wilt Chamberlain, and the Golden Age of Basketball, says that Baylor was much more aggressive than that, at one point shouting: "Tell Bob Short to fuck himself!" Baylor doesn't remember the particulars of the incident, only that there was no way he was taking the court. Baylor had stood up by sitting out before.

The owners eventually caved, the game was played, and that Sunday afternoon in Boston should be better remembered than it is.

Still, the countless wars that Baylor and West fought together did not crystallize into a moment that they wanted to share—a championship. The so-close-yet-so-far-away story line went on and on like a bad dream, through the addition of Chamberlain, through a seemingly endless cycle of postseason failure, through as much agony as two talented teammates have ever felt.

*"When we got K.D., it allowed some
of the opposite to creep in."*
—STEPH CURRY

CHAPTER 3

Shopping in the Hamptons

When Steph Curry was a freshman at Davidson in 2006, he closely followed the stats of Kevin Durant, who was in his first year at the University of Texas. They had first laid eyes on each other in an AAU tournament in Charlotte in their preteen years, and Durant was, well, confused, because he couldn't decide what color the skinny North Carolina kid was. "Where I come from, we don't see the light-skin guys," says Durant, a D.C.-area native. "It's all guys like me."

By the time they got to college, almost nobody was following Curry, but almost everybody was following Durant. But Curry knew how good he was—or how good he thought he was—and he had set his sights on Durant, the gangly kid from the D.C. area who was both prolific scorer and rebounder.

"I sort of knew K.D. would leave after one year and I wasn't going to," Curry told me in 2017. "So I'd only have one year to follow him. We were even for a while, but then he got me." Actually, Durant got him pretty good, finishing with 25.8 points per game as compared with Curry's 21.5, and against superior competition. (This seems like the appropriate time to mention that anyone who thought, even back then, that the number two draft pick Durant wouldn't be a better pro than the number one pick Greg Oden out of Ohio State wasn't watching closely.)

Ten years later, in the summer of 2016, July 1 to be specific—just eleven days after the Warriors had blown a 3–1 lead to lose the championship series to LeBron's Cavaliers—Curry was among those who knocked on the door of Durant's hideaway home in the Hamptons. If the Hamptons seems like a peculiar place for a young NBA superstar to decamp during the summer months, well, Durant, a lover of PB&J, also has a Hamptons kind of style. By this point he had already made his way into an offbeat *New York Times* story about the Hat Shop in SoHo, where he ambled in one day and bought four fedoras. "They matched with my style," Durant told the *Times*. "I'm very happy with them."

The Curry crowd—and it was a crowd—wasn't there to talk hats. Primary owner Joe Lacob, coach Steve Kerr, and general manager Bob Myers rang the bell along with Curry, Draymond Green, Klay Thompson, and Andre Iguodala. *San Jose Mercury News* columnist Tim Kawakami would coin a name for this foursome plus Durant: "the Hamptons 5." It's a wonder they didn't arrive by cable car. Durant, agent Rich Kleiman, manager Charlie Bell, and father Wayne Pratt knew some Golden State reps were coming, of course, but they weren't expecting that number. Not even enough fedoras to go around.

The Warriors had brought along a few bells-and-whistles ideas, but in the end showed only a photo of the prospective Chase Center and made a few pitches about Silicon Valley opportunities. Even those seemed directed to Kleiman and Bell, though Durant no doubt heard them, and subsequently learned a lot from savvy investor Iguodala. Soon after Durant got to the Bay Area he bought into an investing app called Acorns, which rounds up credit and debit card purchases to the next dollar and invests that money, and soon after that he had his own YouTube channel. And by November, Durant was watching the presidential election results at the home of Apple executive Eddy Cue with Apple CEO Tim Cook.

The Warriors hadn't been the only Durant free-agent suitors, of course. The Boston Celtics, for example, had enlisted Tom Brady (though strangely not wife/supermodel Gisele Bündchen) in what turned out to be their futile pitch. (Myers later quipped that the Warriors should've brought along 49ers immortal QB Joe Montana.) But the most serious competition for Durant was obvious—his own team. In the past Durant had made quite a lot of noise about staying in Oklahoma City and building a championship Thunder team with Russell Westbrook.

Exactly when the Warriors had begun recruiting Durant was a story of endless fascination around the league. And continues to be. According to NBA rules, it is illegal for a player to "entice, induce or persuade" another player who is under contract with another team to enter into negotiations. So the first time that Durant could've been legally contacted about joining the Warriors would've been that July 1, the beginning of the free-agent period. Green denied prematurely contacting Durant about jumping ship while also noting, "I think everyone in the world talks to their friends," and later adding that he recruited Durant "like a crazy girlfriend."

ESPN's Adrian Wojnarowski (then with Yahoo!), who dishes out more scoops than Dairy Queen, reported that Thunder players were irritated by Durant's communication with Draymond during the 2015–16 season. Golden State was a *serious* rival, after all, in many ways *their* rival. En route to the NBA Finals, the Warriors had barely scraped by the Durant-Westbrook Thunder by winning the last three games of the Western Conference finals. Plus, Green had been involved in two knee-to-groin incidents with Thunder center Steven Adams—Green as dispenser, Adams as receiver. That's usually how it works with Green.

The Warriors bro-hugged their way out of the Hamptons without a commitment from Durant. Befitting his personality, Myers was pessimistic; befitting his, Lacob was optimistic that Durant would come, though he believed it might take some more schmoozing. First dates, after all, usually require a follow-up phone call.

Curry texted Durant over the next few days. Jerry West spent a long time on the phone with Durant on July 2, emphasizing that, in Golden State, Durant would have the opportunity to showcase his own game and be recognized as something much more than *just a scorer*. West also talked about his own past failures in the post-season, of which Durant had six (though far fewer than West). The Logo had always loved Durant's no-nonsense ways because he himself was a no-nonsense player. (Exactly how much West had to do with getting Durant to the Bay Area is a subject for later.)

Durant called Myers on the Fourth of July and gave him a nifty head fake.

"I just want to tell you that you guys are a first-class organization," Durant told Myers, "and I appreciate who you guys are, *but . . .*"

Myers later said: "He said the word *but* and I thought, *Aww, man . . .* but *is not a good word.*"

"But," finished Durant, "I'm coming to the Warriors."

And the Warriors lost their mind.

Then the NBA lost its mind.

If you like your NBA season spun out in bits by the social-media grinder, juicy morsels to be chewed up, spit out, and reconstituted, then the Durant-Westbrook Breakin' Up Is Hard to Do saga was for you. For others it grew redundant and gloomy, a sad postscript to what had been the eight years they spent together in Oklahoma City as both of them matured into perennial All-Stars.

Framed as a tale of integrity or morality or loyalty or courage or some damn thing, the breakup came to define the early part of the Warriors' season. Durant shouldn't have left, it was said, because he had pledged fealty to Oklahoma City. Durant shouldn't have left, it was said, until he completed the mission of winning a championship. Durant shouldn't have left, it was said, because he was joining a team that had just beaten his previous team. Durant shouldn't have left, it was said, because Golden State was already powerful enough. Durant shouldn't have left, it was said, because, *goddammit, he shouldn't have left.*

But, then, this uncivil war might've been inevitable, given what Durant meant to Oklahoma City. In a story written long after Durant inked his free-agent deal, Anthony Slater, who covered the Warriors for the *San Jose Mercury News,* talked about what a crushing psychic blow it had been when Durant took his leave. "To so many in the state, Kevin Durant wasn't just an athlete," wrote Slater. "He was a symbol. This wasn't Shaq bolting from Orlando. This was the Liberty Bell leaving Philadelphia."

Slater knows of what he speaks; he himself was, essentially, part of the Durant deal, the *Mercury News* having hired Slater away from *The Oklahoman* after they signed Durant. When Slater made that move, OKC center Enes Kanter photoshopped Slater's face onto a photo of Durant. This is where we are with superstar athletes—they have the power to fill newspaper staffs.

Predictably, the Warriors defined the complaining about Durant as sour grapes. Some in the organization were authentically offended that they were being accused of doing something so . . . so . . . what exactly? Legally underhanded? But others weren't all that unhappy that the popular tide had turned against the erstwhile lovable Warriors. Put Curry in that camp. Curry is aware that in some quarters of the league he's considered not quite substantially badass, which plugs into the whole gestalt of the Warriors, a team of finesse, not ferocity. "When we got K.D.," Curry told me in 2017, "it allowed some of the opposite to creep in." What he meant was: The Warriors were no longer America's Student Council team. "You saw how we handled it, right?" Curry said with some amount of glee. "We had a party." Yes, early in the season most of the team gathered at Curry's house and posed for a photo under giant balloons that spelled out "Super Villains." Even that, though, seems like a classic Warrior smartest-guys-in-the-room response. Small wonder they didn't make dry ice and spell out the message in smoke.

But nothing gets a team more united than adopting an us-against-the-world posture. Adam Silver helped them do that about a week after the Durant signing when, during a press conference at the Las Vegas Summer League, the commissioner said that he did not like the idea of the NBA being dominated by "super teams," apparently including the LeBron-led Cavs.

But "super teams," however you define them, are not new. When anyone uses the term "super team" pejoratively, he is referring to teams formed from superstar free agents, not teams strung together through wise draft picks and trades. The Celtics of Auerbach were sure as hell super teams in the fifties and sixties. So was the West-Baylor-Chamberlain team assembled to win a championship in the late sixties. So were the Kobe-and-Shaq Lakers, who were put together by West when he was general manager. Player movement is not new. In 1996, on the event of its first half century, the NBA selected its top fifty players, and more than half of them played for at least two teams. The list is further skewed by the inclusion of so many Celtics (Russell, Cousy, Bill Sharman, Sam Jones, Bird, Kevin McHale, and John Havlicek) and Lakers (Mikan, West, Magic, and James Worthy) who stayed with one stable and winning organization.

Granted, the movement back then was mostly via trade, but players lobbied to be moved and there was ring-chasing, too—witness Robertson joining forces with Abdul-Jabbar in Milwaukee. Wrote Dave Zirin in *The Nation:* "We never had a problem with those [older] super teams because they were put together by old white guys in suits."

The reality is that the league has become a diaspora. "Fans root for laundry" is the way Guber puts it, just as Seinfeld used to joke that fans "root for clothes." But in Oklahoma City, Durant was far more than laundry.

West criticized Silver, publicly and privately, for his comments, partly because he had helped lure Durant to Golden State, partly because he wanted to show franchise unity, and partly because he still thinks more like a player than a team executive. Something else was going on, too. West never forgot what he saw as the financial indignities visited upon him by Cooke when he was a player, and to a lesser degree by Jerry Buss when he was a GM. He doesn't forget anything.

"Some of the things I was put through, I tell you," West said in 2017, "they were whor-a-bull. There were times that—hell, yeah—I would've loved to have gotten away from Jack Kent Cooke, to have walked into his office and said, 'Mr. Cooke, I want you to trade me.' I really liked him when he first got there, but I came to very much dislike him.

"But, look, I'd be crazy to complain. All things considered, I was glad to be a Laker." He thinks for a moment and adds this rejoinder: "Except, of course, for all those times we came up short. They were hard."

"Here in California / Fruit hangs heavy on the vine /
There's no gold, thought I'd warn you /
And the hills turn brown in the summertime"
—KATE WOLF

CHAPTER 4

1969: A Summer of Discontent

As some of you may remember, even hazily, the summer of 1969 was an eventful one in these United States of America. On July 18 a twenty-eight-year-old woman named Mary Jo Kopechne, a former secretary for Bobby Kennedy, drowned on Chappaquiddick Island in Massachusetts. Kopechne had been riding in a car with Senator Ted Kennedy, who swam to safety after he accidentally drove off a bridge.

Two days later, Neil Armstrong set foot on the moon. Three weeks after that, some four hundred thousand humans, none of them senators or astronauts as far as we know, set foot on a dairy farm in upstate New York for the Woodstock Music & Art Fair.

Out in Los Angeles, however, the citizenry was paying scant attention to the peace, love, and bad acid trips that were going on at Woodstock. Three days earlier, on the morning of August 9, in a luxury home at 10050 Cielo Drive in Benedict Canyon, just north of Beverly Hills, the body of actress Sharon Tate, eight and a half months pregnant with the child of husband/director Roman Polanski, had been discovered. Four others had been murdered with her:

celebrated hairdresser Jay Sebring (even back then hairdressers were celebrated in L.A.; Sebring had been flown in, for a fee of $25,000, to cut actor George Peppard's hair); coffee heiress Abigail Folger and her lover, Wojciech Frykowski; and Steven Parent, an eighteen-year-old kid who was simply in the wrong place at the wrong time.

Just as the shadow of Chappaquiddick never left Kennedy, so did the shadow of Charles Manson and his followers, a dystopian version of a Hollywood family saga, hang over L.A. for years. The media scurried to ask Steve McQueen, Connie Francis, and Tony Bennett (yes, *that* Tony Bennett) what they thought of the murders. It turned out that the Manson family homestead was on the site of a former movie studio owned by Howard Hughes. Only a few days after the mayhem, the name of Sharon Tate was moved to the top of the marquees advertising *Valley of the Dolls* and *The Fearless Vampire Killers,* the latter being the movie where she met Polanski. Never a star in life, Tate became an A-lister in death.

The Mansons touched the Los Angeles Lakers, too. One of the figures in the murderous puzzle was Terry Melcher, a well-known record producer who was the son of Doris Day, at that time the Lakers' number one fan, a cheery, blonde, good-girl-next-door star who had sat courtside for Lakers games ever since Cooke opened what he insisted be called the *Fabulous* Forum in December 1967. (Day was even more of a Dodgers fan because she had a relationship with shortstop Maury Wills, an interracial affair that was looked upon unfavorably by management.) Day's son had rejected Manson's music, and there was conjecture that Melcher had been a Manson target, or at least that the house on Cielo had been targeted because Melcher used to live there with his girlfriend, the actress Candice Bergen.

Acknowledging an awkward segue, one presents the portrait of Jerry West in this violent summer of 1969, a man who managed to be both at the top and at the bottom of his profession. As West was beating himself up after another frustrating loss to the Boston Celtics in the '69 Finals, he noticed from time to time that a car seemed to be following his white Ferrari. He didn't think much of it. "Kids often trailed me home from games," West said, "so maybe it was just some young fans." It was only later, when it came out at trial that members of the Manson family had followed around a white sports car and also had a vague plan of killing celebrities, that West wondered if he had been a target. "I still don't know," says West today, "but I know this—they wouldn't have caught me." (Jonathan Coleman, who co-wrote West's autobiography, would later send him a novel based on the Manson clan called *The Girls*. "Jerry was obsessed with the whole Manson thing," says Coleman.)

West was ambivalent about fame, suspicious of its demands while attracted to its benefits, among them the availability and participatory spirit of female companionship, a major reason that his first marriage blew up. West was not a Here-I-am! star along the lines of, say, Magic Johnson, but neither was he a social recluse in the mold of the early Bird, the prototypical superstar hayseed. West could accurately be described as "shy"—still can to an extent—but that doesn't mean he didn't like the spotlight.

Stardom, after all, wasn't new to West when he came to L.A. in 1960. He was nothing less than a deity back in his home state, where a coach named Ken Loeffler wanted his services so badly for Texas A&M that he sat on West's doorstep and literally wept for them. The 1950s Villanova star George Raveling played against West in Morgantown and said that the pregame announcement of the Mountaineers star might well have been, "Number 44, Jesus Christ from heaven." Some people honestly thought that West Virginia's basketball team had been named for Jerry West. That's not the case, but for a long while the town of East Bank, West Virginia, did change its name to *West* Bank on March 24 every year; it was on that date in 1956 that West led East Bank High School to the state championship. "Damn, that was embarrassing," says West today. There was—still is—a lot of West fetishism in West Virginia. Years after he bled profusely during a game at the University of Kentucky—he still remembers looking down and seeing that his white sneakers had turned red—West received in the mail the bloody towel that a fan had scooped up after West was done leaking into it.

At the time of the Manson murders, West was a mess. Sports had undergone a revolutionary upheaval at the beginning of the year when Joe Namath's New York Jets toppled the Baltimore Colts in Super Bowl III. By August, the upstart New York Mets were on their way to the World Series title they would win in October. Championships by the Jets and Mets represented nothing less than the coming Apocalypse to traditionalists. But in pro basketball it had been more of the same. Old-time Boston Celtics beat showy Hollywood Lakers. West great but not great enough. Same time next year.

Wilt Chamberlain came to Los Angeles in 1968 to join West and Baylor, not as a third wheel but as the base of the triangle that would presumably get the Lakers their first championship since 1954, back when Mikan was taking his sweeping hook shots in his Chuck Taylors and Minneapolis owned the pro-hoops world.

Seven seasons had passed since Wilt achieved the unachievable: On March 2, 1962, in half-full Hershey Arena, where his Philadelphia Warriors were playing the New York Knicks, he scored one hundred points in a single game. The site was this quaint arena in Chocolate Town because the Warriors were trying, as were most NBA teams at that time, to attract regional audiences; it was Philadelphia's third game in Hershey that season.

As the teams warmed up, the public address system blared out Wilt's rendition of "By the River." There is some existing doubt that the voice is indeed Wilt's, but he had appeared on *American Bandstand* two years earlier and lip-synced it. Chamberlain laughed as he listened. The recording was forgettable. The evening was not.

A little over a month later Baylor would have that brilliant sixty-one-point game in the Finals at Boston Garden, but on this night Wilt Chamberlain became immortal, swam with the gods, ascended Everest in sneakers. One hundred points in a single basketball game. Roll it over and over in your mind. In the 1998–99 NBA season, as the game had slowed to a crawl with an unsightly isolation style, only one *team,* the Sacramento Kings, averaged over one hundred points a game for the season. In high school and college ball, one hundred still stands as a magical goal for a team. *Free tacos if we score a hundred!*

It was a strange night, mystical in some respects, made more so by how little it was chronicled. No New York writer had bothered to make the Hershey trip, and only two print journalists from Philadelphia, Jack Kiser from the *Daily News* and Jim Heffernan from the *Evening Bulletin,* were there. We have only the inimitable voice of Warriors radio announcer Bill Campbell, crowd noise rumbling in the background, to remember the moment:

One minute and one second left and he has ninety-eight points. In professional basketball! I'll tell you, that's a lot of points if you're playing grammar school kids. Rogers throws long to Chamberlain. He's got it. He's trying to get up. He shoots, no good. The rebound, Luckenbill. To Chamberlain. He shoots. Up, no good, in and out. Rebound Luckenbill. Back to Ruklick. In to Chamberlain. Good! He made it! He made it! A Dipper dunk! He made it! Fans are all over the floor! They stopped the game! One hundred points for Wilt Chamberlain!

The game came in the midst of Chamberlain's most Herculean season, when over an eighty-game campaign he averaged 50.4 points per game, 25.7 rebounds, and, most amazingly of all, over forty-eight minutes played. The Warriors played seven overtime contests that season, and the only minutes Wilt missed came when, with eight minutes left, he was ejected from a January 3, 1962, game against the Lakers in Los Angeles. (The Lakers won 124–123; Baylor didn't play and West scored forty-four points.)

Wilt's statistics are so overwhelming as to be phantasmagorical. A website called BasketballOnSteroids.com took a heavy sabermetric dive into Wilt's 1961–62 season and concluded that it "may represent the greatest individual season any athlete in the modern era, in any sport, has put forth."

Consider:

Wilt's scoring average of 50.4 is 31.59 percent greater than the second-best mark, Baylor's 38.3 one season earlier. Applying that margin of superiority to baseball batting averages, Ted Williams would've had to hit .518 in 1941, instead of .406, to be that much ahead of the second-highest average, Tony Gwynn's .394 in 1994.

The site makes interesting statistical transfers to other sports, too, and they're all remarkable.

A letter writer to the *New York Times,* Jack Stutman, brought up another point—that Wilt may have routinely achieved a triple-double in points, rebounds, and blocked shots, which were not officially calculated until after Wilt retired. Wilt averaged 8.8 blocks per game in the 112 games from his career in which blocks can be documented, writes Stutman, and the vast majority of those are from later in his career. In the three instances when blocked shots were discussed during the 1961–62 season, Wilt had nine, twelve, and "at least twenty." Wilt's blocked shots are sometimes mentioned in postgame press reports, and he frequently opined that he had more than he was given credit for.

Oscar Robertson once said that Wilt single-handedly saved the league because everyone was so curious about a player who could score one hundred points in a single game that they began to follow the sport. That might be a bit strong. But Gary M. Pomerantz, in his book *Wilt, 1962: The Night of 100 Points and the Dawn of a New Era,* is accurate when he posits that the one-hundred-point game was among the loudest announcements that African-American athletes were starting to take over in America's sporting culture. At the time of Wilt's three-digit game, Jim Brown was in the process of setting the template for NFL running backs, and Muhammad Ali, a 1960 Olympic boxing champion, was noisily rising through the ranks.

The takeover had clearly begun to scare White America. Calls to raise the basket or mandate that big men play farther from it came from all quarters, while Wilt himself was often treated as more pariah than star.

Wilt's later comment that "nobody loves Goliath" was treated with scorn, but the man had his reasons for making it. Consider this column by a celebrated journalist that appeared in *Sports Illustrated* early in Wilt's career as he began shattering statistical norms.

Basketball is for the birds—the gooney birds. The game lost this particular patron years back when it went vertical and put the accent on carnival freaks who achieved upper space by growing into it. Who can applaud Wilt the Stilt or his ilk, when they outflank the basket from above and pelt it like an open city? These fellows are biological accidents who ought to be more usefully employed, like hiring out as rainmakers and going to sow a few clouds.

That bit of analysis, astonishing both for its atrociousness of style and its soullessness, came from the typewriter of Shirley Povich, considered one of the most astute sports journalists of his day. His son Maury is the longtime host of a television version of a true freak show.

It is entirely in keeping with the Chamberlain narrative that the NBA's most valuable player the year that Wilt went for 50.4 and 25.7 was—of course—Russell, who averaged thirty-two fewer points and two fewer rebounds. For that matter, Russell also got the nod over Robertson, whose celebrated triple-double season milestone was just replicated by Durant's worthy frenemy, Westbrook. One could reasonably argue that the one-hundred-point game and the fifty-point scoring average in fact worked against Wilt. Even at that early point in his career—1961–62 was his third season—Wilt's playing reputation had been set, maybe not in stone, but in soon-to-harden concrete: He was phenomenal as an individual but didn't make the team better. That was nonsense, of course—he made his teams *much* better.

But always there was Russell.

If there were geographic justice, the Boston immortal would've performed his winning magic for the Warriors in the Bay Area. He was nine when he came to Oakland with his parents, who were part of the great African-American migration from the South chronicled in Isabel Wilkerson's critically acclaimed book *The Warmth of Other Suns*. The African-American diaspora included the parents of Huey Newton, who would head the Black Panther party, and Jimi Hendrix, who would reverb the hell out of his guitar and set it on fire. The gangly son of Charles and Katie Russell became a revolutionary of a different sort, though he knew Newton and no doubt dug Hendrix.

The Russells came from Monroe, Louisiana, where they had faced the typical Jim Crow indignities. Charles once had a shotgun stuck in his face at a gas station because he didn't seem to be "waiting your turn," and Katie was once told by a policeman to go home and change because she was wearing "white woman's clothing." Katie died when Bill was twelve, and life in the Oakland projects was difficult. Russell was a diligent athlete who practiced hard in both basketball and track. His long-legged athleticism was apparent but so was his two-left-feet awkwardness. He stuck with it, became an outstanding high jumper at McClymonds High School— one of his rivals was a future crooner named Johnny Mathis from Washington High in San Francisco—and a serviceable though low-scoring basketball center, whose teammates included future Hall of Fame baseball player Frank Robinson. The only college interest Russell got came from the Jesuits at the University of San Francisco.

At USF, Russell kept improving, and coach Phil Woolpert kept tailoring his defense to take advantage of Russell's exquisite shot-blocking. Teamed with Woolpert's leading perimeter "swarmer," K. C. Jones, who would later be a Russell teammate on the Celtics and then an assistant to Sharman on the Lakers streak team, the USF Dons eviscerated offenses. They disrupted tempo with full- and half-court pressure, and, when the offense managed to break through, Russell was usually there to swat away or at least change the shot, which, in turn, engineered a fast break. Widely ignored in the East, the Dons set what was then an NCAA record of sixty straight victories and captured NCAA championships in 1955 and '56, Russell's last two seasons.

There are many ways to mark revolutionary moments in the evolution of the game, and reasonable people may disagree on what those are. But consider these five:

- In 1891 James Naismith nailed up his peach basket and told the lads to have at it.
- In the 1920s, a group of Chicago-based African-American players, already ostracized from the mainstream outlets of

the game, formed a team called the Savoy Big Five because they played—more accurately "performed"—before concerts in the Savoy Ballroom. The SBF became the Harlem Globetrotters, who disseminated the game around the world.

- In the 1930s, a product of the San Francisco playgrounds named Hank Luisetti began taking a running one-handed shot, a fundamental change that turned the game into a more rhythmic whole and began the demise of the stop-and-measure set shot that was gone from the game by the late 1950s.
- In the fifties along came Russell, the first man to turn defense into offense. Big men were firmly entrenched by the time Russell played for Woolpert and then Auerbach, but they were almost always thought about in terms of offense.
- And decades later along came the long, long shooting of Steph Curry.

That's a lot of revolution for northern California.

Wilt and Russell had much in common—their size, their menacing goatees, the night-to-night responsibility each carried onto the court, the obstacles they faced being black superstars in white 1950s America. It wasn't only the dramatic incidents of segregation that united them; it was the utter banality of racism they faced on an almost daily basis. In Robert Cherry's excellent bio, *Wilt: Larger Than Life*, he quotes Sonny Hill, Wilt's boyhood friend and still a media personality in Philadelphia, talking about a normal day walking down the street with the teenaged Wilt. "My God," a passerby might say, not even bothering to lower his voice, "look how tall that n—er is."

You read about Wilt and Russell, and in some cases even remember them going against each other in real time (as this reporter can do), and it's hard not to find yourself, however subtly, favoring one over the other. You're not necessarily making a basketball choice but more of a personal one. They approached life and the game so differently, their personas mismatched for two giants who were doppelgängers to each other, judged against each other, and measured eternally against each other.

Wilt was the magnet, drawn to the spotlight, the spotlight to him; Russell was the one who stayed in the shadows but always emerged at the right time. On the court or off the court, Wilt was *palpable*; Russell was a cougar, silently stalking. Wilt's teammates look back with affection on his predilection for making more claims than a Gold Rush prospector. He said he set a world record on a pinball machine, wrestled with a mountain lion, bowled with a ball that didn't have finger holes, beat Jim Brown in arm wrestling, threw a football over a hundred yards, outshot West in practice games, drove from New York to Los Angeles in thirty-six hours (never bothering to relieve himself or stopping for gas because his Cadillac had "auxiliary gas tanks"), drank thirty-six glasses of orange juice at a single sitting, and whipped Lucille Ball's ass in backgammon. Who brags about whipping Lucille Ball's ass in backgammon? And there was something about twenty thousand women in there someplace. "Yeah, Wilt put a little honey on his stories," says Jim Cleamons, who was a rookie on the 1971–72 Lakers streak team, "but he wasn't so over-the-top that you couldn't enjoy it. And he could laugh at himself and not take himself so seriously."

Comparable stories about Russell from his Celtics teammates? There are none.

By the time they strode to midcourt for Game 7 of the 1969 Finals, Wilt and Russell were not on friendly terms. In his book *The Pivotal Season,* author Charley Rosen writes that their relationship had always been "phony" and "one-sided," theorizing that Russell had long suckered Wilt into being a friend basically so he could outwit him during games. That is simplistic. They were most assuredly friends early in their careers, bonding over slights and humiliations endured only by seven-foot-tall black men who were public figures in a color-conscious country.

But 1968 had been a choose-your-side year in America. Russell had chosen his. Along with Jim Brown and Ali, Russell had become one of the faces of athlete activism. (Author Taylor pointed out in *The Rivalry* that Russell spent the summer of 1968 living with Brown in Hollywood, news from the chaotic Democratic convention washing over them like a tidal wave.) It was a moment America had never seen before, three major players in three major sports speaking out on civil rights issues, prompted by a hundred things but certainly by the black-gloved salute and the inevitable backlash that followed Tommie Smith and John Carlos in the 1968 Mexico City Olympics.

Chamberlain, by contrast, had chosen . . . Richard Nixon? The Veep and the VIP (Very Important Pivotman) had first met on a cross-country flight in the early sixties and hit it off immediately, finding common ground over the shared assumption that an un-washed public considered them to be (a) losers unable to win the big one, and (b) dumb. As paranoid as that might sound, it does have the ring of truth. Nixon, remember, was years away from win-ning the 1968 election, and Chamberlain had already begun his second-banana act to Russell.

Chamberlain bristled about many things in his life, but perhaps nothing got him as exercised as the opinion that he was dumb. "People say Muhammad Ali is smart because he's such a good talker," Wilt wrote in his 1973 autobiography co-authored with David Shaw, *Wilt: Just Like Any Other 7-Foot Black Millionaire Who Lives Next Door*. "Well, Muhammad's a good friend of mine, but if you get him off two subjects—religion and boxing—he doesn't know enough to string three intelligent sentences together."

Chamberlain had been deeply affected, he said at the time, by the assassination of Martin Luther King on April 4, 1968. No rea-son to believe otherwise. In fact, Chamberlain and Russell had pe-titioned, to no avail, to get the following day's Game 1 of the Celtics-76ers Eastern Conference finals postponed. But Wilt's re-sponse to the murder was hardly typical—it moved him, he said, to join the GOP for the 1968 election campaign, thereby making Wilt perhaps the only person in American history to inhale Martin Lu-ther King and exhale Richard Milhous Nixon.

"I kept asking myself, what can I do to help America, and par-ticularly my people, reach the mountaintop and see the promised land that Dr. King so often talked about," Chamberlain said in July 1968 to the *Los Angeles Sentinel*, a black-owned L.A. daily. "Some-thing came over me at that precise moment. As I walked with thousands of others from the Ebenezer Baptist Church to his final resting place, I quietly walked up to [Nixon] and told him I liked his program and wanted to join his team." Wilt actually went to the GOP convention in Miami in an effort to excite black delegates for Nixon, and made prerecorded speeches that went like this:

> This is Wilt Chamberlain again. . . . Black is beautiful. . . . Richard Nixon is a vote for black people to determine their own destiny.

Russell was disgusted by Wilt's political positions, and even lobbed this strange insult at his rival: "Notice how little [Chamberlain] smiles," Russell told the *Los Angeles Times*. "That's not because he's angry all the time. It's because he's lonely. An outsider." Of all the insults Russell could've hurled at Chamberlain, lack of smiling would seem to be near the bottom since Russell himself was not Mr. Sunshine.

Russell was Russell, Wilt was Wilt. Russell had not been a basketball prodigy—he worked for what he had gotten—while Wilt coasted on his talents. Russell's school (San Francisco) came out of nowhere to win; Wilt's school (Kansas) came out of the skylights to lose. Wilt played a year for the Globetrotters; Russell dismissed them as a circus act. Wilt deejayed at his campus radio station; Russell discussed physical fitness with President Eisenhower. Wilt flashed the Black Power salute from time to time but only as a hello; Russell never flashed it but signaled so much more with just a glower. Russell was handed the keys to the Celtics coaching kingdom in 1967; Wilt's entreaties to coach the Philadelphia 76ers were ignored. Wilt came across as a man-about-town, talking about "fine young things" and "copping a lady"; Russell came across as a citizen of the world.

It came to this: Wilt was sizzle, Russell was steak.

There was something else at play, too—Wilt's utter hopelessness at the foul line. Russell was no marksman—he made only 56 percent of his free throws and only 44 percent of his shots from the field, which is relatively horrible for a big man with limited range—but he wasn't a joke. Wilt's free-throw shooting *was* a joke. Those who would tear him down for just about anything had a credible case when it came to the foul line, where he shot just 45 percent for his career. Moreover, Wilt shot almost *four times as many* free throws as Russell. It was like the old line: The food is terrible and there's so much of it.

The reasons Wilt gave for his inability to make free throws were numerous (injuries, weight-lifting, fatigue, physics related to his height), and, as with what started World War I, one could cogitate about them for hours and still not figure out which are valid. It's painful to watch a video of Wilt shooting from the fifteen-foot line in the latter stages of his career. At one point he decided to stand at the extreme right side of the line and hurl a line-drive missile at the basket, virtually guaranteeing a miss. Eventually, he started shooting quickly, almost as if he believed he could get the trial over with and get back to playing before anyone noticed.

Wilt made numerous references to Russell's offensive abilities vis-à-vis his own, this one being the clearest. "Bill Russell couldn't score as well as I could if he had a stepladder, three basketballs, and a cannon with a range-finder," he wrote in his autobiography. But every time Wilt did it, he sounded defensive about his offense because Russell almost always won.

But surely Russell would not win in 1969. The Celtics had finished in fourth place in the Eastern Conference, and, as L.A. saw it, lucked their way into the Finals. Despite some injury concerns surrounding West and Baylor, the Lakers had been dominant, having easily disposed of the Warriors and the Hawks in the West. Anyway, this Game 7 was at the *Fabulous* Forum, not haunted Boston Garden. Oddsmakers had even made the Lakers a favorite despite the glaringly obvious history—the five occasions when they had come up short against the annoyingly efficient Celtics.

Down in San Diego, a tall, still-developing sixteen-year-old, entranced by the incantational voice of Hearn, remembers being nervous before that series but believing that, yes, it would at last be time for the Lakers. "Everything about Chick from the moment I listened to him were these two messages," Bill Walton told me in 2017. "First, the greatness of Baylor and West. And, second, how are we going to beat the Boston Celtics? That was supposed to be the year."

Before the game Celtics guard Sam Jones noticed a bed of balloons hanging from the ceiling held back by netting. They were obviously put there in anticipation of a victory, a bit of premature celebratory ejaculation by Cooke. Jones relayed this information to center-coach Russell, who laughed his cackling laugh.

West noticed the balloons, too. His thought process was different: *What has that asshole Jack Kent Cooke gone and done now?*

With about six minutes left, the Celtics led 103–92. Baylor was hobbling with a customary aching knee, and West was in worse shape, playing on a leg that was shot up with Novocain for a hamstring pull he had suffered in Game 5. ("I promise you," says West today, "that injury would not even be an issue today.") Inevitably, though, West had begun to heat up. Then Wilt went up for a rebound on a John Havlicek missed shot and came down off-balance, most of the impact centered on his right knee. He got an injury time-out, and trainer Frank O'Neill froze his knee with what color analyst Jack Twyman said was Freon. Wilt stayed in the game, but, after West drew a foul, Wilt signaled to the bench that he wanted a replacement.

It was one of the most stunning moments in Game 7 history, still deconstructed, comparable to Pippen's much-maligned migraine in the 1990 Eastern Conference finals. After about a minute Wilt told teammate Tommy Hawkins to tell Coach van Breda Kolff that he was ready to go in. "We don't need him," Hawkins recounts van Breda Kolff as saying, and stuck with his replacement, Mel Counts. Wilt told him again. To which VBK reportedly said, "We're playing better without you." No sideline reporters were there to verify exactly what was happening.

(The relationship between VBK, who had coached at Princeton, and Wilt was doomed from the start. Though he liked his drink and was fond, according to some Lakers, of engaging in farting contests, VBK was an unyielding perfectionist as a coach, without the diplomatic touch that would be shown later by Sharman. VBK once complained that his star player, Bill Bradley, wasn't "hungry enough" when most coaches would've amputated a limb with a penknife just to have shared a bench with All-Everything Bill. Wilt didn't go much for unyielding perfectionists, and he and VBK just did not get along; West calls their relationship "one of the most bizarre I've ever seen.")

West, playing with an impressively bulky volume of tape around his left thigh, was carrying the Lakers. His thirty-ninth and fortieth points brought the Lakers to within five points, at 103–98, and his two free throws made the score 103–100. As well as he was playing, a fleeting doubt might've crossed West's mind, which was always full of doubt. *We should've taken them out earlier in Boston Garden. Never give Bill Russell life in a Game 7.*

Still no Wilt. If the television audience was waiting for an explanation, it never came. Twyman mentioned Wilt's name only in reference to Counts being a better defender than Wilt away from the basket. The sloppiness of the game in the final minutes cannot be overemphasized. It was a comedy of errors rescued only by West, who would finish with forty-two points, thirteen rebounds, and twelve assists. It was a phenomenal performance considering (a) his injury and (b) the fact that the other Lakers, excepting Wilt, made only nineteen of sixty shots.

With the Lakers seemingly ready to take the lead, Keith Erickson knocked the ball away from Havlicek. Improbably, it landed directly in the arms of Boston forward and future Warriors coach Don Nelson, who launched a jump shot that, more improbably, bounced high off the back rim and into the basket. It was the kind of shot that was supposed to go in at Boston Garden but nowhere else. And it killed the Lakers. With Wilt still on the bench, fuming and frustrated, Boston won 108–106.

West walked off the court, pale as a mourner, his face spasmed into a theatrical tragedy mask. It didn't matter that almost every Celtic came into the Lakers' locker room to shake his hand or that he won the MVP award. All the championship losses came back to him, the five previous ones to Boston, and even the 71–70 loss to Cal in the 1959 NCAA final when the ball was in his hands and he didn't have enough time left to take a shot that might've won the game. "My life and career always tilted toward the tragic side," he wrote later in his book. And nothing, apparently, was going to change that. "Hope is thin and despair is thick," Viet Thanh Nguyen would write decades later in his Pulitzer Prize–winning book *The Sympathizer*, and West felt nothing but a deep, broad band of despair, certain that he'd never be a winner.

Meanwhile, the balloons stayed in place, the USC pep band, hired by Cooke to play "Happy Days Are Here Again," stayed silent, the celebration programs were shredded, Auerbach laughed and blew stale stogie smoke into the Forum, Russell waxed uncharacteristically emotional after his last game, and West, unmoored, quietly left the Forum to beat himself up in private.

The inevitable comparisons between Russell and Wilt, already set in stone, now became the equivalent of rabbinical text. Russell won, Wilt lost, Russell endured, Wilt quit. Wilt's burden, then and forever, was to have his championship record compared unfavorably to Russell's. But Russell saw it another way, believing that too often he heard that Wilt would've been just as successful had he played with the Celtics. Russell had always managed to keep that feeling under wraps until he went on a lecture tour after that final game in 1969. When the subject came up at one stop, Russell went off on Chamberlain, saying he couldn't believe that Wilt would leave a Game 7 with an injury. It further cleaved their relationship, which was not repaired until NBA commissioner David Stern made it his business to get them together years later.

One of the fairest assessments of Russell and Wilt comes from Tom Meschery, a former Warrior, a Wilt teammate, and, partly owing to his romantic sensibility, an unabashed Wilt admirer.

"Wilt was a wonderful guy," says Meschery, "the most misunderstood guy on the planet. Sweetest, kindest, gentlest guy I've ever known. Horniest, too, I might add. Russell was hard-nosed, persnickety. Always had a chip on his shoulder. He could be a bright and funny man, too, but there was something serious about it.

"Now, to be sure, Russell won championships with great players. And maybe Wilt would've won more with Russell's teammates. But he wouldn't have won as many. Russell was the heart of that team. Russell's dominance on defense, and the defense that he demanded as a player? Wilt just did not have that effect on his teammates. Wilt's personality could rub players the wrong way. Wilt would've won maybe three or four championships, but that steady stream? No way. That was Russell."

Perhaps the best indication of the almost surreal power that Russell held over the Lakers comes from this West observation. He talked about staring at a photo of Russell that showed him standing with his hands on his hips at midcourt. And West said: "He looks almost regal." What a strange thing for the Logo to say.

The defeat sent West into a tailspin. In *West by West* he compares a photo of himself walking off the court after Game 7 to the iconic shot of a bloodied Y. A. Tittle after the New York Giants quarterback was knocked silly during a game against the Pittsburgh Steelers in 1964. Tittle suffered a concussion and a cracked sternum; West had no palpable physical wounds but more severe psychic pain than Tittle ever suffered.

Even the Dodge Charger that West had won for being the MVP served as a motorized rebuke—it was roughly the color of Celtics green. Once while West was jogging during that summer of '69, he overheard someone utter the word *choke* as he passed by. West says that he had to restrain himself from beating the guy up, a throwback to the days of rage he experienced growing up in a household with an abusive father.

Late in 2016, West was asked if he ever considered quitting after that loss in 1969.

"I came very close," he said. "I didn't like myself very well. I just couldn't cope with the horrible feeling I had, the idea of going back into a locker room that was about losing. I kept thinking: Is this all there is? I was so frustrated. I was *so* frustrated. Basketball wasn't bringing me any joy at all. None.

"You know, *pity* and *envy* are two horrible words. But I associated them with myself. I know people pitied me, and I hated that. And I used to say to myself all the time, *Why the hell can't we get to where we want to go? Why can't we get the right bounces?* And that was envy."

As West spoke, you could feel the man's pain, still visceral fifty years after so many other triumphs.

"I thought it was all over for us. I really did," says West. "I thought I'd be labeled as a loser for life. And who thought we would even stay together as a team? I certainly wasn't sure about it. And with all that happened, it's kind of amazing that we did."

"But when I got to Oakland? It was . . . Brooklyn."
— CHRIS MULLIN

CHAPTER 5

Curry's Unhappy Draft Day

In the spring of 2009, by which time Durant was already on his way to becoming an NBA All-Star, Davidson junior Curry declared for the NBA draft. The basketball world didn't take a lot of notice. Curry was not coveted across the board as was Blake Griffin, the consensus number one pick, a cartoonishly athletic power forward from Oklahoma. Curry was even projected in some analyses to be as low as a midteens pick. He was undersized—how many NBA players had as their idol growing up the 5'3" Muggsy Bogues, as Curry did? He hadn't played in a major conference, and, besides, it was a draft rich in backcourtmen—Arizona State's James Harden, Memphis's Tyreke Evans, and USC's DeMar DeRozan, along with a couple of small point guards whose value had to be sized up next to Curry: Jonny Flynn from Syracuse and Ricky Rubio, a phenom who had played in his first Spanish ACB League game when he was fourteen years old.

Team Curry (himself, his father Dell, and agent Jeff Austin) believed that playing fast was Steph's best—maybe his *only*—chance of being an NBA star. "We knew what [then Knicks coach] Mike

D'Antoni had done with Steve Nash in Phoenix," said Austin, "and it seemed like a perfect fit." The Knicks had the eighth pick, so getting Curry seemed like a reasonable scenario if the Knicks wanted him. And D'Antoni wanted him.

One problem: The Golden State Warriors, who were picking one spot ahead of the Knicks, wanted Curry, too. Well, one person did, anyway—general manager Larry Riley. As we already know, Curry wanted no part of the Warriors, which was not a minority opinion around the league at that time. But Riley, an old NBA hand with a folksy manner, loved him some Curry. He firmly decided that Curry was his man, ironically, after being in the stands for one of Curry's worst college games, a 76–58 loss to Purdue on December 20, 2008, at Conseco Fieldhouse in Indianapolis. Curry missed his first eight shots and scored only thirteen points on 5-of-26 shooting. Riley didn't care.

"I wanted to see how he would hold up under pressure," Riley said in a 2017 interview, "and I knew Purdue would beat the shit out of you because that's the way the Big Ten played. The other knock was that Curry was a two-guard, not a point. I never believed that. I thought he was a point guard, and the fact that he shot so well only made him more valuable. Well, in that Purdue game he made the long pass, made the short pass, knocked down some shots, and stood up to everything they threw at him. They got their asses beat, but I walked out of the arena saying, 'This kid is for real.'"

That was the message Riley communicated to Don Nelson, the Warriors coach and general franchise overseer. Always the iconoclast, Nelson agreed that an undersized kid who would bomb three-pointers might be perfect. So Riley let Team Curry know of Golden State's interest and that he and Nellie would love to have Steph work out for them.

The answer from Austin was clear: *Thanks, Larry, but we don't want to work out for you. And we don't want you to draft Steph.*

It wasn't a decision made just by the old guys. "I can't lie," Curry told me in 2017. "I was hell-bent on New York. I wanted to play for D'Antoni, and I didn't want to play here." At the time he was sitting at the Warriors' practice facility in Oakland, the one with the

2015 NBA championship banner hanging from a wall with another one (though he didn't know it at the time) due soon. Curry smiled. "I guess it was one of those cases of being careful what you wish for, right?"

Twenty-five years earlier another college player, this one named Chris Mullin, had been in Curry's position. The Warriors wanted him, but he wanted the Knicks. There has never been a clearer Knick wannabe than Mullin, Brooklyn-born and St. John's–honed, a city kid who talked New Yawk and played New York. Mullin should've come out of the womb with a Big Apple birthmark on his shooting arm, which was his left.

But Mullin had no chance of joining his hometown team, the 1985 draft notable for being the one that included the first draft lottery. The Knicks got the top pick—the fact that they did is still a favorite of conspiracists who believe that Commissioner Stern guided the lottery that way—and that prize was going to be Patrick Ewing.

That draft was replete with other big men besides Ewing, at a time when centers were still considered the key to success, so Mullin knew he was also going to be drafted behind players like Wayman Tisdale, Benoit Benjamin, Jon Koncak, and Joe Kleine. He didn't know where he was going to go, but *please don't let it be Golden State at number seven, please don't let it be Golden State . . .*

"I had just dreamed of playing with the Knicks," says Mullin now, relaxing in his office on the campus of St. John's, where he is the head basketball coach. "Clyde Frazier was my guy. He's still my guy. I had never left New York and certainly didn't know much about Oakland.

"But they called my name and that was that. What was I going to do, play in Europe? Yes, I was very disappointed. But I was the first player picked who wasn't a center or a big forward, so I bet everybody in the Bay Area was disappointed with me, too. Yeah, it seemed strange when I got to the Bay Area. I had never left New York except for a basketball trip or two, and what I thought of as

California was maybe I'd be lying on the beach looking at palm trees. But when I got to Oakland? It was . . . Brooklyn.

"The only thing about the Warriors I knew was Rick Barry. Coach [Lou] Carnesecca [Mullin's coach at St. John's] had coached Barry in the ABA. He told me, 'Rick was a great, great player. But sometimes he couldn't get out of his own way.'"

Ah, a perfect way to describe the tortured history of this franchise, speckled with more whimsy than wins. Even the 1975 championship was a strange one, befitting the off-kilter aura of the NBA in the seventies. Scheduling for the Western Finals games had already been fouled up because of arena commitments for—you're going to love this—the Ice Follies and a kung fu exhibition. So the top-seeded Washington Bullets were given the option of either a 1-2-2-1-1 format, or opening on the road and playing Games 2, 3, and 4 at home. They chose to open at home, lost that game and promptly got swept by Barry's Warriors. (Golden State owner Franklin Mieuli, a man for whom the word *jaunty* seems to have been invented, used to ride around the city with the championship trophy in the back of his convertible. Whenever he made a stop, he left it in the unlocked car, confident, he said, that no one would steal it. No one did.)

But then the downhill slide began for the Golden State franchise. Bad karma and bad personnel decisions started to pile up. In compensation for the free-agent exit of Jamaal Wilkes to the Lakers, for example, the Warriors received the number five pick of the 1978 draft. They selected Purvis Short, who turned out to be a nice player, while with the next pick the Boston Celtics selected Larry Bird, who turned out to be Larry Bird.

Even when the Warriors did something good, it turned out bad. They had the sense to grab center Robert Parish with the eighth pick of the 1976 draft but four years later sent him and a first-round draft pick to the Boston Celtics in order to trade up to get two picks. Those picks turned out to be Joe Barry Carroll (memorably monikered as "Joe Barely Cares" by hoops scribe Peter Vecsey) and a so-so guard named Rickey Brown; the other pick the Celtics got turned out to be McHale. So the Warriors assembled the

Bird-McHale-Parish frontcourt that was the foundation of three Boston championship teams in the 1980s. Between what Auerbach did to the Lakers in the sixties and what he did to the Warriors in the seventies, the state of California should've charged the annoying genius with grand larceny.

That was not Golden State's only center-centric move that seemed to have been made by kindergarteners doodling on a draft board. In 1983 they ignored Clyde Drexler, Dale Ellis, and Derek Harper to pick Russell Cross, a 6'10" center from Purdue. He became just one of Golden State's crosses to bear, playing only forty-five games before exiting stage left. Later, the Warriors managed to get a really good center . . . after he had stopped being one because of aching knees. That was Ralph Sampson.

Drugs were never far away from the Warriors franchise. "You walked more than thirty feet in either direction in the Oracle," says Bay Area media personality Ray Ratto, "and you were high." (To be fair, that still prevails in many areas of the Bay Area.) Pot was just part of Oakland's rock-festival charm, but cocaine was something else, a problem that hit the NBA in the late seventies and lasted well into the eighties. It seemed worst of all in the Bay Area. Perhaps something sinister wafted in with the fog from the bay. John Lucas, Bernard King, Micheal Ray Richardson, and Chris Washburn were all wearing Warriors colors in troubled times. (In 1983 Golden State traded Micheal Ray to the Nets for Sleepy Floyd, prompting Bill Simmons to later write: "Anytime you can turn a cocaine addict into someone named Sleepy, you have to do it.")

Even visiting players sometimes fell hard on a trip to Warrior Land. The Oakland Hyatt became to basketball what the "Riot House," a Hyatt on Sunset in L.A., was to rock 'n' roll. (See *Rock Star, Almost Famous, This Is Spinal Tap*.) During a western road trip in that era, Atlanta Hawks coach Mike Fratello chose to keep his team in Los Angeles for a couple of days after a game against the Lakers rather than have them fly out early for a game against the Warriors, memorably reasoning: "I'd rather have them fuck themselves to death in L.A., rather than spend an extra couple days in Oakland."

And then there was the time in 1997 when Warriors guard La-trell Sprewell choked his coach, P. J. Carlesimo, another milestone to be excised from the franchise history reel.

There were moments of hope along the way—the "Run TMC" (Tim Hardaway, Mitch Richmond, Mullin) teams of the early nine-ties that played up-tempo and suggested a time in the near future when NBA teams might actually start fast-breaking again, and the "We Believe" team of 2007, an eighth seed that defeated a top seed (the Mavericks) in the first round of the Western Conference play-offs. But both turned out to be chimerical, a flash of thigh.

Through it all, a knowledgeable fan base was always part of the Warriors, no matter how feckless they might've been on the court. It plugged into the gestalt of an area where your cabdriver might be a Berkeley Ph.D. and where former Warrior Meschery did po-etry readings with Beat heroes Lawrence Ferlinghetti and Allen Ginsberg. "It was a great basketball town before it was a great Warriors town," sums up Ratto.

But in 2009 Curry wasn't thinking about the town. He was think-ing about the team. Now, Golden State wasn't the only place he didn't want to go. He refused to work out for both Memphis and Minnesota even though the Grizzlies, who had the second pick in the draft behind the Clippers, would've almost surely taken him.

"Jeff, my bosses won't let me take Steph unless he works out," Austin was told by Kenny Williamson, the Grizzlies assistant gen-eral manager, who was known in basketball circles as "the Egg-man," a nickname given to him by his grandmother because he sold eggs door-to-door while growing up in Harlem. (Williamson died in 2012.)

"Sorry, Kenny," Austin told him. "We're not coming."

But Riley didn't care about an audition. He remained steadfast, for that was his nature. In 1997, as he waited to board a flight from Cincinnati to Detroit for a scouting trip, he says he heard a voice telling him to go home. He rebooked on a flight back to Vancouver, where he was working as a scout for the Grizzlies. The Detroit-bound flight, Comair 3272, went down in a blizzard, killing all twenty-nine souls aboard. Riley says he had a "guilty complex" for a while, but it turned him into a man of strong faith.

Riley admitted that he would've taken Griffin with the first pick, but, had the Warriors been second in line, he would've still taken Curry, a move at the time that would've drawn almost universal derision. "I listened to everything Dell and Jeff had to say," Riley remembers. "They made their case, and I made mine. I told them, 'Steph doesn't have to work out for us, and you don't have to like us, but we're taking him. And we're going to make it work.'"

So the Golden State Warriors called his name and David Stern shook his hand, and there was Curry at his first Warriors press conference, facing an uncertain future with an uncertain franchise, so young-looking that he appeared to be waiting for a prom date, a vision that probably left most Warriors fans thinking: *Well, we can always come to watch the other team, just like we always do.*

"Let's get out of here. Jerry's down there going crazy again."
— CHICK HEARN

CHAPTER 6

Fame and Glory but No Ring

LAKERS

Jerry West had a practice ritual. He would stand with his back to the basket, begin to count down from four seconds, *one thousand four, one thousand three . . .* , turn, and release a jump shot to beat the hypothetical buzzer. He wrote in *West by West* that he always gave himself "enough time to take maybe one or two dribbles to get somebody leaning." Like many great players he seemed to have a clock in his head.

West hit several buzzer-beating clutch shots in his career, but he remembers one in particular because it came against the Celtics. In Game 3 of the 1962 Finals, his first against Boston, he made a steal with time running out and the score tied 115–115. As his teammates yelled for him to take a jumper, the clock in West's head told him that he had enough time to speed in for a game-winning layup, which he did.

He also remembers it because it occurred during the first of those six Finals defeats to the Celtics in the decade of the sixties.

On April 29, 1970, West made another buzzer-beater, this one an enduring YouTube classic, this one a seemingly impossible launch, this one a shot that lifted West to immortal status (if he was not there already), this one . . . another dagger in his heart?

Game 3 of the Finals, this time the Knicks as the opponent. New York forward Dave DeBusschere makes a jump shot from the foul line with three seconds left to put New York ahead 102–100. Chamberlain grabs the ball, stabs one foot out-of-bounds—in later years Wilt always noted that he didn't have both feet out-of-bounds, so his inbounds pass was illegal—and shovels to West. Everyone thought it was over. Walt Frazier would say later that he was in the process of walking off the court. But West takes three quick dribbles—*one thousand three, one thousand two*—and takes off from several feet behind the midcourt line, probably sixty feet from the basket. It's a desperate shot, to be sure, but one taken in reasonable rhythm, and down it swishes, as DeBusschere, by now back on defense, puts both hands on his head in a classic *holy shit!* gesture.

This is what happens after the shot goes in. West simply starts walking toward the bench, takes a quick glance at the scoreboard to confirm, that, yup, we're heading for overtime (no three-point shot back then), accepts the hugs from his teammates, and sits the hell down.

"I don't even like to talk about it," West said in 2017, as he has told dozens of interviewers over the years. "You know why, don't you?"

Yes. West missed five shots in OT, the Lakers lost the game and, eventually, the series. West despises the fact that so many associate him with heroics that occurred in a losing game. It only highlights, as he sees it, the number of occasions that the name Jerry West is associated with losing. It's hard to imagine how desperately West would've despised his sixty-footer had it come against Boston.

The Lakers had followed up their haunting 1969 defeat to Russell's Celtics with more failure, losing to the Knicks in '70 and in the Western Conference finals to Milwaukee (the eventual champion) in '71. That meant Robertson had gotten his championship before West did. That had to hurt.

West should've been comfortably cast as a kind of Lion in Winter by the 1971–72 season, particularly considering the injuries and the agony of losing that weighed upon his soul. Curiously, though, he seemed to be getting better. He never won a regular-season MVP award, but he should've gotten it in 1970 when he averaged 31.2 points per game along with 7.5 assists and 4.6 rebounds. He was clearly the best player in the league. The MVP was New York's Willis Reed, and, no offense to The Captain, but he wasn't even the best player on the Knicks. That was Walt Frazier.

What made West so successful?

"First of all, he was a really unique athlete," says Pat Riley from his office in Miami. "Jerry had a great vertical, hops, long-ass arms, I mean *loooong* arms, great hands. And his competitive desire was off the charts. It was a quiet competitiveness. He was a very, very humble man, antisocial to an extent, and I think he channeled everything into competition."

West was a terrific shooter, back when shooters weren't all that terrific; aside from centers such as Chamberlain and Abdul-Jabbar, shooting percentages generally hovered in the 30s, and West finished his career with a .474 percentage. West told me, "I had to become a great shooter because, back in West Virginia, if I wasn't, the ball rolled down a damn hill and I had to chase it." That sounds like a delicious bit of mountain folklore, but West didn't seem to be kidding.

And West added this: "I was much more likely to create shots for myself on the road," he said. "I thought we needed them more in those situations. I always considered myself a better road player than a home player."

But West's rep as a shooter came mostly from his performance in the clutch and his ability to get off his jumper in traffic. "I seemed to concentrate more when defenders were all around me," West says. "I kind of compare it to baseball. I liked the heat, rather than the off-speed pitch. And I always thought two shots, the jumper and the drive, were enough. No use wasting around with the left hand. The dominant hand is enough. Players should use the rest of the time to work on defense."

Had West played in a later era, though, he would've had to develop more of a left hand, not so much for shooting (Bird used to launch a left-handed shot now and again just for the pure damn hell of it, and LeBron, Curry, and Kyrie Irving do it once in a while, too) but for dribbling. West would've faced much more pressure before he got into shooting mode because increasingly sophisticated defenses would've wanted, God knows, to take the ball out of his hand. Even when West went left, he often dribbled with his right hand, though he may have had a reason for that. In a 2015 story that Chris Ballard of *Sports Illustrated* wrote about West, he quotes the Logo mulling Curry as a dribbler:

> What if Curry dribbled with his right hand, rather than his left when he brought the ball up the left wing? He'd be able to see everything behind him and, when he made a pass to a cutter down the middle, it would be a shorter, two-hand pass, rather than a looping lefty one.

West bristles at the notion that he always went right (just as one of his Hall of Fame contemporaries, Lenny Wilkens, always went left), and he says that he increasingly went left as his career went on. But most observers remember him as most deadly going to his right.

"The first game I ever started was against Jerry," says D'Antoni, a native West Virginian who is good friends with West. "I was playing with Kansas City–Omaha [which became the Sacramento Kings] early in the '73–'74 season. Phil Johnson, our coach, is going over the scouting report and he tells me, 'Mike, you got Jerry. You know he only goes right. But don't worry because no one has stopped him yet, and you're sure as hell not going to do it.'"

Jim Barnett, who played against West and today is the color man for Warriors broadcasts, tells of the time late in West's career— Game 1 of the 1973 Western Conference finals at the Forum—when he was determined to make West go left.

"We're tied 99–99. I pick up Jerry, make him go left. He doesn't get his shot off but he's looking for it. I keep pushing him left, all the way left, make him terminate his dribble. I had him. I'm at his side where I can block the shot. But I'm afraid to go up with him because they'll call the foul and he'll sure as hell make two free throws to win it. But it doesn't matter, I figure. He can't make the shot from that angle. He's in the corner with his dribble stopped. I'm right on him. He's not in rhythm. So I let him shoot it. He makes it. They win. That's Jerry West."

What is undoubtedly true is that West's defense set him apart from most other guards. With Chamberlain, Abdul-Jabbar, Havlicek, Frazier, Hakeem Olajuwon, Jordan, Kobe, Tim Duncan, and LeBron—other nominees are welcome—he remains among the greatest two-way players in basketball history.

"I think defense was the thing that made me different," West says. "And no one really emphasized it growing up. In college, Fred Schaus didn't start thinking about defense until halfway through the season."

In *The Pivotal Season,* author Rosen gets a great comment from Baltimore's Jack Marin, a sharpshooting contemporary of West's, about the Logo's defense. Marin says that if West was back on defense in a 2-on-1 situation, it was a team rule that you just took it to the hole and hoped for the best. "West had such long arms that it was impossible to pass the ball anywhere near him without him reaching out and getting a piece of it," Marin told Rosen. Lenny Wilkens added this: "He had hands that were as quick as a snake's tongue."

In *Jerry West,* Roland Lazenby's bio, the author consults a longtime Lakers scorekeeper named John Radcliffe, who notes that West would undoubtedly be the NBA's all-time steals leader—"with little hope of anyone catching him"—had the league begun keeping steals stats before 1973–74, West's last year. Radcliffe says that West routinely had six steals a night and ten or more on numerous occasions. Jack Ramsay, who coached against West in both college and the pros, told Lazenby this: "Jerry was the first player I ever saw that would trail his man, and when the player went up to shoot the jump shot, he'd take the ball off his hand from behind. He did it repeatedly."

The fact that West remained so formidable as a defender had something to do with the arrival of Chamberlain in 1968. "If you beat Jerry," remembers Geoff Petrie, an outstanding offensive player with the Portland Trail Blazers, "he never gave up on you. He always followed you, chased you, and he could block your shot from behind. But let's say you get by him and now you have Wilt, who was such a gigantic figure in terms of the space he took up and his athleticism. So you have Jerry lurking and Wilt looming . . . what the hell do you do?"

With all of his talent, West's *look* had a lot to do with his legend. His face was an unreadable mask during games, stolid expression, every hair in place, a gentleman assassin. I quizzed West as to what he wore on his hair to keep it so tamped down. "Hell, I don't know, maybe a little hairspray or something," he answered and didn't want to pursue it further. His son Ryan still calls him "Cement Head," a reference both to his stubbornness and that unmovable hair.

In what has become Pat Riley's go-to anecdote about West's intensity, he remembers being in West's room on the fiftieth floor of a Kansas City hotel after a loss to the lowly Kansas City–Omaha Kings. He noticed West gazing out the window. "Don't do it," Riley said. Chick Hearn's widow, Marge, told West's co-author Coleman that every time the Lakers lost, her husband would say, "Let's get out of here. Jerry's down there going crazy again."

Strangely, West rarely lost his temper during games. Maybe his body furnace would've been better if he had let it out once or twice a game . . . or even once or twice a season.

"I came close to really losing it only one time," West said. "It was with Guy Rodgers." Rodgers was an outstanding playmaking guard whom his Warriors teammate Chamberlain considered, with an obvious slight directed at West, to be the best ever at setting him up. "Guy took a swing at two or three guys when their backs were turned. Sucker punched them. If he would've hit me, hell, I might've killed him. That's the result of being brought up in an abusive household. You don't give a damn what you do sometimes. I never let it come to that, because I was too scared at what I might do.

"I only got two technicals in my entire career, and they came in the same game in Phoenix [during the 1972–73 season]. I deflected the darn thing, went to get it, took one dribble, somebody stepped on my heel, and I went skidding across the floor. I looked at Darell Garretson and said, 'That's a foul.' He says, 'You tripped yourself.'

I say, 'You're a fucking idiot.' He gives me a T. I say, 'You might as well give me another one because you are a fucking idiot.' "

Remember that story. We shall return to it.

Going into the 1971–72 season, the Lakers were still looking for that coaching savior, some kind of West Coast version of Auerbach. Cooke had replaced van Breda Kolff with Joe Mullaney, who, like VBK, had come from the college ranks, in Mullaney's case, Providence. No one exactly blamed Mullaney for the Finals loss to the Knicks or the conference finals loss to the Bucks, but they didn't exactly *not* blame him. So Cooke, Schaus, scout Bertka, and Hearn, who by then had become a de facto team executive, gathered to discuss the dismissal of Mullaney and the coaching prospects.

Wooden, midway through his Wizard of Westwood act that would produce ten NCAA championships in twelve seasons, was a perennial candidate, even though he had let it be known that he had no interest in coaching the Lakers. That did not stop Schaus from haranguing the Wizard into taking a meeting at Cooke's house. As West and Coleman write in *West by West,* Wooden showed up and politely declined the offer. Cooke then pushed over a piece of paper that had a dollar figure on it, and Wooden said, "No coach is worth that money." At this point, Cooke threw Wooden out of his house. But let's not necessarily place Wooden in the company of angels; in making that decision he was choosing his campus bully pulpit and the support of deep-pocketed UCLA booster Sam Gilbert over the checkbook of the tweedy Cooke. (That wasn't the only time Cooke didn't get his way, incidentally. When he divorced from his first wife—he was married five times, twice to the same woman—he had to pay $42 million in what was then the largest divorce settlement in history. The presiding judge on the bench for the trial was none other than Joseph Wapner, who went on to fame on *The People's Court.*)

So the Lakers hierarchy looked elsewhere, ending up with the man who in 1975 would co-author a book with Wooden called *The Wooden-Sharman Method: A Guide to Winning Basketball.*

"Fred, who's the best coach in basketball right now?" Cooke asked his general manager at a meeting after the Wooden rejection.

"Bill Sharman," answered Schaus quickly. "He's an up-and-comer." As far as Bertka, the lone survivor from that meeting, can remember, no one mentioned the cold reality that Sharman was also an ex-Celtic, the shooting companion for Cousy in the NBA's first great backcourt duo.

Sharman had coached the Cleveland Pipers to the American Basketball League championship in 1962. He then moved to the Bay Area and coached the San Francisco Warriors into the 1967 NBA Finals, where they lost to Chamberlain's 76ers. (That was the same year, by the way, that a Haight-Ashbury pot bust at the home of the Grateful Dead was front-page news. Read a story in the *Chronicle* that could only have been constructed in the sixties: "The raid—on The Dead's way-out 13-room pad at 710 Ashbury St.—also led to the arrest of the group's equipment manager, two business managers and six girls, variously described as 'friends,' 'visitors' and 'just girls.'") For a lifestyle contrast, Sharman then moved on to Salt Lake City, where he coached the Utah Stars to the 1971 ABA title.

"Okay, I want Bill Sharman to coach the Lakers," said Cooke, as if he were announcing he wanted that particular eye roast on display in the meat case.

"Well, he's under contract," said Schaus.

"I want Bill Sharman," said Cooke.

"He's under contract with the Stars," repeated Schaus.

At this point Cooke turned to Hearn and, in his best scrotum-shrinking voice, said, "Francis. Tell. Fred. Schaus. I. Want. Bill. Sharman. To. Coach. The. Lakers."

"There wasn't a lot of doubt in his voice," remembers Bertka.

So Schaus made the call, Cooke made the terms of the deal, and Sharman became a Laker, eventually winning a court case against the Stars, who had sued for breach of contract. Whatever Cooke wanted, Cooke got, it seemed, except for a conquest of the Celtics. At the introductory press conference, Cooke, dripping with unctuous formality, announced him as "William. Walton. Sharman." The *Los Angeles Times* headlined it this way: "Free Throw Champion of the Universe Meets Basketball's Favorite Bridesmaids."

The generally positive stories about Sharman that followed the announcement contained only one dissenting view, that from one Rick Barry, who had played under Sharman for one season with the Warriors. Barry liked him as a human being, he said, but hated him as a coach, an opinion that continues today, forty-six years later. "He made basketball like my job instead of fun," Barry told me in 2017. "No time off, too serious."

As West recalls it now, he was comfortable with the decision to hire an ex-Celtic. "I didn't think much about the connection," West said. "But I also didn't know if he'd be a great coach. What I did know was that he was a terrific competitor." Their playing paths had crossed only briefly—Sharman retired after West's rookie season—as West remembers it there had been talk about the Lakers trading him to Boston, right after he was drafted, in exchange for Sharman becoming the first coach of the Lakers in L.A. Auerbach nixed the deal. (West says that he came close to being traded only one other time, this in the late sixties when he was unhappy about his contractual dealings with Cooke and a possible trade to Phoenix for Charlie Scott was discussed. It never seemed to be serious from the Lakers' perspective.)

Riley, however, remembers that West was apoplectic about the thought that a Celtic would be leading them. West's high school team in West Virginia used to pretend they were Celtics—West, a terrific rebounder, was center "Easy Ed" Macauley—but that infatuation had long been replaced by a deep and lasting disaffection with the team in green. "Jerry couldn't believe we had gotten Sharman," Riley said in 2017. "It drove him nuts." Plus, Sharman had fought with Cooke to bring along an assistant as his defensive specialist, one K. C. Jones, still *another* Celtic and, further, one whom some of the Lakers considered to be a dirty player, probably because Jones had tortured them so much over the years. "I wouldn't exactly use the word *dirty*," says West today when asked about Jones. "K.C. was very athletic, very difficult to play against. He grabbed, he held, he did everything. It was a big adjustment playing against him."

Cooke pushed back against the assistant request, asking why Sharman should have an assistant when he didn't have one. In point of fact, Cooke had a dozen assistants, considering the monarchial manner by which he ran his business. But an assistant coach was an unknown quantity in the NBA back then. What the hell was he going to do? Throughout the sixties and well into the seventies, an NBA bench looked spare: the players, the head coach, and a trainer, whose job it was to keep track of fouls, tape ankles, arrange travel schedules, and locate the bars with the highest percentage of female clientele. Bertka had lobbied Sharman for the assistant job, too. No, insisted Sharman, I want Jones. He wanted him to work particularly with Gail Goodrich, an outstanding scorer but reluctant defender who would be West's backcourt partner. Cooke finally relented and the following year even allowed Sharman to make Bertka the NBA's first "second assistant."

West had never played against Sharman in the Finals, but K.C. had faced off against the Lakers four times in the championship round. More pain for West—Jones would be a living, breathing reminder of West's ultimate frustration. *Two former Celtics telling me what to do,* West thought. *How the hell is that possibly going to work out?*

*"I live and breathe this twenty-four hours a day.
This is the most exciting thing you can ever do.
It's every man's dream. I am a Warrior."*

—JOE LACOB

CHAPTER 7

When Peter Met Joe

After Steph Curry's name was called on Draft Day 2009, there was absolutely nothing to indicate that anything productive, never mind magical, would ensue for Golden State. Consider what the other principals who would later be a part of a phenomenally successful franchise rise were doing at the time.

- In 2008 Joe Lacob had earned a championship ring with the Boston Celtics, where he had been a part owner and third in command. But he had sold his chunk and was looking around for new opportunities where he could be the capo. Warriors owner Chris Cohan was ready to sell—something he should've done years earlier for the sake of the franchise—and Lacob was intrigued. The Warriors were near his Silicon Valley base, after all. Perhaps he could get a group together to buy the Warriors. But even for a VC risk-taker like Lacob, Golden State did not look like a particularly sound investment.

- Peter Guber was involved in his usual thousand things and was looking on with interest as Los Angeles Dodgers owner Frank McCourt dug himself a deeper and deeper financial hole with lavish personal spending. Guber thought: *Maybe buy into Major League Baseball if the Dodgers become available?* He wasn't thinking much about basketball and certainly not about the Warriors. He was not a huge hoops fan. Guber was also working on his third book, teaching business courses at UCLA, and executive-producing four movies that made it onto TV screens that year, all from books by the prolific romance writer Nora Roberts, a close friend of Guber's. God only knows what else he was up to.

- Steve Kerr was in his final year as general manager of the Phoenix Suns. He was disappointed that Larry Riley was not going to give up Curry, but it wasn't like he was passing up a revolutionary player, right? Kerr figured they might get a long-armed defender at number fifteen named Earl Clark, which turned out to be the case. (Clark batted around the league for six years and was never successful.)

- Bob Myers was a highly respected player agent at the Wasserman Media Group. He had learned his lessons well from his mentor, Arn Tellem, and had no thoughts of running a franchise.

- Mike Brown, who would be Kerr's chief assistant on the 2017 champions, had just wrapped up a superlative 66-16 season as head coach of the Cavaliers. But Dwight Howard was a monster in those days for the Orlando Magic, and Brown's (and LeBron James's) Cavs had bowed out in six games in the Eastern Conference finals. Brown's job was in perennial jeopardy; one sideways look from LeBron and he could be gone, which he was the following season.

- Kevin Durant was wrapping up his second year in the NBA, having already experienced the disorientation of moving—his Seattle SuperSonics had become the Oklahoma City Thunder after his rookie year. OKC finished with a miserable 23-59 record, but Durant had played splendidly with a scoring average of 25.3 points per game. He also had obvious chemis-

try with a quicksilver rookie named Russell Westbrook.
Could they become the NBA's next great tandem?

- Klay Thompson had completed a modest freshman year at
Washington State with a 12.5 scoring average. Nobody
thought much about him other than he was the son of former
Laker Mychal Thompson. If you wanted a quote from the
quiet and reserved Klay—and you probably didn't—you
would have to settle for one about Klay from his talkative
dad.

- Draymond Green was finished with a freshman year at Michigan State that could not even be described as modest. He averaged 3.3 in both points and rebounds and took exactly one
three-point shot the entire season, which he missed. He was
on no one's draft board.

- Jerry West was getting antsy. Two years earlier he had left the
Memphis Grizzlies, where he had run the show for five years,
and was back in Los Angeles. He was playing golf and even
became executive director of the Northern Trust Open, a PGA
Tour stop. But it wasn't enough. He continued to take phone
calls from everyone, kept his eyes and ears open, gracefully
handled the seductions from NBA teams. He watched with
much agita as the Celtics beat the Lakers in the 2008 Finals,
then watched with joy as the Lakers won back the championship in 2009. He had never really stopped being a Laker. But
he needed a gig.

- As for the Warriors team on Draft Day 2009, well, they
were just happy that the season was over. The "We Believe"
team of 2006–07 had been forgotten, replaced by a chemical
mess of an aggregation that had won twenty-nine games in
2008–09 and didn't believe in anything. Strangely, it was one
of the most balanced scoring teams in NBA history, with
eight players who averaged in double figures for points per
game and a ninth with 9.5. But that was part of the problem.
It had no leadership, no identity, no personality.

Curry looked around and saw nary a simpatico teammate. There
was Stephen Jackson, whose series of off-court troubles included a

charge of criminal recklessness for firing a gun outside a strip club (he pleaded guilty and paid a fine). There was Monta Ellis, a talented offensive player who was moody and inconsistent. There was Corey Maggette, who was that rare Duke product to be a certified underachiever through much of his career.

(In fairness, though, Jackson and Ellis were Golden State fan favorites. The former would be brought back for franchise appearances often during the 2016–17 season and evinced a few smiles when he admitted to a fondness for ganja and told of Don Nelson's willingness to look the other way. As for Ellis, we will soon see what happened when management opened the front door for Curry and showed Ellis out the back.)

Team Curry's worries about the Warriors went beyond personnel. There were rumors that the franchise would be sold, which always casts an unsettled air. Then again, perhaps a sale would be a good thing. Golden State was still under the control of Cohan, who over the years had excelled in only one area—litigiousness. A 2002 *Chronicle* story revealed that, at that time, Cohan was involved in at least six lawsuits, three of them against old friends, two of whom had been in his wedding. (One disenchanted Golden State diehard wrote on a Warriors fan website: "I hate Chris Cohan. I hate his wife. I hate his mother, his children, his grandchildren and his dog. The biggest mistake in human history was when Cohan's mother met his father.") Cohan had become disengaged from the team and handed most of the day-to-day over to a man named Robert Rowell, who was not in any way, shape, or form qualified to run a basketball team. "Cohan was a dreadful guy," says Meschery, the old Warrior who had begun to stay away from the team during the Cohan years. "All he cared about was money."

Golden State . . . where dreams go to die.

Joe Lacob arrives, to quote our president, "bigly." At about 6'0" with an average build, he is neither small nor large, but his presence manages to be oversized, as are so many of those who made their millions in Silicon Valley. Stern refers to Lacob, fondly, as "a tire-kicker." Says Stern: "Joe was always looking for a team. He'd come in, take a look, kick a few tires, come back a year later and do the same thing." In 2006 Lacob stopped kicking and bought in, becoming part owner of the Celtics. "Russell, K. C. Jones, Havlicek, Sam Jones," says Lacob. "They were the guys I grew up watching."

It seems like the Celtics, then, would've been his dream buy-in, but they weren't. "I'm an all-or-nothing type of guy," says Lacob, "not a limited-partner type of guy. I was living in California, and it's hard to run a team when you're not near it. Being involved with the Celtics was a great thing in many ways. I learned a lot about how the league operates. But you just have to be *there,* and I wasn't there."

The Lacob family had headed west before Joe was in high school. He was a go-getter, tossing peanuts to fans in Angels Stadium, where he began working part-time as a high school freshman. "You showed up in the parking lot every day, and if you did well selling you got picked the next day," Lacob told me in a 2016 interview. "I was a Red Sox fan who became an Angels fan." And, more unusually, a Celtics fan who became a Lakers fan. "That's much more complicated," says Lacob.

Lacob studied biology at the University of California–Irvine and got a master's in public health from UCLA. Along the way he found out that his real talent was entrepreneurship (he didn't get into the top medical schools), so he got an MBA from Stanford. He used that and his medical background to start numerous medical-related companies by the time he was thirty, and he ended up being one of five managing partners at Kleiner Perkins, one of the world's largest venture-capital firms, arguably *the* ur-VC firm in Silicon Valley. While Guber was working with Hollywood stars, Lacob was doing the same thing with the pantheon of Silicon Valley. "We've done some of the biggest companies in the world," says Lacob. "I've seen everything. I was here when Sergey came in to make his first pitch." That would be Sergey Mikhaylovich Brin, co-founder of Google. "I was just the right guy at the right time," says Lacob. "When everyone else was out chasing women, I was doing something else. But no matter how much money I made, always back here [he taps his head] was swirling this idea of owning a sports team. That was my endgame."

Lacob is a certified, full-throated fan. "I always loved sports," says Lacob, who still plays a weekly pickup hoops game at Stanford. "I'm a six-foot Jewish guy, so I had limitations. I played a lot of sports, including basketball, but I wasn't that good.

"Look, I know this sounds crazy, but the first time I ever saw a basketball court—I was maybe nine years old—at the Boys' Club, I was enthralled by it. The hardwood caught my imagination, and I thought, *I want to be rich enough to own a team. Maybe baseball but probably basketball.* I could never get hardwood out of my head." (And, yes, he is a bit of a hardhead.)

Lacob was one of those fathers that everybody, especially his own family, wants to boot out of the gym. "He lived to come to my games, and I mean he was at *every* one," says Kirk Lacob, now the Warriors assistant general manager. "He sat at midcourt yelling at me. 'Look up! Pass the ball! Hit the shot!' At one point my mom got so mad she made him go watch from the hallway. During timeouts I could look out there and see him talking to himself.

"By the time I started playing in high school I had developed this ability to stop hearing him. I mean that honestly. I could hear everything else going on in the gym, including the stands. But not my father's voice."

Peter Guber arrives "youngly," appearing suddenly from around a steep corner in his driveway, putt-putting his personal golf cart directly from Bel-Air Country Club, which he can reach on a private path from his home in Brentwood. His Mediterranean Revival sits on ten manicured rolling acres overlooking the city. Guber bought it in the early nineties from Grant Tinker and his better-known wife, the late Mary Tyler Moore. "I can ride this path directly to the breakfast room," Guber says. Of course he has a pathway directly to Wolfgang Puck's breakfast room at Bel-Air; figuratively speaking, Guber has a pathway directly to almost everywhere.

Guber is seventy-five but looks at least a decade younger, maybe more. Somewhere, Dorian Gray–like, there might be a photo of Peter Guber getting older.

For almost a half century Guber has been a fixture in Hollywood as a movie executive (he was studio chief at Columbia when he was twenty-eight) and producer, responsible to some degree over the years for films as diverse as *The Last Detail, Close Encounters of the Third Kind, Shampoo, Taxi Driver, Midnight Express, Rain Man, The Color Purple, Flashdance, Missing,* and, well, the list goes on and on. If he's not on the Mount Rushmore of Hollywood moguls, he's in the conversation.

Among his other production credits is a little thing called *Batman*—the original 1989 version with Michael Keaton and Jack Nicholson—which explains why the original Batman costume sits in his home office, silent guardian of all the treasures that lie within— a screening room that seats twenty, an art deco billiard table, four Academy Awards, dozens of personally signed photos from Hollywood royalty as well as regular folk like Nelson Mandela and Hillary Clinton, gold records (he formed Casablanca Record and Filmworks), a collection of autographed baseballs by Cy Young winners (and one from Cy himself), a wide assortment of movie posters (there's one in French for *Le Couleur pourpre*), and replicas of all the major trophies and awards won by the Warriors, such as Curry's back-to-back MVPs.

Perfectly understandable, then, that the creaky gate that admits you to Chez Guber is the original gate that stood at the entrance to Jurassic Park. He didn't have anything to do with the movie, but, when you're Peter Guber and you want a certain gate, you get the damn gate.

Like Lacob, Guber, the son of a junk dealer, grew up in Massachusetts. One summer he even heard Auerbach give a clinic. His family was close with Maurice Podoloff, the first NBA commissioner, and Guber was a Celtics fan, scoring free albeit obstructed-view seats to watch games at the old Boston Garden. "To this day," says Guber, a storyteller of the first order, "people ask me why I move my head around at games, and I tell them: Because I have years of sitting behind a post."

"I'm guessing your seats have gotten better over the years," Guber's guest says.

"Better," he answers, "but much more expensive."

Guber's primacy as a movie mogul moved him into the circle of the Showtime Lakers in the eighties. He has been a longtime friend of Pat Riley's—the Rileys and the Gubers once took a trip together to the Grand Canyon—and in the early nineties Guber went into business with Magic Johnson. Guber is the one to whom Magic pitched the idea of opening movie theaters in underserved African-American areas around Los Angeles. They're still in business together, owning a little thing called the Los Angeles Dodgers, the name partners in Guggenheim Baseball Management, which paid $2 billion for the franchise in 2012.

Guber was not—still isn't to a large degree—a die-hard sports fan à la Lacob. He likes to buy things and turn them into profitable businesses. Hell, he tried to buy NBC when he was running Sony, but the government ruled that a foreign company could not have control of an American broadcasting company. He was never the kind of guy to buy a team so he could wave the pom-poms. "I wasn't after sports teams," Guber says. "I was after the media and the venues." He holds the same pragmatic notions about movies. "It's called show *business*," he says. "It's not called show *show*."

Guber went to Lakers games because he knew Riley and it was, as he says, "just part of the L.A. culture," part of what a plugged-in L.A. guy does. From his courtside seat he could exchange pleasantries with legit superfan Jack Nicholson, whom Guber helped convince to sign on to *Batman* as the Joker. When Guber began buying into sports he sunk his money into the much less glamorous business of minor-league baseball, where he could, and did, turn a profit. He almost bought the Lakers, the Kings, and the Forum from Jerry Buss only because he was trying to buy Prime Ticket, a regional sports network owned by Buss, and those entities had to be part of the deal. (It fell apart because Guber's deal partner, Bruce McNall, was being investigated for banking practices and was later convicted and served nearly five years for bank and wire fraud.)

Guber thought he had a deal to buy the Oakland A's in 2001—again, it was to make money, not because he liked to swap Reggie Jackson and Sal Bando stories—but that deal also fell through. A few years later he met Lacob, who had also failed in an attempt to buy the A's. Now the duo decided they wanted to buy the Dodgers, and thought they had them until McCourt swooped in and bought the team alone.

But then, near the end of 2009, came an opportunity that got Lacob more excited than usual, and he is an excitable guy—the Warriors were going to be sold in an auction. Cohan had at last decided definitively to get out. In 2007 the IRS said he owed more than $160 million in back taxes and penalties.

Lacob couldn't believe his luck. *Basketball. That magic hardwood. Right in his neighborhood!* He was already a season-ticket holder, screaming his lungs out at the frustrating failures of a franchise that took two steps backward for every one step forward. So Lacob called Guber. "I'm working on this deal, and I think we can get it," he said. "I'd like you to join with me."

The main don't-go-near-this-team sign was obvious—the Warriors stunk, reeling under mismanagement that was more like non-management. It was a franchise steeped, simmered, and stewed in failure. But Lacob saw a hometown team in his grasp, and Guber saw a devalued product with potential, kind of like a mediocre film that could be made better with the injection of a star performer and an experienced director. "You have to have the belief and conviction you can change the trajectory of the franchise," says Guber. "How do you know you can do that? Well, you never know for sure, but the business that you're going into, apart from your franchise, has to be in an upswing. The NBA, I believed it was. So did Joe.

"Then we looked at the market. The Bay Area is a rich basketball market with a robust fan base. And we thought we had the skill set to improve the business. So we dove in."

From the beginning Lacob has been the majority partner. At league meetings Lacob takes the lead seat, Guber the secondary one, and Lacob speaks for the franchise. "I wanted to be the Guy," says Lacob, who put in somewhere over $100 million of the $450 million purchase price. "I wanted to be on the firing line. I looked at this as kind of my second game in life. I wanted to have a lot on the line and put my money where my mouth is." That was fine with Guber, who put in about $30 million. He had enough money in other ventures, and, anyway, he knew that something else would come along for which he would need capital. (Which turned out to be the Dodgers.)

"Joe is a basketball guy," says Bob Myers. "He's not someone who made a lot of money, bought a basketball team, and only then decided to like the game. If he didn't own the Warriors, he'd still have a season ticket."

"I don't think they necessarily looked at it this way at the time, but they were the perfect team," says Rick Welts, who was hired by the new owners to be Golden State's president and chief of operations. "Joe is a financial genius who is driven by basketball. Still plays, loves being around the coaches, loves talking basketball, loves being in the draft room, the whole thing. Peter is focused on completely different things. He adds value on the player side because he's a great talent manager and has spent his whole life managing stars. But his real focus is on the experience that fans have. That's his background from someone who's been in movies and music. He thinks about the audience."

The $450 million purchase price broke the NBA record—banker Robert Sarver had the previous mark of $401 million, which he paid for the Phoenix Suns in 2004—and in most circles was roundly derided as an absurd amount to pay for an in-the-doldrums franchise. "There's no doubt that Joe and Peter overpaid for the team," says Austin, Curry's agent. Even Lacob and Guber knew that, but they were going against Larry Ellison (the founder of the company that in 2006 paid for naming rights to the arena) and really thought that they could turn the Warriors into a financial winner. "There's a certain amount of luck involved," says Guber. "You have to be the highest bidder at the right moment. Nobody thought we would beat out Ellison. There was a headline in one paper: 'Ellison Wins Bid.' It was 'Dewey Defeats Truman' all over."

Lacob and Guber didn't do it alone. A number of Lacob's Silicon Valley playmates came aboard, reflecting a trend in sports—basketball was becoming the tech world's new favorite playtoy.

"Increasingly people who have made substantial wealth are

looking for investments that bring not only profits but fun," says David Stern. "Plus, basketball seems to have that ability to turn things around quickly for an investor if you're any good. Given the NBA's digital and global footprints, that's a very attractive strategy for a business."

The deal went through in July 2010. Joe and Kirk Lacob, who would soon be working for the Warriors—his father and friends call him "Rain Man" for his facility at remembering basketball facts and figures—were taking a trip through Greece and were on their way to visit the Oracle at Delphi. On that day there were a lot of quips about the Oracle, where the Warriors play their home games, and also where, in his office, Larry Ellison was getting used to the idea that he had finished second in something.

"The deal wasn't a cure for cancer," said Guber at the time, "but it was a cure for Cohan."

Life didn't change all that much for Guber, who is so absurdly busy that one suspects he is cloned. He just bought an e–sports team (whatever that is), he's in the middle of a group building a stadium in downtown Los Angeles, and he's still teaching. You want to get Guber really wound up, don't ask about Robert De Niro's Method acting or Durant's post-ups; try grade inflation in today's institutions of higher learning. "I may not be the smartest guy around," Guber said to me in 2016, "but I am a motherfucker hard worker. My feet, my tongue, my heart, and my wallet go in the same direction. I am blessed. My mom died at ninety-eight, my dad died at ninety-six, and I had an aunt who died at a hundred and five." Guber's clear point was that he expects to be working that long. "You know what counts? Aliveness. I have a lot of *aliveness*."

Behind the scenes, these two high-powered men have had some dustups; given their oversized personalities, it's amazing they have not been made public. Mostly they're about process. Guber is a visionary, Lacob is a man who has a P&L and sticks to it. But mostly they stay in their respective lanes.

Lacob's life changed more dramatically after the purchase. He decided that he would remain on the thirteen boards on which he was active, but he pledged to go to no new business meetings, review no new deals, and get in on no new funds. As the more active

partner, he would begin a schedule of seeing about seventy-five percent of Warriors games live. When he comes home at night he looks
at box scores from around the league, not the Nikkei Exchange.

"I don't care about the market anymore," he said. "I live and
breathe this twenty-four hours a day. This is the most exciting thing
you can ever do. It's every man's dream. I am a Warrior.

"I love everything about this, and I really want us to be the best.
The *best*. I want to *dominate* the NBA every year. I will be at every
important meeting; I will be in that locker room. I know what these
guys are thinking, and I let them know what I'm thinking."

Good thing Lacob approached it like that, because there was
much work to be done. The team was coming off a 26-56 season.
The idea of even making the playoffs seemed absurd. The first
regular-season game that Lacob and Guber saw together was October 27, 2010. The Warriors beat the Rockets 132–128.

Despite the win, Guber, watching the game from a producer's
perspective, wasn't happy. "It was absolutely the worst fan experience I ever had," he says.

But Lacob, who knew basketball, or thought he did, was cheered.
The kid Curry looked pretty good with twenty-five points, but the
real star was Curry's backcourt mate, Monta Ellis. He had forty-six
in the win. Moving forward, Lacob thought, Ellis looks like the
Guy. And you always need the Guy.

"It's sort of a shame. I can only imagine what Elgin and Jerry went through all those years against the Celtics."

—PAT RILEY

CHAPTER 8

Elegant Elgin Exits

Nine games into what turned out to be one of the most extraordinary seasons in NBA history, an extraordinary moment occurs at a Los Angeles Lakers' practice session at the Forum. The site in itself was unusual because the team usually worked out at a local college, Loyola Marymount. The date is November 5, 1971. The Lakers are 6-3 at the time, and first-year coach Bill Sharman is dissatisfied with their play. He's threatening to fine everyone, including himself. Jerry West missed all three of those losses with an injury.

As his teammates work out at one end, Elgin Baylor stands, hands on hips, talking to Sharman and general manager Fred Schaus. There are no raised voices, there is no drama. Baylor was never about drama unless he was up in the air holding a basketball and figuring out what to do with it. Neither are there any cameras to record the moment. These days a reporter would've seen Baylor walk away, caught up to him in the hallway, talked a minute or two, and sent out a tweet that, through retweets and other avenues of social media, would've reached millions of people within thirty minutes. "Elgin Baylor Retires" would've most assuredly *trended*. But it didn't happen that way four decades ago.

Baylor nods and leaves practice, never to suit up again in the Lakers' colors of purple ("Forum blue," as Cooke insisted it be called) and gold. The Lakers play that night with second-year forward Jim McMillian in Baylor's stead. They beat the Baltimore Bullets 110–106.

And don't lose again for sixty-five days and thirty-two games.

What exactly was said in that meeting remains a matter of conjecture, the stuff of Lakers legend. The official word that has drifted down through the years is that it was Baylor's decision to retire when Sharman told him that he had gotten too old, that the ball was "sticking" when it got to him, that he was the impediment to the fast-break style that the coach wanted to implement.

Over the years Sharman described the meeting in a couple of different ways. One went like this: "Elgin, I feel terrible, but I know you have a bad leg that's bothering you very much so I thought I'd bring you in as a substitute. Elgin told me, 'I don't want to be a substitute and I'm still injured, so it's best that I retire.'"

On another instance Sharman said it came down this way: "Elg, I'm not going to start you for a while and let's see what happens because if you don't play as much you might be faster and play a little better and have more fun. Elgin was disappointed, no doubt about it, and said, 'Bill, I've had a great career. I'm just going to hang it up.'"

Here's what Baylor told this interviewer in 2016:

> The things I used to do I could no longer do as well. I knew it was time. I didn't want to embarrass myself. I was talking to Sharman, and he said, "How would you feel about giving McMillian a chance to get more minutes?" He wasn't going to take me out of the lineup. He didn't say that in so many words.
>
> It would've been selfish to keep playing. And it was tough because I thought we could win it that year. Hey, Russell had retired, right? So I made the decision to retire.

Other versions have been given, on and off the record, and here's the one that seems the most credible:

Sharman, with the backing of management, had become convinced that McMillian had to play and Baylor had to sit. But he immediately sensed Baylor's resistance to sitting. There are few things more potentially damaging to a team than a superstar who isn't in the rotation, so it was clear to Sharman that Baylor should retire to spare himself embarrassment and also to get away from the team, where he might be tempted to snipe from the bench. In exchange for stepping away, Baylor's retirement would be treated as if he were being cut—that is, Cooke would pay him. Now, spending an extra nickel he didn't have to was not in Cooke's DNA, but the honeymoon phase between owner and coach had just begun. Sharman, who was handpicked by Cooke to win a championship, wanted Baylor gone. So Baylor would be gone.

And one wonders:

Was that the exact moment that Elgin Baylor—an icon of the early days of the NBA, a player way ahead of his time, a man who stood up to racism—tumbled from the Lakers' temple like an outcast angel? Or was it later, in 1986, when he signed on as general manager of the Clippers? Or did it come about as a more gradual process, the result of being away from the Lakers, turning into a version of that once-important patriarch who becomes less and less of a welcome sight at family reunions?

Pat Riley partly blames Baylor. "I think Elgin could still have helped us a lot coming off the bench, but he refused," says Riley. "Then they were going to pay him to be an ambassador, but he turned his back on the team. I didn't feel it so much, because I had just joined the Lakers. But guys like Jerry and Wilt, guys he had played with, resented the fact that he just left and almost never came around.

"It's sort of a shame. I can only imagine what Elgin and Jerry went through all those years against the Celtics. As great as they both were, that had to be very painful. And they also had to look at each other in the eye and think, *We're not doing enough for each other to help us win. We need somebody else.*"

West got his somebody else in Chamberlain; Baylor never did. He never even got a playoff share from the Lakers' championship season of 1971–72. And when the franchise began to put up statues in front of the Staples Center like latter-day Greeks, the name of Elgin Baylor did not come up. Or at least never got very far. There was an early suggestion that West and Baylor be joined in one statue, recognizing their binary significance to the franchise. But that idea went nowhere. West went up alone. So did Kareem Abdul-Jabbar, Magic Johnson, Chick Hearn, and Shaquille O'Neal, with Kobe Bryant due in 2018.

Baylor conceded during the 2016 interview, that, yes, he would've liked a longer and deeper relationship with the organization he helped get to the top. "But I don't think about it a lot," he was careful to add.

How about the statue? Do you think about that?

"He thought about it," cut in Elaine Baylor, "because I brought it up. But it didn't go anywhere."

She is furious that her husband's legacy seems to go unrecognized.

As for Elgin?

"What's important is what you accomplished on the floor," he says. "Anyway, why do I want a statue out there and have the birds messing with it." *I used to sneak some helium in my sneakers.*

The statue of West went up on February 17, 2011. Among those who spoke at the ceremony were Kareem, Magic, and Riley. Along with Elgin Baylor.

There was positively, absolutely no sign that this Lakers team, 6-3 when Baylor departed, was going anywhere. The problems had started with Wilt and Elgin. Both liked to station themselves on the left side of the basket and operate from a post-up position on that block. They got in each other's way quite often, and that happened off the court, too. For almost a decade Baylor had been the dominant presence in the locker room, leader of discussions, dispenser of nicknames, de facto chairman of the poker games. That ended when Wilt, the quintessential Big Personality, came aboard. "When Wilt got there," says Keith Erickson, "all of a sudden he was the biggest, the loudest, and the strongest."

Remember that Wilt existed on a different level of stardom than anyone else, even the beloved Laker twins Baylor and West. As a Globetrotter, Wilt had met kings and princes. He was always the biggest show in town, literally and figuratively. On a Wilt team, everyone was middle management except for Wilt. After Wilt arrived, Baylor's nicknames weren't so much fun anymore, and as Baylor's physical skills diminished along with his command of the team, it started to eat him up inside.

As for West and Wilt, all seemed to be fine. But in this, his third year with the team, Wilt had begun to resent what he saw as a protective shield placed around West. Chamberlain had already come to the Lakers with the notion that neither West nor Baylor wanted him there, believing that the team had voted 9–2 against getting him in a trade. "I guess guys like Elgin Baylor and Jerry West were afraid I'd come to Los Angeles and take some of their glory away," he later wrote in his autobiography.

West dismisses this as nonsense and doesn't remember any team vote. "They asked me about it, and I said, 'Of course we should go after Wilt Chamberlain.'" Baylor says he doesn't remember a team vote either, and said he was fine with Chamberlain coming, though given how they got along there is reason to doubt that Elgin was fully behind the addition. On or even deep off the record, West is still reluctant to bash Wilt, preferring to remember him as "complex and lonely." He speaks fondly of dinners they had together on the road in Wilt's hotel room. West considers himself the Eternal Laker, and Lakers don't bash Lakers. (They do bash Lakers owners from time to time, though.)

Wilt praises West in many parts of his autobiography but always seems to find a way to belittle him, too. Certainly Wilt resented that some of West's popularity derived from his unwillingness to be confrontational or, put another way, from his determination to be neutral in most situations. Since West was a team leader and a major figure in the NBA, Wilt believed that West should've taken it upon himself to have spoken out more, and that he did not do so for political reasons, not because of a quiet nature.

Remember the double technical that got West ejected from the game in Phoenix? Chamberlain wrote this in *Wilt:* "He [West] thought the official had screwed him, and he said so. But he wouldn't criticize the official in public. When reporters asked him about what had happened, he put on his contrite, little-boy-next-door look and said, 'I have never been so embarrassed in my life.'"

Again, this came out over a year after the 1971–72 season, and it may have been co-author Shaw who reminded Wilt of it. But Wilt certainly endorsed the sentiment. Chick Hearn's excessive admiration for West had a lot to do with Wilt's feelings that, no matter what he did, he would be considered a second-class citizen in West World. "He [Hearn] has one slight problem; he thinks Jerry West is Jesus Christ," Wilt wrote. There is little doubt that Chick's praise of West was indeed fulsome. Then again, George Raveling had said the same thing about West, in lighter terms, when West was still at West Virginia.

It was all of a piece, a lifelong Nixonian theme, as Wilt saw it. He would never be fully appreciated. That was for other players, Caucasians, those who played it safe, solid citizens like West. One can only imagine how Wilt felt when none other than Russell had flown in to help celebrate Jerry West Night at the Forum during the 1970–71 season. Wilt did call West "one of the most unprejudiced guys I've ever known," but he also resented the fact that West was among those considered to be the proverbial Great White Hope. There was never anyone celebrated as the Great Black Hope.

As always, there were personal distractions swirling around Wilt at the beginning of the 1971–72 season, the most bizarre having ended right before training camp began. That was his planned boxing exhibition against Ali.

Wilt had long been a boxing aficionado and seemed receptive when he was approached about fighting the Greatest. Wilt and Ali sometimes referred to each other as friends, but they were not close. There was always an edge to their relationship. Both needed and commanded the stage. Ali considered Wilt somewhat of a carnival joke, while Wilt considered Ali pretentious and not, as we already know, as smart as he pretended to be.

Several irresistible YouTube clips exist in which Wilt and Ali, nicely dressed in suits and ties, discuss with Howard Cosell their planned fight. Ali could get under anyone's skin, and Wilt, though he held it together pretty well, was no exception. At one point, Wilt pulls out a pen from his sport-coat pocket and urges Ali to sign.

"Just hold on to your pen now . . ." Ali says.

"How long?" Wilt says. "How long do I wait?"

"Don't start popping off now," Ali answers.

Cosell gathers them together and calls in Ali's trainer, Angelo Dundee, and his handler, Bundini Brown. Brown measures the comparative wingspans, Wilt's coming in at ninety-two inches, Ali's at seventy-eight. It was great theater.

"Reach don't mean nothing if you can't find anything there," says Ali, reasonably. "This don't mean nothing," Ali says later. "David slew Goliath." To infuriate Wilt, Ali adds, "I got Bill Russell to be one of my sparring partners." Then he points to Wilt's goatee and says, "Cut that beard off because I'm not fighting a billy goat." Ali won a unanimous decision, as he almost always did in verbal sparring matches, but Wilt took it all in with an easy grace and didn't appear intimidated.

The match was eventually set for July 26 in the Houston Astrodome, and there was even a prefight presser. Asked what he thought the result would be, Ali said, repeatedly, "T-imm-beerrrr!"

Eventually, negotiations fell apart because, according to Chamberlain, Ali's people reneged on a verbal agreement to pay him $500,000 after taxes. (Ali was to get $1 million.) Chamberlain even includes a photo of that page of the contract in his autobiography. The Lakers were, of course, relieved. Cooke never did want Wilt to go along with it. "That fight crowd's a sleazy crowd," Cooke told him. "You don't want to get mixed up with them." That advice was dispensed soon after Cooke had put up the money for the first Ali–Joe Frazier fight in Madison Square Garden.

With the fight talk behind him, Chamberlain turned his attention to another major distraction: the house he was building on three acres atop the Santa Monica Mountains, overlooking the San Fernando Valley and the Pacific Ocean. It was an oversized palace for an oversized king, oddly triangular-shaped. An account of the construction of the house suggests what Egyptian slaves went through to build the pyramids. Five railroad cars full of redwood, for example, were taken to the top of the mountain. In the style pages of the newspapers it was invariably referred to as a "sybaritic paradise," careful attention devoted to the custom-made seventy-two-square-foot bed. The one thing Wilt liked to go on and on about was the nose fur from seventeen thousand wolves that was used to make his bedspread and rugs. It is relevant to point out that People for the Ethical Treatment of Animals did not come along until 1980.

But the big question mark for the Lakers was about this guy who was going to replace the legend that was Baylor. Jim McMillian? What's he, an Irish bartender? McMillian had been Bertka's draft choice. Bertka had seen him play in the Quaker City Tournament in Philadelphia and was impressed by his intelligence, feel for the game, and ability to play away from the basket, both on offense and defense.

Still, Bertka knew that McMillian would be a tough sell. McMillian played at Columbia, and, while Ivy League pros weren't all that unusual (Princeton's Bill Bradley was already a solid pro entering his fifth season with the Knicks), they still raised an eyebrow. More to the point, McMillian didn't *look* like a star and certainly didn't look like Baylor. At 6'5" and two hundred and twenty-five pounds, he was short-legged and wide-bodied. *Chunky* was the word Bertka used to describe him. Bayne says in his Baylor bio that Elgin called him "Floyd Butterball," alluding to both his build and his resemblance to boxer Floyd Patterson. Chamberlain shortened it to "Butter." But they weren't asking Jimmy Mac to be in a beauty pageant, and Bertka sold McMillian to Schaus.

The draft in those days was a low-key affair, barely on the media radar screen, so when the Lakers announced that with the thirteenth pick of the 1970 draft they had chosen "Jim McMillian from Columbia" there was neither outcry nor affirmation. But someone was concerned. Shortly after they made the pick, Bertka heard Cooke's unmistakable voice boom over the intercom summoning Schaus to his office. (Cooke loved to use the intercom as an instrument of power; in the three years that West coached the Lakers in the mid-seventies, he loathed it when he heard, "Jerry West please report to my office!") Bertka accompanied Schaus. Cooke informed them that he had just taken a call from Ned Irish, who ran the Knicks, Madison Square Garden, and just about everything basketball-related in New York City at that time.

"Fred," intoned Cooke, "Ned Irish wants to know how we possibly could've drafted a fat kid from Columbia. Are you sure he can play?"

"Well," said Schaus, "Bill thinks he can." That's sometimes a scout's job description—get thrown under the bus.

"Let's hope he's correct," said Cooke, dismissing them.

CHAPTER 9

The Logo Signs On

In the spring of 2011 a small contingent from the Golden State Warriors took off from the Bay Area on Joe Lacob's private plane, bound for L.A. on a mission of seduction. Their target was primed to be seduced. Jerry West had picked the spot, Valentino, a fine-dining Italian restaurant in Santa Monica. West likes some old-school L.A. establishments, like the clubby Dan Tana's in West Hollywood, but this night was not for prying eyes.

Four years earlier West had left Memphis, where he had been moderately successful as director of basketball operations for the Grizzlies, his personnel moves having turned an also-ran into a playoff team. West cut quite a figure around Memphis. He was a legit celebrity in a town with a distinctly yesteryear feel—W. C. Handy, Elvis, Sun Studios, B. B. King, Booker T. & the M.G.'s. Midway through West's five-year tenure, a couple of stalkers, possibly fed up with Elvis's continued refusal to surface, set their sights on West. They were so aggressive that West eventually needed a security guard. "One woman even went so far as to buy a wedding dress for the happy life she envisioned we would have together," West and Coleman wrote in *West by West*.

Despite West's moves and his celebrity, the Grizzlies had failed to win a playoff game in three tries and were frequently in ownership turmoil. Anyway, the Home of the Blues had seemed like a way station for this King of the Basketball Blues. Jerry West in Memphis? It was like putting Elvis in Sheboygan. For the better part of forty years West had been synonymous with Los Angeles, where he had played, coached, and general-managed. (And, as we now know, to where he is returning as a consultant with the Clippers.)

West was ready for a new challenge. He was in reasonably good health for a man who had taken so many pills over his lifetime, battling depression and an arrhythmic heart. He had more money than he had ever dreamed of. His marriage was solid. The two sons he had with Karen—Ryan and Jonnie—had followed West into the basketball profession (imagine Shakespeare's progeny deciding to pick up a quill)—and both were astonishingly well-adjusted. "Credit their mother for that," says West, unnecessarily.

Both of the boys played basketball, but West rarely worked with them or attended their games. "Obviously you'd want someone like that to give you advice and push you to a certain extent," says Jonnie, Golden State's director of player programs. "But my father was very hands-off. Part of it was the attention he gets. If something isn't about him, he hates for the attention to be on him. I never faulted him for that."

In fact, Jonnie did the unthinkable—he played at West Virginia. He had been offered a scholarship by then–Mountaineer coach John Beilein, who liked his shooting and high basketball IQ. Jonnie red-shirted his freshman year and didn't see much action after Bob Huggins took over when Beilein went to Michigan. But he thoroughly enjoyed the experience. There is more West Virginia in him than in any of the sons. "Part of getting used to being 'Jerry West's son' was going to West Virginia," says Jonnie. "My dad would've preferred I go elsewhere. But he never said, 'Don't go there.'"

Early on, Ryan felt more resentment about his father not attending his games. He couldn't understand it. But as he got older he preferred that Jerry not attend, because of his withering critiques. (Ryan didn't play at Loyola Marymount, where he went to college.) Still, these days the two sons and the dad are close, united by basketball, hoops junkies to the core. There's something so right about seeing the three Wests sitting together at the 2016 Las Vegas Summer League, the sons cracking jokes about ol' Cement Head, the father, sitting in the middle, pointing out little tips about a certain player's flawed footwork.

"I know there are people on the outside looking in who sometimes feel bad that we didn't grow up with the prototypical father-son relationship," says Jonnie. "But I don't blame my dad for anything. I know who he is and I know what he grew up with and I know how that affected him. So to me he's the best dad there is."

The new Golden State ownership group seemed promising to West, but still, the first season under the Lacob-Guber administration had produced only a 36-46 record. And from watching the Warriors on TV, West could see obvious chemistry issues between Curry and his high-scoring backcourt mate Ellis.

Lacob was shimmering with excitement about the prospect of talking hoops with West. Even though Lacob had grown up in Celtics country, West had been one of his boyhood heroes. Several years earlier Lacob had played on a team coached by West at a Magic Johnson fantasy camp in Hawaii, and he was eager to rekindle that memory, too. A meeting with Sergey Brin at Kleiner Perkins may have netted Lacob a bundle, but the Google founder didn't burrow deep into Lacob's soul, the way West did. Alas, the fantasy camp conversation didn't last long. "Jerry didn't remember what I was talking about," said Lacob, laughing. "I guess he sees lots of guys like me."

Myers, Golden State's assistant general manager and obviously a fast-rising star in the organization, knew West from Memphis. Myers would come into town to visit player-clients signed to his then-boss, high-powered agent Arn Tellem, who was extremely close to West. (They had a kid named Kobe in common, as we shall see.) West would sometimes pick up Myers at the airport and put him up at his home. Myers trusted West implicitly but still had understandable reservations about adding West to the team. From Myers's perspective, it was like he was about to take over producing the Beatles as George Martin strolled into the recording studio.

But West, who was about to turn seventy-three, made it clear that he wasn't going to horn in on the day-to-day. He had no desire to study the salary cap, think about a player's Bird rights, or get back into the grind on a full-time basis. And West had his own concern. "I told them I wouldn't accept the position if there was going to be any resentment that I was there," West said.

Myers's minor hesitation aside, the invite was a no-brainer for the Warriors, who were adding both a legend and a legendary mind to a franchise short on both. "Getting Jerry gives us cover of darkness," Guber said, which has since become an oft-repeated line within the franchise. What he meant was: Whatever mistakes are made by the new ownership, fans will cut them some slack because West is there.

The pitch was solid, and most of all it offered new challenges for a man who desperately needs them. After a series of follow-up negotiating calls between West and Lacob, the Logo decided to get back in the game. His contract was never made public, but it was believed to be about $2 million per year with some deferred money that West used to buy into the franchise.

But why do it? Why keep on going? West's answer is more along the lines of: Why not?

"Life is a big damn puzzle," West told me in 2016. "If you don't understand that, you're nowhere." He took both hands and put them on a table. He was speaking at a closed bar in Las Vegas, site of the NBA Summer League, in the late morning. West is a renowned card player at Bel-Air Country Club, but he was in Vegas only to scout players. It's something he has always loved. (Later he will abruptly conclude the interview by saying: "I have to go watch the Thon Maker kid.")

"You got a piece here and a piece there and maybe they fit together, but then you got an idiot piece over here," says West. "Well, you have to get rid of the idiot piece or figure out some way around him.

"I was more a thinker than a performer as a GM. Lots of guys make a show about thinking, but they don't really sit down and work it out. Same thing when I played. I analyzed the players and teams I played against. It was very much like a puzzle. If you don't have the corner pieces, the whole thing doesn't work."

He stopped short. West will brag a little, a right that he's certainly earned, but then he gets worried that he's bragging too much.

"All I'm saying," says West, "is that I've had pretty good success at putting that puzzle together."

True to his word, West never horned in on the daily business of the Warriors. He almost never went to away games—except when Golden State played the Clippers or the Lakers at Staples—and limited himself to a dozen or so home games. But he stayed on top of things, and he loved nothing more than talking to the Golden State players, before or after games and sometimes at practices if he was in the Bay Area. That was his great gift. That has *always* been his great gift. He has been nothing but management for the past forty years, yet he somehow always registers as *player*.

"You know what was a big deal for me?" says David West, a key frontcourt reserve for the Warriors. "That Jerry West knew my name. It made me feel, I don't know, wanted here.

"The things he goes over with you are basic things, staying on balance, following through on your shot, playing with confidence, things like that. Obviously his pedigree is partly what you respond to, but with players he doesn't come across as grouchy, you know? He comes across like he's talking *with* you, not down to you."

Another Golden State rotation player, swingman Shaun Livingston, says much the same thing. He and West ran into each other often over the years because they were both rehabbing knee injuries at the Kerlan-Jobe Orthopaedic Clinic in Los Angeles. (Livingston's, as every NBA fan knows, was serious. It's a miracle he's playing. West's injury was not.)

"You just feel that experience when you talk to Jerry," says Livingston, who came to the Warriors in 2014. "And you feel his competitiveness, too, feel his fire. He brings examples from his playing days because that's how he relates to today's game. But it never sounds old. He has a good grasp of what's going on today, and a lot of old players do not. Talking about today's game is out of their comfort zone, but that's not the case with Jerry. You know what? He's a Renaissance guy. That's how I think of him."

Did your father follow him as a player? Livingston is asked.

"Well, more like my grandfather," he answers.

As vague as this sounds, it did become evident early in the Lacob-Guber tenure that at long last Golden State's ownership was Serious About Winning. They would lose about $25 million in their first year—"We did not buy into a well-run business," says Lacob wryly—but they had a plan. They knew what kind of people they wanted for the front office: intelligent, forward-thinking, untethered to old ideas, basketball people but not necessarily those who had been doing the same thing for their entire adult lives.

It was Lacob's Boston connection, specifically with Celtics GM Danny Ainge, that first drew the Warriors to Myers. Or, more accurately, Myers to the Warriors. Myers sent an email to Lacob, who probably responded only because Ainge had told him about Myers. Their first meeting seemed to go nowhere—in an interview with Tim Kawakami, Myers said that he told his father, "I have no opportunity there"—but Lacob eventually called back and offered him the job of assistant general manager.

Larry Riley, The Man Who Loved Curry, was still in the top job, but from the moment Myers showed up Riley started to get the feeling that he wouldn't be there long. "They told me I was supposed to train Bob, and I knew he was going to replace me, and they knew I knew," says Riley. "Is that weird? Well, kind of. But the other option was, 'Get your ass out of here.' So I stayed." Such a personnel move might be commonplace in the business world, but not so much in the sports world, where new owners immediately bring in their own guys and fire the *other* guy's guys.

Myers had earned a curious fame at UCLA, being a walk-on for the 1995 team that won an NCAA championship. His ex–Bruin teammates still call him "Forrest Gump" for his ability to be in the right place at the right time. Warrior blood also ran through Myers, who was born in the Bay Area. "The first team I remembered was

Joe Barry Carroll and Larry Smith and Terry 'Long Socks' Teagle, and Sleepy Floyd and Sarunas Marciulionis," Myers said. "I loved Run TMC, but people forget how brief that was. There was a great energy in the building, and Nellie and the brand of basketball were entertaining. But we were never going to win it all. We were always a stepchild, always the next tier behind the Bulls and the Lakers and a lot of other teams. It was frustrating to be a Warriors fan."

Becoming the lead front-office man for a championship team seems like a no-brainer now, but when Myers came aboard he was leaving a lucrative job as an agent with Tellem's powerful firm for an uncertain future. Put in draft terms, the Warriors were at best a mid-second-rounder. "Our first goal was just making the playoffs," says Myers. "That would be our championship. And remember that sixteen teams make the playoffs. It was a modest goal." He smiles. "But it was *our* goal."

Shortly after they got Myers, the Warriors hired the estimable Rick Welts, who had just resigned his position as president and chief executive of the Phoenix Suns. Like Myers, Welts talks like someone with a Ph.D.—business? psychology? English?—but came to the job with much bare-knuckle history, if that metaphor can be extended to a front office. Welts had been a ball boy and then an assistant trainer for the Seattle SuperSonics, fetching shots, handing out towels, and taping ankles for players like Tom Meschery. He went on to become one of David Stern's most trusted lieutenants in the early eighties when the NBA was trying desperately to gain traction as a corporate player. It was Welts—at first the NBA's director of national promotions and eventually its executive vice president, chief marketing officer, and president of NBA Properties (third from the top behind Stern and deputy commissioner Russ Granik)—who came up with many of the marketing ploys for All-Star Weekend, as well as the idea of placing jumping-bean Ping-Pong balls in a plastic dome for the draft lottery.

Stern and Welts both get teary-eyed when they talk about the importance each played in the life of the other. "David and I went through the wars together," says Welts.

A couple of months before he was hired by Lacob and Guber, Welts had been the subject of a May 2011 *New York Times* page-one story in which he came out as gay. Many of those who knew Welts were aware of his orientation, but, incredibly, no one had ever brought it up to him, nor had he discussed it with anyone in the basketball world. Such were the strictures against being gay in pro sports, especially male pro sports, and such was the isolation Welts felt in his world.

And what was the reaction to that *Times* story?

"Frankly, I was astonished," said Welts. "I expected, maybe, ninety–ten in favor. But it was a hundred–zero. *Zero!* It was the most amazing experience I ever had in terms of what I expected and what happened. I have binders full of emails and letters, literally thousands of them, and there is not a single negative one. It defied any kind of logic or expectation."

In the summer of 2016 the NBA Board of Governors met in Las Vegas to discuss, among other things, the 2017 All-Star Game scheduled for Charlotte, North Carolina. Welts was among the speakers. Everybody knew this was a man who had been responsible for many of the innovations that had grown All-Star Weekend, a man who had a seminal role in selling the NBA when so many didn't want to buy. Welts's message was clear: If the game remains in Charlotte, where Governor Pat McCrory's controversial bathroom bill had just been passed, he wouldn't be comfortable attending. There was no fiery rhetoric or threatening tone—that isn't Welts's style. But when he was done, the NBA's decision to turn its back on Charlotte was an easy one.

People like Rick Welts didn't exist in sports operations a decade ago; in many places they *still* don't have a Rick Welts. Business-side people acted as almost quasi–hatchet men for the owners, dispensing orders like warlords. Jack Kent Cooke didn't have a Welts, or for that matter a Myers. But both fit the image Lacob and Guber wanted for the Warriors—contemporary but appreciative of tradition, collegial with an edge, competitively indefatigable.

Welts's task on the business side was formidable—change the culture of losing that permeated the organization. "Everybody came to work expecting that the same thing would happen that always happened," says Welts. "We would lose, and people wouldn't want to do business with us. I had to get across the message that we weren't going to lose anymore—of course I wasn't sure that was true—so let's be ready. If you've done things right within your organization, you can take it from zero to sixty overnight."

Welts, a veteran of the days when the NBA was toxic to advertisers, also seems to understand, to a much greater degree than Lacob, why all this is possible.

"There are people in my business who believe they are the reason for the success of their teams." Welts made it clear that he was not talking about Lacob, who has been accused of doing exactly that. "Well, a secret I learned early on was that those guys playing and coaching are the reason these enterprises are interesting. It's not the men and women in suits. All somebody like me can do is get the organization prepared for when the team gives fans a reason to really, really care. And that's what we did."

For public relations, the Warriors already had their man in tireless veteran Raymond Ridder, who has a kind of old-school philosophy about public relations in that it's actually supposed to involve "relations." He orchestrates postgame media sessions like a frantic but friendly auteur, sending his callow but competent assistants on various missions. "Okay, Draymond's at the podium, Klay's next, Brett, we got Steph over here but only for ten minutes, he's gotta run, and Matt, we have K.D. over there but he's got a TV thing so make it fast. . . ."

Ridder jokes about how far the franchise has come. "I used to be that annoying voice calling up reporters and saying, 'Listen, our defensive efficiency has really increased over the last two weeks. You should think about doing a story on us.'" These days Ridder, who got a $100,000 share from the players after the Dubs won the 2015 championship, does very little pitching and a lot of catching, though Connor Letourneau, who covers the Dubs for the *San Francisco Chronicle,* says that Ridder will sometimes offer story angles, albeit for the lesser-known players. So there is a comity between players and press that does not exist on most other teams, even in the NBA, which is among the most media-friendly of leagues.

Some find the public relations in Warrior Land, though, to be a bit oppressively non-oppressive. Journalists can feel like they're trapped in a giant jar of artificial sweetener, everybody cooperating, everybody saying the right thing, a kind of one-size-fits-all style of communication. Even Draymond's hell-yes-the-earth-could-be-flat! soliloquies come across as more Eddie Haskell than burn-down-the-house. Klay Thompson has been presented, accurately, as someone who shies away from the press; GM Myers says that Thompson is "like the first Terminator, the one who doesn't say anything," and *Slate* did a brilliant tongue-in-cheek piece about him headlined "Is Klay Thompson a Robot?" But Thompson's reluctance to talk is mixed in with a good-guy affability, present particularly after games, when he is liable to converse about his beloved bulldog, Rocco (who once dropped a deuce on the infield at Dodger Stadium while his master was taking batting practice), or the positive effect that sunshine has on his game, all offered while munching on a piece of pizza or slurping down a beer. He's the frat brother you enjoy living with even if the dishes don't always get washed.

Going to Golden State was once a rare trip for basketball journalists, usually undertaken to cover the other team, but these days national writers are much more likely to be in the Oracle than in Madison Square Garden. (Especially in May and June.) "Oakland—not New York or L.A.—is now the basketball media capital of the world," wrote *The Ringer*'s Bryan Curtis in a piece headlined "The Best Locker Room in the Biz." Former Knicks writer Scott Cacciola of the *New York Times* covers the Warriors almost like a full-time beat, and the *Washington Post* literally moved NBA writer Tim Bontemps to the Bay Area. "At this point in time," Bontemps says, "where else would you be?"

The bottom line is that Warriors access, homogenized at times, is much, much better than most. When, before a game in December, Kerr joked that he wanted his own sound track as he walked in for a pregame press conference, Ridder ordered up Elton John's "The Bitch Is Back." And isn't it nice to have a PR man who pulls aside a coach before a post-practice interview session and reminds him to send out a good word for Shelley Smith, an ESPN reporter who had suffered a ministroke in the Golden State locker room after Game 1 of the Western Conference finals? That's what Ridder did with Mike Brown, who then sent out a team-wide message to Smith.

"It is literally easier for me to get fifteen minutes with Curry than it was for me to get the backup quarterback when I was covering Cal," says Letourneau. The *Chronicle* beat man, younger than some of the players, understands how fortunate he is to be, at twenty-six, covering one of the world's coolest sports teams. "Even though I work all the time," he says, "it's like a dream."

Myers is known for working all the time, too, or at least going on what he described to *Sports Illustrated*'s Chris Ballard as "work benders," eighteen-hour-a-day, nonstop sessions that usually come along during the free-agency period. If Myers felt at all unnerved by West, he didn't show it and consulted the Logo often early in his GM tenure. "It's very rare when you speak to someone and every time there is something profound in that conversation," Myers told me. "Jerry has the ability that in the course of any conversation he leaves some bit of knowledge that only he can impart."

Part of that knowledge included handling game stress. Before one game in the 2015 Western Conference finals against Houston, Myers called West and told him he might not be able to handle watching the game from the arena. A bad case of nerves had gotten to him. West assured him that he shouldn't feel guilty about leaving, although Myers eventually decided to stay and has not yet left an arena midgame.

With the possible exception of obstetricians on call, no one knows more about leaving games than West. When he was GM of the Lakers, he almost never went on the road and, as you know, never considered going to an away game in the Finals. But he even frequently left home games at halftime or even earlier, unable to stomach the suspense, the mistakes of his players, or both. In *West by West,* he conjures up a specific time that he skipped out on a game and slipped into a darkened theater to watch *Gladiator.* (Says West to himself as he munches on popcorn: *Nothing happens to anyone that he is not fitted by nature to bear.*) Mitch Kupchak, the Lakers assistant GM under West, encountered many fans over the years who showed up late for games and were stunned when they came upon the Logo on his way *out* of the Forum. "Jerry would often stop and talk to them," says Kupchak. "He'd vent to the average fan, too. 'I can't stand watching so-and-so. He's just terrible.'"

Myers doesn't have a Westian personality. He doesn't rant and rave about players in public. Still, Myers sees commonalities between them.

"You shouldn't have to leave," Myers says. "You should have enough perspective to realize that it's just a basketball game. But I understand Jerry's behavior because I'm subject to it. The pain of losing and holding himself responsible is what kills him. And he does it against all logic. He would've made every single shot in an individual game in the NBA Finals and still would've held himself responsible in a loss. That's who he is. That's probably what made him so great but also what's cost him some of his joy." (*Joy* is a favorite Warriors word.)

"We actually share a lot of the same philosophies. Jerry has extreme difficulty when he sees people lose focus because he rarely loses focus himself. But I understand that. I feel the same way. I love people who care that much. In any business it's much better to have someone who cares too much than cares too little.

"Jerry gets so wrapped because he's a perfectionist. Yes, he's very hard on everyone, but he's harder on himself. What he expects of you or me is less than what he expects of himself. Everything inside of him is what he feels about himself, and he's projecting it outward. He puts the struggle with himself out on other people." (Man, it would be tough to sit on a chair across from Myers. He'd negotiate your contract *and* psychoanalyze you. But his assessment makes a lot of sense.)

As time went on, Myers became less and less dependent on West, which is to be expected. Myers grew into the job. He was not involved in the decision to cut West's compensation; that was Lacob's call. Myers made a call to West to urge him to stay, and they've spoken by phone since the breakup. But maybe he understands, more than most, why West has to move on.

"I've known Jerry for over twenty years and value tremendously the time that we worked together with the Warriors," says Myers. "I consider him a great friend and certainly wish him well with the Clippers. Jerry is an unbelievable model. I'd like to be his age and doing something I love. At least I think I would. Why not?"

Why not, indeed? Only West can answer. But, man, sometimes, it seems hard to be Jerry West.

Jerry West remains a god in West Virginia, where, during his college years, says George Raveling, he could've been announced as "Jesus Christ from heaven."

West and Elgin Baylor, shown here with Coach Fred Schaus, who later became the Lakers' GM, were a devastating tandem throughout the decade of the sixties.

West and Oscar Robertson, above, at a college all-star game shortly before their graduations from West Virginia and Cincinnati, were the first two picks in the 1960 draft.

No matter how prodigious the numbers put up by Wilt Chamberlain, he usually finished second to Boston's Bill Russell.

West felt that Robertson was more prepared immediately for the NBA, but that as time went on he could more than match the Big O.

West (far right) liked Lakers owner Jack Kent Cooke (shown in 1966, shortly after he bought the team) at first, but grew to despise his miserly and autocratic ways. Also pictured are mid-sixties Lakers guards Archie Clark (left) and Walt Hazzard.

The steady coaching of former Celtic Bill Sharman, with or without his voice, was one of the major reasons for the Lakers' success in the 1971–72 season.

Happy Hairston goes in for a layup against Phil Jackson, but for the most part the power forward concentrated on rebounding and defense.

The incomparable Chick Hearn sold pro basketball to a Southern California audience that, at first, had no use for it.

Looking a little bit like the Logo silhouette, West drives against New York's Dave Stallworth in the 1970 Finals. West always claimed that he went left as often as he went right.

Jim McMillian, shooting a jumper over Milwaukee's Bob Dandridge in the 1972 Western Conference finals, was a kind of early version of Golden State's Draymond Green.

West, at near left, slipping a pass around Bucks defenders to Jim McMillian, had more playmaking responsibility under Sharman in 1971–72.

Slithery southpaw Gail Goodrich, above, had a variety of shots and a way of "squirreling it up there," as teammate Jim Cleamons put it. Goodrich and West formed what is still the highest-scoring backcourt combo for a single season.

No one knew it at the time, but Pat Riley (driving in the 1972 Finals) and Phil Jackson (defending) would later coach the Lakers to a combined seven NBA championships.

Wilt (between Bill Sharman and assistant K. C. Jones) could certainly big-foot a team, but West (at right) respected the effort he gave during their championship season.

The 1971–72 streak/championship team. Front row (left to right): Jim McMillian, Jim Cleamons, Pat Riley, Wilt Chamberlain, Coach Bill Sharman, LeRoy Ellis, Willie McCarter, Earnie Killum, Flynn Robinson. Back row: Assistant Coach K. C. Jones, Elgin Baylor, Keith Erickson, Gail Goodrich, Fred Hetzel, Roger Brown, Rick Roberson, Malkin Strong, Jerry West, Happy Hairston, trainer Frank O'Neill. (McCarter, Killum, Hetzel, Brown, Roberson, and Strong weren't with the team by the time the season started, and Baylor retired the day the streak began.)

After he was bizarrely announced as "offensive coach," West preferred to leave the X's and O's to the bespectacled Pat Riley and left for the front office.

One of West's best GM moves was getting Kobe Bryant with the thirteenth pick of the 1996 draft. Then–Lakers coach Del Harris is on the right.

Jerry Buss congratulates West on the day of his statue unveiling at the Staples Center, but there was never much Lakers interest in a statue for Baylor (left).

CHAPTER 10

And a Celtic (?) Shall Lead Them

When Bill Sharman accepted the Lakers head coaching job before the 1971–72 season, he was forty-four years old, recently divorced, but now remarried. Just as Karen West would prove to be a stabilizing force for Jerry several years later, so did Dorothy Sharman help neutralize the sharp edges of this competitive man. (Dorothy died of cancer in 1974 at age forty. Sharman later remarried, and Joyce Sharman, who is still alive, was another stabilizing force for the rest of his life.)

But what about the team he was coaching? Were the Lakers stable?

That was another question.

Sharman has a fascinating backstory, his own Moonlight Graham tale. After starting in the Dodgers' class-A minor-league team, outfielder Sharman worked his way up to the big club near the end of the 1951 season, primarily so the regulars could get some rest with what looked like an insurmountable lead in the National League. But the New York Giants kept winning, the Dodgers kept losing, and Sharman never got his chance.

"I was dying to get into a game," Sharman said in 1971, the year he took over the Lakers. "In the outfield, as a pinch hitter, anything. And five times Charlie Dressen called on me to pinch-hit. But strange things kept happening. Before I could get up to the plate, somebody would hit into a double play to end the inning, or somebody would get picked off a base." Sharman and several of his benchmates did get tossed from a game by umpire Frank Dascoli for arguing a call. "So I never got in a Major League game," Sharman used to say, "but I did get thrown out of one."

The future shooting guard was in a familiar place—sitting in the dugout—when Bobby Thomson hit the "Shot Heard 'Round the World" to give the Giants the pennant. Sharman did make one contribution—he kicked dirt on infielder Eddie Stanky and manager Leo Durocher as they rolled around on the ground in joy. Sharman decided to concentrate on basketball after that season and found championship success with the Celtics.

Sharman, who wore a set of long sideburns like some early-day hipster, was a tangle of contradictions. One might've expected him to be one of those back-in-my-day drones who relentlessly quoted maxims from Auerbach. He wasn't. Now, he could be a grind. As a player who depended on shooting, he was known to spin basketballs to find the roundest ones and check the rims to make sure they were straight. But he seemed to know when he was being a control freak and tempered that aspect, as Lynn Shackelford found out in his frequent dealings with him as broadcaster/traveling secretary.

"I would tell him that the bus was coming at six-fifteen, and Bill would say, 'Well, Lynn, sometimes you get traffic over there at that intersection, and maybe we should think about making it six.' And I'd say, 'Let's make it six.' And Bill would say, 'Good idea, Lynn.'"

Sharman was also forward-thinking, an early proponent of the three-point shot, someone willing to discuss raising the basket, staying up-to-date on video (it was "film" back then), constantly on the lookout for ideas that would improve the game.

Called "Willie" by most of the Celtics and his friends, Sharman was also color-blind, a friend to black players. He and Earl Lloyd broke into the NBA together in 1950 with the Washington Capitals (who later disbanded), and Sharman used to pick up Lloyd for practices and games. "Remember, Washington was in the South in the back-of-the-bus days," Lloyd, who died in 2015, told *Pro Hoops History* several years ago. "I've been asked, of all the players from those days, if there was one I admire most. Let me tell you, it was Bill Sharman. He was my friend, and think of what that meant at the time."

Sharman was also a brawler. In *Jerry West*, author Lazenby quotes reporter Doug Krikorian recalling a fight that Sharman had with a 6'6" tough guy that Sharman "beat the shit out of." The other guy? Earl Lloyd. Boxing was one of five sports at which Sharman excelled—basketball, baseball, track, and tennis being the others. "I don't know if I've ever met a kinder, gentler man," said Cousy in a film about the 1971–72 Lakers, "but on the floor Willie turned into a terror."

Another odd thing about Sharman, which wouldn't be odd at all today, was his embrace of physical fitness. He was like one of those Christian missionaries ripping off a set of sit-ups before morning prayer. Cousy used to urge him not to let Auerbach see him down on the floor lest "he'll have us all doing that." He and Schaus frequently played a couple of sets of tennis at six a.m., about an hour after Chamberlain was getting to bed, and, at a time when jogging was considered unusual, Sharman was a zealous practitioner. When his wife needed a break on a long drive, Sharman would jog down the highway as far as he could get before she picked him up. He carried vitamins in his suitcase, sipped afternoon tea, and had a drink concoction that he claimed gave him energy. This was at a time when a drink concoction to most players meant a Manhattan.

As he settled in as Lakers coach, Sharman realized that his task was as much diplomatic as strategic. First, he had to negotiate his way around Cooke, who, after all, had fired two coaches in four years, both of whom had gotten teams to the Finals. Cooke was not a patient man. He was already tired of losing to the Celtics, and his Los Angeles Kings, who shared the *Fabulous* Forum, were not drawing spectators or winning games. "I knew Los Angeles had more expatriate Canadians than any place in the world," Cooke used to moan, "but what I didn't know was that they were all the ones who hated hockey."

Cooke had a right-hand lackey named Jim Locher, who began almost every sentence to a Lakers employee with "Mr. Cooke would like you to . . ."

There were variations on that to the outside world. On one occasion NBA commissioner Larry O'Brien requested that the Lakers move a tip-off time to noon to accommodate prime-time TV viewing. "Mr. Cooke does not move his starting times," Locher informed the NBA. (That was in the era before Stern came along. His answer would've been: "Commissioner Stern says that Mr. Cooke *does* move his starting times unless he wants to be fined an unconscionable amount of money.")

Stern remembers attending a deposition at Cooke's office when "he was very, very harsh to the African-American who was attending him and serving him coffee, treating him almost like his manservant." Stern thinks for a moment, then adds: "Cooke was also very abusive to the lawyer on the other side, so maybe more than a racist he was probably just a general ass." Jerry Colangelo remembers that, when he was running the Phoenix Suns, he was meeting with Lakers GM Schaus in a hotel room about a possible trade when Cooke, pasha-like, made a grand entrance wearing an extravagant robe.

In a tribute film about the streak team, Cooke was not remembered in tender terms. Claire Rothman, who was hired by Cooke to run the Forum, said that he "was the most miserly rich man who ever lived." She also recalled that Cooke used to send his chauffeur out to find a place to re-bristle his hairbrush, which sounds like something out of P. G. Wodehouse. The most oft-repeated quote about Cooke, uttered behind his back, of course, came from Hearn: "He's the only man I've ever known," Chick would say, "who would like to die in his own arms."

But Sharman had leverage with Cooke. The owner's people had told him, after all, that Sharman was the best coach in the land. He brought with him the Celtics' magic. Cooke was desperate to win. While he treated Sharman's request for a new projector like he had been asked to provide ermine-lined warm-up suits, he did grant him K. C. Jones. And the evidence points to him paying off Baylor to allow him to retire.

"The best NBA coaches are the ones with clout and leverage," says Shackelford. "Sharman, because it was his first year and because he came so highly recommended, had it. Fred Schaus was as frugal as Cooke. We always thought that he got a bonus for beating the budget. Well, Sharman overpowered everyone in that first season." Riley puts it this way: "Even Wilt recognized that something fresh and new was coming in."

Anyway, as a coach of the Cleveland franchise in the American Basketball League, Sharman had an owner named George Steinbrenner. So what if Rod Hundley told author Lazenby that Cooke "was the number one asshole that ever lived"? Sharman knew his way around assholes.

But what about his troika of superstars? A basketball team is a relatively small unit. Today, almost a half century after Sharman took over a West-Baylor-Wilt team, franchises are still hesitant about taking on three superstars. (The current Warriors don't have four, remember. They have two—Curry and Durant, with Thompson and Green being "merely" all-stars.) The twosome of Bryant and Shaquille eventually overwhelmed the Lakers. In 2012 the Durant-Westbrook Oklahoma City Thunder let James Harden, a transcendent offensive talent, escape because they worried that there weren't enough balls to accommodate three offensive-minded stars.

The key, as Sharman saw it, was Chamberlain. Sharman had a deep and abiding respect for West, and the desire to coach him was a major reason he accepted a job that many of his friends had advised him to reject. He was a little less sure about Baylor but considered him to still be a reliable scorer. But what he needed to achieve real success was for a fully committed Chamberlain to be a zealous rebounder/defender, a supporting cog on offense, a willing outlet passer to ignite what he saw as a potentially lethal fast break, and a uniting force in the locker room. For all his success, West was still the classic lead-by-example guy, and Baylor had largely checked out on his leadership responsibilities.

Sharman didn't approach Wilt warily, as many coaches had done. He didn't refer to him as "the Load," as van Breda Kolff had. Sharman liked Wilt's game. When he was coaching in the ABA he tried to convince Wilt to jump and play for him. Given Wilt's love of being the contrarian, it's surprising that didn't happen.

Sharman had a major advantage going for him in his dealings with Wilt. Though he rarely voiced it, Wilt envied the enduring relationship that Russell had had with Auerbach. While coaches came and went in Wilt's life with the frequency of girlfriends—Al Cervi, Neil Johnston, Frank McGuire, Dolph Schayes, Alex Hannum, van Breda Kolff, Mullaney—Russell had worked only for Auerbach and then himself. Wilt longed for that stability. Plus, theorized Shackelford, in the eternal battle of one-upmanship that Wilt waged with Russell, he would be eager to demonstrate to Sharman that he, Wilt, could be a better team player than Russell.

Sharman also got lucky in this respect: Wilt had started to love Los Angeles even more than he did New York City, his first adopted home, and Philadelphia, his birthplace. Before the deal to get Wilt was done, he and Cooke had held secret meetings, probably against league rules at the time, about the possibility of his being traded there, Cooke enjoying the code name that Chamberlain had for him—"Mr. Norman."

To put Sharman's basketball philosophy in perspective, some NBA history is necessary. While we rightly sing hosannas to the contemporary Golden State offense, which led the NBA in scoring with an average of 115.9 points per game during the 2016–17 season, we should also note that the Warriors were outscored by the old-school, Converse-wearing, short-short-sporting, gravity-limited Celtics of the fifties and sixties. In the 1959–60 season, the Celts averaged 124.5 points per game. The following season, Sharman's last as a player, they averaged 119.7 points. Those numbers were achieved, remember, without the three-point shot, which didn't come into the NBA until 1979.

The Celtics were unusual only in their *efficiency*, their ability to generate points off of Russell's defense—he blocked a shot, retrieved it, started the break with an outlet pass, and sometimes *finished* the break with a layup. Sixty years ago in the NBA almost *every* team played fast. The Lakers had always played fast, even given Baylor's predilection to study the defense and slither through openings off the dribble. West had always played fast, even at West Virginia under Schaus. In those days whoever had an open shot usually took it, even if that player was not identified as a "shooter." Successful teams recognized which players to get the ball to, of course—Wilt's teams looked for him, the St. Louis Hawks looked for Bob Pettit, and the Lakers looked for Baylor and West—but there was precious little isolation, that is, clear-out patterns designed for only one player that turn the other four into traffic cones. In the old days, lots of players got up lots of shots. (In an immortal example of masonry, Sharman and Cousy each launched twenty shots in Game 7 of the 1957 Finals and made a combined five. Curry and Thompson could shoot that percentage blindfolded.)

Sharman came from the school that dictated: *We run whenever we can. And one player does not hold on to the ball.* If Sharman had a mantra that was it. He wanted the Lakers to run like his Celtics had run a decade earlier. Baylor getting old? West coming off surgery? Wilt more comfortable setting up and simply calling for the ball in the post? Goodrich looked dumpy and nothing like a guy who could tear up and down the court?

Too bad. The Lakers were going to run, even though he knew it might be a tough sell to Chamberlain. The offense usually went *through* Wilt and didn't whiz *by* him.

Sharman wanted something else, too. He wanted the ball in West's hands. One of the oddest things about West's playing career is that it's hard to discern whether he was a point guard or a shooting guard. Those terms didn't come along until much later, perhaps even with the Showtime Lakers when Magic was always identified as a "point guard," James Worthy as a "small forward," and Kurt Rambis and A. C. Green as "power forwards." Physically, West profiles as a shooting guard, not to mention the fact that he shot a lot and scored a lot. But West was also a brilliant passer and a player who had the ball in his hands a lot. He averaged 6.7 assists for his career, a high number for someone who also averaged twenty-seven points.

"One day in the preseason Bill said to me, 'Jerry, instead of leading the league in scoring, why don't you lead the league in assists?' "

West explained to me in 2016. (For the record, West led the NBA in scoring only once, in 1969–70, when he averaged 31.2 points per game.) "We didn't break it down as much as it's done now. You were just a G, a guard, in the score book. But teams, smart teams anyway, always got it to the player they felt was the best ball handler. To be honest, I thought ballhandling was the weakest part of my game. But if you're talking about someone who was *safe* with the ball, I think it was as safe with me as anybody."

That is accurate. West was not slick with the ball. For that matter, neither was Oscar Robertson. They didn't cross over much or go behind their back. "We didn't *expose* the ball to the extent they do today, and we didn't take as many chances," West says. "Today the ballhandling skills are so much better than what they were, and anyone who says they aren't is crazy."

West, Robertson, and others were *strong* with the ball, shielding it with their big bodies, warding off potential larcenists with sharp elbows. As he watches today's Warriors, nothing drives West to distraction more easily than watching Curry, who is a hundred times more adept at handling than West ever was, put on a dribbling show and then throw a harebrained pass for no apparent reason. "I just don't know why he does that," West will say over and over.

As for Sharman's desire to run, West says it was never an issue for him. For one thing, he had begun to get in the best aerobic shape of his life. He and newcomer Riley had struck up a friendship, and Pat, hungry for playing time, had them running the Santa Monica Stairs. Plus, West thought that playing up-tempo made strategic sense. "The tendency is to think that old teams don't want to run," says West, "but it's just the opposite. You're a more efficient runner because you don't make as many mistakes. And you're not working so hard for baskets. If you can go down and get a basket within five seconds you are *saving* energy." (Years later D'Antoni would preach the same sermon when he took over the Phoenix Suns.)

Sharman began instituting his running philosophy during training in Hawaii, where the Lakers encamped every year only because the team got free accommodations in exchange for radio and TV plugs about tourism. (The franchise's close relationship with the island—many Lakers players have owned condos there over the years—continues today.) The Lakers practiced in a National Guard Armory that had little ventilation. Sharman had done research—or claimed he had—showing that four or five key minutes would decide almost every game. He wanted the Lakers to be in the best shape possible to dominate that time frame, whenever it would occur. Practically every Laker came back from camp with some version of this quote that West gave to the *Los Angeles Times:* "I went to Hawaii with a suntan and came back without it."

The endless running was supplemented with old-fashioned calisthenics, jumping jacks, sit-ups, and toe-touches. At times a Sharman practice looked like an adult gym class. As part of a jumping exercise, Sharman had each player take a running start and see how high he could touch on the backboard; the joke was that the 6'1" Goodrich—"Stumpy," as Baylor called him—could barely reach the net. There's an actual video of that drill, and it's not far from wrong regarding Goodrich.

And there was detail. Sharman kept stats of scrimmages. Rookie Jim Cleamons was cheered to learn that he had been the second- or third-leading scorer and one of the top rebounders, but that was before he was taken to a far end of the court by Sharman and given this message: "You're not going to play much this year. I've got a veteran team. I'm going to play my veterans first. If it gets to around Christmas and I have to make some changes I may reconsider what I'm doing."

That never happened, of course. By Christmas the Lakers had won twenty-seven games in a row.

Yes, things were different in Laker Land—straightforward, serious, intense—and there was no open revolt, or even a sign of one. Wilt was pretty much being Wilt. He expended minimum energy, and let Sharman know, *Okay, I'm buying into this program for now, but it better work.* But he always showed up.

Sharman's Big Ask, however, was still to come.

In the first few paragraphs of the various Sharman obituaries written after his death in 2013, the word *shootaround* was likely to appear. Or, as Rick Barry put it, the *goddamn stupid* shootaround. For all his accomplishments, Sharman is best known for having come up with the idea that teams should climb out of bed on the morning of home and away games, walk, drive, cab, or bus over to whatever gym was available, and "get out the kinks." It was his implementation of the shootaround with the Lakers that has gotten the most attention through the years, but he had actually started it, Barry says, with the Warriors in 1966.

Shackelford remembers Hearn mentioning in the preseason that Sharman wanted to practice on game days. "Bill told Chick that he didn't want to call it a practice because Wilt doesn't like to practice," Shackelford says. "I said, 'Well, what do we call it?' Chick thought a minute and said, 'Oh, we'll just call it a shootaround until we think of something better.'" Like so many other things in Laker Land, the term *shootaround* apparently came from Chick.

Some would assume that Sharman did it mainly as an attempt to curtail drinking and general carousing the night before; if you had to be at a ten a.m. shootaround, went the reasoning, you might consider getting home at two instead of, say, four. That might've been part of it. But Sharman was nothing if not a creature of habit. He had long been doing it himself, believing that he felt sluggish if he sat around all day with a game looming.

Also, he had a theory, as he explained at the time:

"Shooting is muscle memory. If you have a speech to give at night, you rehearse it during the day. If you have a game to play that night, you prepare for it during the day." Sharman also believed—well, *hoped*—that the extra practice might improve Chamberlain's free-throw shooting.

The shootaround has endured, and rare is the player over the years who has said, "Damn, now *this* is a good idea." But it has gotten considerably easier. NBA teams have dedicated facilities that have become more or less a second home for the players anyway. In Sharman's day it was different. Teams often had to trek to strange places, YMCAs, Jewish Community Centers, high schools, even the occasional grammar school. And that was often for home shootarounds. The road was a who-knows? proposition. Bill Bertka remembers more than one morning shootaround in Buffalo (the

Buffalo Braves existed from 1970 to 1978, after which they became the Clippers) when he was tasked by Sharman to smooth out relations with the arena for a shootaround. "I'd be walking around in the snow in penny loafers and a thin jacket with a couple bucks in my pocket, knocking on doors, trying to find a supervisor who could get the hockey ice cleared off from the night before," says Bertka. "Bill was always looking for an edge. He thought the shootaround gave him one."

There are several stories about how Sharman presented the shootaround idea to Wilt. One says that Sharman wooed him in a fancy restaurant, picking up the check; Wilt liked freebies. Others say that Sharman visited Wilt at home. Others say that he just wore Wilt down by mentioning it every day. But everyone agrees that Sharman did it diplomatically because that's how he did everything. Wilt's reported initial response to the idea has the whiff of legend, even as it has the ring of truth.

"Coach," Wilt is said to have uttered in his deep voice, "you can have me in the morning or the evening. But not both." There is no doubt that a morning shoot did not fit Wilt's body clock. Even when he was home at night, he was a roamer, rarely closing his eyes until five a.m. Six years earlier, when Wilt was traded from San Francisco back to Philadelphia, he had insisted that he be allowed to reside in New York City. As Cherry uncovered in his Wilt bio, 76ers practices were held at four p.m. to allow Wilt to make the New York–to–Philly commute.

There are also mixed reports as to how the early shootarounds went down. Some say that Wilt missed the first one, others say that he showed up in shorts and flip-flops.

As Cleamons remembers it, Wilt wasn't present for the first shootaround, which happened at Madison Square Garden before the second game of the season. Either that or he had to be first located and then coaxed into coming. It's difficult to verify. Coverage of teams, even high-profile teams like the Lakers, was much more casual back then, with few reporters even accompanying their teams on the road. If, say, LeBron were to miss a practice or shootaround without explanation these days, the Internet would lose its mind, and it would be Pearl Harbor in one hundred and forty characters. As the season went on and the Lakers kept winning, Wilt seemed to accept the shootaround as just part of the Sharman deal. (There is one small exception to that, which will be covered later.) Now and again he would say something like, "They never did nothing personally for Wilt Chamberlain except make me lose some sleep. But we're winning and I'm not going to do anything to rock the winning way."

Really, that's all Sharman needed to hear.

Sharman liked shootarounds for another reason, too—they got him back in action. Many times he would dismiss the team, and he, K. C. Jones, Shackelford, and perhaps a stray journalist or somebody else would play two-on-two. "K.C. had been a ferocious competitor, but he couldn't have cared less," says Shackelford. "But Sharman? He was sticking elbows into people's ribs. He took it very seriously."

By the time the Lakers arrived back in the mainland for the preseason, Sharman's patterns were established. If practice was at ten, he walked in at 9:56. At the end he whistled the team together, said a few words, and left. He told Bertka that he didn't want meaningless conversations at practice. If he needed to speak to a player, he would do it in private.

His scrimmage teams were set in stone. The first unit was Baylor and Happy Hairston at forward, Chamberlain at center, West and Goodrich at guard. McMillian went against Baylor, Rick Roberson (soon to be gone) against Happy Hairston, LeRoy Ellis against Wilt, Keith Erickson against Goodrich, and Flynn Robinson and Cleamons against West. (Riley was a wild card. He could guard West or one of the forwards. If there were injuries or other absences on a certain day, K.C. could be reliably inserted to raise a little hell on defense.)

West and Robinson were separated because they were the best shooters, but Robinson, a reluctant defender, couldn't contain West with a bear trap. So Sharman often used the young, energetic, and athletic Cleamons to check West. "All I wanted to do was get better," said Cleamons, "and what better way to do that than to have the Logo in front of you? Bill told me that the veterans would get mad at me. 'But you're not trying to impress them,' he said. 'You're trying to impress me.'"

The Lakers' half-court offense was hard to define. Sharman labeled it as "center-opposite," a system originated by USC coach Sam Barry and widely considered to have evolved into the triangle offense refined by Tex Winter and popularized by Phil Jackson. (Jordan had a little to do with it, too.) But that wasn't the key element of it. Sharman told author Lazenby that it was "twenty-five percent Sam Barry and seventy-five percent Red Auerbach." Meaning, he wanted to keep moving, keep passing, and run whenever possible.

"When practice got stagnant, Sharman would say, 'Okay, give me four or five quick passes,'" remembers Cleamons. "He didn't care if it led to a basket. He just wanted us to keep moving, get flowing again."

One small thing Sharman did early was to stop Wilt's habit of grabbing a rebound and slamming it into his palm, an Incredible Hulk move that added nothing and subtracted a precious second or two from the break. *Get rid of the ball and go,* Sharman shouted repeatedly. (Until he could shout no more.)

The Lakers' defense, like every other team's defense in the league at that time, wasn't hard to define. It was basic man-to-man. Some revisionist historians love to talk about how great old-time defenses were, but that is nonsense. To be sure, defenses were tough and hard-boiled. Hand-checking, even grabbing, was allowed. But they weren't sophisticated. Much of the double-teams, switches, and quasi-zones came into the game in the mid-seventies from the influence of college coaches like Hubie Brown. Before that, you played your man hard and battled your way through ball screens.

Sharman did make one defensive change, putting West on the bigger guard most of the time. "When I first got to the Lakers," Goodrich told me, "Fred Schaus didn't want Jerry on the other team's top guy. I guess he didn't want him fouling out. That means I was playing guards like [Boston's] Sam Jones. Jerry was much better equipped than me to play guys like Jones. Jerry is one of the best defensive players ever, every bit the match of Walt Frazier, who people used to talk about being the best." (West said in 2017 that Frazier was somewhat overrated as a defender, a tremendous "ball hawk" more than someone who bodied up on people and stopped them. To balance it out, West, ever the diplomat, also says that Frazier "was very much *underrated* as an offensive player.")

Another Sharman innovation was a system of plusses and minuses, which most teams have in place today. Plusses for offensive rebounds, blocked shots, assists, steals, diving after loose balls, drawing offensive fouls. Over time they came to be put up on some scoreboards as "hustle points." Minuses were offensive fouls, turnovers, not getting back on defense. Sharman used to holler them out to trainer Frank O'Neill, who kept track. There was a monetary value attached to them, ten bucks, five bucks here and there. West was still talking enthusiastically about the system in 2017. "We would even fight over it once in a while," West said. " 'Hey, that was my steal and you gave it to Gail.' I was getting checks for a couple hundred bucks sometimes. That was real money back then."

The Lakers eventually traded Roberson and signed John Q. Trapp, who would become the stuff of minor legend. Phil Jackson says, "John Q. had this kind of scary cross-eyed look to him." Another reporter, in what must've been considered an exotic reference, describes Trapp as "looking like an Islamic sage with his bristly muttonchop sideburns and fierce demeanor." Asked one day where the Q in his name came from, Trapp responded: "Quincy. That's what my mom and dad laid on me. They thought I'd be president or something." That did not happen, and the ultimate fate of John Q. remains an eternal mystery of the streak team.

Trapp's signing gave L.A. an 8-4 racial mix. Chamberlain, Baylor, Hairston, McMillian, Ellis, Robinson, Trapp, and Cleamons were black, and West, Goodrich, Riley, and Erickson were white. It wasn't a startling breakdown for the time, but it was atypical. Cleamons noticed it and was always grateful for how he was treated by the white players. "Jerry West picked me up at the airport when I came to town," remembers Cleamons. "And when we went to New York for the first time, he and Pat said, 'Come on, Rook, you're going clothes shopping with us.' "

The net effect was that under Sharman the Lakers became a very professional team in the best sense of that word. Focused, intense, and cohesive. "We didn't have choirboys," says West today. "Today's Warriors, with maybe the exception of Draymond once in a while, are choirboys. That wasn't us, not with players like Wilt and Happy and John Q. But we were extremely professional when we got on the court."

A few things, however, furrowed Sharman's brow as the season began, most of them surrounding Baylor. He was worried about the relative shortness of his forwards—Baylor and McMillian were both only 6'5" and Hairston was 6'7". Chamberlain and Baylor never really did straighten out who commanded the favored left side of the court. Also, Baylor was reluctant to run, and, when the Lakers did get into the half-court, he tended to hold the ball and work for his own shot. (Think of Carmelo Anthony in today's game, only Baylor had been twice the player that Anthony ever will be.) Things that worked when Baylor was twenty-five weren't working when he was thirty-five, and it's difficult for a player to accept that. Sharman was also concerned about Baylor's interior defense and his tendency, like many great players, to go for steals instead of bodying up on his man. With Baylor around, practice sessions were not as intense. Aging, injured superstars are unlikely to run through a wall. That was understandable but still didn't sit well with the coach.

The Lakers were at 6-3 when Sharman made his decision. Baylor had to go. The coach had already publicly commented about the Lakers' lack of hustle in certain games. "I warned them that they can expect some fines, some really big ones, too, if this trend continues," Sharman said. "If I can't get the message across, then I will be fined, too. I'll be at the top of the list." It was classic Sharman: He really didn't think he should be fined, because God knows he was hustling, but if he was going to throw his players under the bus he would crawl under there with them.

Following a 109–105 loss to the Warriors at the Forum, Sharman had four days to think about what was going on, and he kept coming to the conclusion that the main problem was Baylor. He came to his firm decision on November 4.

The following day Baylor was gone.

The newspapers were cautious in their assessment of the situation, no inferences about how Baylor might be angry, no speculation about whether he was put out to pasture. When Baylor retired he was the third-greatest scorer in NBA history behind Chamberlain and Robertson. Mal Florence of the *Los Angeles Times* provided the most fitting obituary to Baylor's career. "He and Jerry fought the good fight," he wrote, leaving out the obvious . . . *but never won*.

*"I'm happy to take all the grief that anybody feels
about the deal. It had to be done."*
—JERRY WEST ON THE TRADE OF MONTA ELLIS

CHAPTER 11

Steph Stays, Fans Fret

It's hard to pinpoint exactly when the word *culture* began to get volleyed around the sports world like a tennis ball. It's a fairly recent phenomenon. The Celtics sure had a damn good culture when they won sixteen championships over thirty years, even if we didn't call it that. This observer never heard it said about the Showtime Lakers or the Jordan Bulls either. *Culture* might've started creeping into the conversation with the New England Patriots in the NFL and the San Antonio Spurs in the NBA, two teams with similar "cultures."

But with the Golden State Warriors the word *culture* really settled in, often preceded by *healthy,* as if it were a breathing organism whose vital signs are taken on a daily basis. Which in a way it is. Players and coaches come and go, but the culture, once established, remains constant. Until it doesn't. "We need a culture reset here," said Toronto Raptors president Masai Ujiri after his team was swept by the Cavaliers in the 2017 playoffs. Simple translation: Things are going to change.

Culture is created over time by some delicious bit of magical alchemy, takes hold like benevolent bacteria, strengthens and endures. It's a thing bigger than the sum of its parts, able to withstand even moments of bad juju, as, say, when the foot of Draymond Green, a big part of that positive Warrior (also warrior) culture, begins finding opponents' nutsacks with astonishing regularity; or when Green "pushes the wrong button" and sends out a Snapchat photo of his penis; or when your primary owner suggests that the folks in the Warriors organization are a good bit brainier than anyone else in the NBA, as Lacob did in a 2015 *New York Times Magazine* piece; or when your superstar angrily hurls his thoroughly masticated mouthpiece into the crowd, as Curry did during Game 6 of the 2016 Finals; or when the wife of your superstar tweets that the NBA Finals "are rigged for money," as Ayesha Curry did during that same game.

Other teams recognize good culture and pine for it. "When you find lightning in a bottle like the Warriors have found," says Pat Riley, "that combination of forward-thinking management, great coaching, great fan base, young, hip, and all that, behind a team that is capturing the imagination of everyone in sports? When all that fires at the same time, you have something very unique. You want to keep that going as long as you can."

In an effort to change the Warriors' losing culture, Lacob and Guber did a complete analysis—some would call it an autopsy—of every aspect of the Warriors' business. David Lee, now with the Spurs, was on the Golden State roster then, and the owners picked his brain about how things were done with the New York Knicks, where Lee had begun his career in 2005. Imagine being so thirsty for intelligence that you ask how James Dolan does things. "The way they looked at it," says Lee, "the Knicks were a high-expense team, did things in a first-class way, hotels, restaurants, all that kind of thing. They were thorough."

Only after Lacob and Guber had the info did they begin lopping off heads in the front office in areas like promotion, marketing, ticketing, arena management, et cetera. "Eighty percent of the management that was here on day one is not here anymore, and fifty percent or more of the employees are different," Lacob proudly told me in 2016. Without context that certainly sounds like a chapter right out of *Bottom-Line Management: A Textbook for Arrogant Owners*. Yet their moves didn't seem like cost-cutting wet kisses to stockholders. They not only refilled positions but also increased the workforce. They even added two men to the equipment staff. One of their additions as general counsel and vice president was David Kelly, who had been a popular Chicago rapper known as Capital D before he dropped the mic and started shuffling legal briefs from behind a desk. You know you have the apotheosis of a modern culture when your corporate suit can lay down rhymes and impress Draymond, as Kelly has done.

Sometimes, when it was least expected, Lacob and Guber elected to stay with the status quo, as with their decision to retain Jim Barnett, the long-time color analyst who was sixty-seven and had been with the team since the mid-eighties.

"Did you think they'd get some thirty-year-old whiz kid to replace you?" Barnett was asked.

"It crossed my mind," said Barnett. But though Lacob and Guber can throw a lot of Silicon Valley and a lot of Hollywood at you, they are not young men. They understand the importance of institutional memory. Which is also what they got with West.

Guber went to work on his specialty—the entertainment part of the game. "When you came into Oracle Arena," he said, recounting his first Warriors game in 2010, "you got treated like you were a criminal. Every touch point was awful. Music, video board, food, even the way you were taken to your seat. The things I saw weren't low-hanging fruit; they were fruit on the ground.

"And sound? Are you kidding? Would you go to a Broadway play if you sat in the balcony and you couldn't hear the actors? That's how it was at a Warrior basketball game. Stupidest goddamn thing I ever heard." Or didn't hear.

So the Warriors hired from the marketing/tech world a man named Kenny Lauer—who concedes "I'm not a basketball guy"—to oversee what on most teams is called "Game Ops" but around Golden State was changed to "Game Experience."

"Before games, we don't say, 'It's game time,'" says Lauer. "We say, 'Okay, it's time to put on a show.' Before the new owners, the Warriors were digitally illiterate, which is ironic considering how ideally positioned we are near Silicon Valley. Peter wanted to change that. In fact, after my interview with Peter and Rick Welts, Peter sent me up to Google to be interviewed because no one else here knew what questions to ask me."

If you're at a game with the Warriors mobile app loaded, you might get pinged about a special on a player's jersey at the team store. So you turn left instead of right, which will also take you past the place where you can order up a bánh mi sandwich of brisket, snap peas, Thai basil chimichurri, taro stem, and yuzu pho broth. (One order and you would've blown through West's 1971 nine-dollar per diem.) Or you might be riding the escalator to a nose-bleed seat and suddenly a message appears that reads "You could be riding down now instead of up! Ticket upgrade possible!" The Warriors used to beg people just to come in the door; now they have hundreds of fans rushing to get in on the Zaza Pachulia poster special. "We have a Harry Potter bag of tools to build fan experience," says Lauer.

This brave new world is by no means the sole province of the Warriors. In a recent survey of the most tech-savvy teams in pro sports, the Warriors ranked second behind the Kings, whose owner, Vivek Ranadivé (who originally bought in with Lacob and Guber and was the Warriors vice chairman before he bought the Kings), is considered the genius who digitized Wall Street with his Teknekron Software Systems. But so what? The Warriors are the Warriors, and the Kings are the Kings.

As for the sound issue, the Lauer team doesn't have that all figured out. Retrofitting fifty-year-old Oracle Arena—it's a matter of some irony that the NBA's oldest venue houses the NBA's hippest team—to the Warriors' tech needs was not always possible, so most of these innovations won't be obvious until 2019 after the move to the Chase Center, a fever dream for a guy like Lauer, a place where every technological bell and whistle will be available. What the organization must hope for, of course, is that Curry and Durant are still in the new arena. (Things change in an instant. Just ask the Oklahoma City Thunder.)

The lone wheel that squeaked now and again belonged to West, who was given to moments of puzzlement about all the new stuff going on around him. While West stayed away from the tired it-was-better-in-my-day sermons that are so common among many of his generation, he does cast a fisheye at the Silicon Valley sense of superiority that surfaces now and again, as well as the sheer volume of employees it takes to run this business. When the Lakers ruled the world in the eighties, they were a lean operation, particularly in the front office, where you could find West, Mitch Kupchak, a secretary or two, a few phones, and little else.

"Jerry West is not a great influence in that being-happy-going-forward way," says Lacob, chuckling. "He's never happy. He has demons. He has a shroud of negativity around him. He's always thinking about what went wrong. But at least that means he's focused on how to get better. I love Jerry. But I could not *be* Jerry."

Guber is asked what kind of mood West was customarily in when they flew up together to games from Los Angeles. "Well, he has his own unique way of evoking mystery," says Guber finally.

Meaning?

"Meaning you never know which Jerry is getting on the plane," he answers. "But he's smart as shit and he knows this business. We talk about everything. Life, basketball, players, personnel. I ask him about people in the basketball business that I should meet. Or I might say to him, 'Jerry, I think we should look into another treatment area besides ice. This whole soaking-in-ice business is bad.' And Jerry West, who spent *hours* in ice, will say, 'Hey, that's interesting. Tell me about it.' Jerry is not a traditionalist about ideas. And he doesn't care where the idea comes from if it's a good one."

In his early days with the Warriors, West was truly invested in basketball ops. He appreciated the message sent by the owners to the basketball people: *You don't quite have a blank check, but do anything you need to do.* Through much of his time as general manager of the Lakers, West had gotten that same message from Jerry Buss.

West found a kindred soul in Travis Schlenk, who had started as a video coordinator with the Warriors and rose to assistant GM. "We see the game similarly," says Schlenk. "We come from the same kind of place, small towns, blue-collar, working-class America, he from West Virginia coal country, me from Kansas farming country." West saw something in Schlenk and made a few calls on his behalf to the Atlanta Hawks, who hired Schlenk to be their general manager near the end of the 2016–17 season. West was overjoyed for him; on the other hand, he lost a front-office compadre when Schlenk said goodbye.

But there was still the product on the floor to think about. Even by the relatively decumbent expectations everyone had for the Warriors after the Lacob-Guber purchase, the team was not performing well. Change—even sea change—would be necessary. If the Warriors were a puzzle, as West likes to think about teams, Curry and Ellis were slightly different versions of the same corner piece, no way to slide one into the other. There was division within the organization as to which explosive small guard should be the centerpiece going forward, and to this day it's hard to straighten out who exactly thought what. After all, who wants to be the dolt who thought Monta Ellis was a better player than a guy who became a two-time MVP?

But there were ten thousand Warrior loyalists who felt exactly that way. As profoundly strange as it sounds now, one cannot overestimate the degree to which Ellis, not Curry, was the fan favorite.

One thing is certain: Larry Riley preferred Curry because he had drafted him. So did West, who had never liked Ellis's playing style. "I got the deal going," Riley says now, "and Jerry helped me sell it." The only one who owned up publicly to preferring Ellis was Nicole Curran, Lacob's longtime fiancée, who was friends with Ellis's wife. On March 13, 2012, when the Warriors dealt Ellis and two non-contributors (Kwame Brown and Ekpe Udoh) to the Milwaukee Bucks in exchange for center Andrew Bogut and Stephen Jackson, Curran took her displeasure public, and Lacob let it be known that his romantic fortunes took a downturn that day. The Warriors had no intention of keeping Jackson on his second goround with the club, and he was shipped to the Spurs a few days later. (After Golden State won the championship in 2015, Lacob let us know that his romantic fortunes were back on the upswing, oversharing that he and Nicole had enjoyed a threesome with the

Larry O'Brien Trophy.) The Ellis-Bogut deal came down thirty-seven games into the 2011–12 season, which was the second for Lacob-Guber, the first for West as an adviser, and the first for Mark Jackson as coach. Golden State had a 16-21 record at the time.

A week after the Ellis trade, the Warriors held a ceremony to retire the number of Chris Mullin, who had served the organization faithfully as a player and exec but who had left three years earlier on bad terms. "One of the first things Joe Lacob said to me after he got the job was, 'I want Chris Mullin's number up there,'" says Raymond Ridder.

Honoring Mullin was smart. Lacob had pledged to do a better job at keeping alive Warriors history than Cohan had done, admittedly a low bar. Lacob's mistake, however, was deciding to emcee the event himself, possibly to assuage the anger of a fan base that was still trying to figure out why a slow-footed Bogut was better than a fleet-footed Ellis. Actually, it was worse than that. At the time, Bogut was a *no*-footed player, trying to recover from a broken ankle that had him hobbling for months. (Although Bogut was the main piece in the Ellis trade and the starting center on the 2015 championship team, the Warriors grew to dislike the Australian center's game, believing that he was soft and not mentally tough. The Warriors practically gave him to Dallas after the 2016 Finals loss.)

At the time of the Mullin ceremony, West was in Charlottesville, Virginia, promoting *West by West*. Co-author Coleman was with him. "I remember the phone call Jerry made because he had just finished giving me crap about my car being dirty," says Coleman. "He said, 'Joe, don't do it. Don't be the one out front. And the fact that your girlfriend was not happy about the deal? Nobody cares. If anybody wants to complain, it's on you. You're the owner of the team. Plus, I'm happy to take all the grief that anybody feels about the deal. It had to be done.'"

Lacob didn't listen, and, as soon as he took the mic, boos from all corners of Oracle Arena rained down upon him. Both Mullin and Rick Barry, who had been invited to the ceremony, urged the fans to be quiet, but the cascade continued. It was a truly embarrassing moment for a man who routinely made billion-dollar deals in the privacy of a Silicon Valley boardroom. "It was definitely a weird evening," Mullin said. "I was having a great time until then, talking to everyone, and I didn't anticipate anything like that. It was wrong, and it had a lot to do with the trade of Monta. But Joe probably has to take some blame. Nothing that positive had happened with the franchise yet, and they were putting the cart before the horse."

Lacob got through the evening and, to his credit, faced the press afterward. But it was not the end of the questioning. From the point of the Ellis-for-Bogut deal until the end of the lockout-shortened 2011–12 season, the Warriors went 7-22. That gave the Lacob-Guber team a 59-89 record over two seasons.

So, what was so special about them? Or Steph Curry, for that matter?

But things kept improving. The Warriors found good pieces in the draft, meaning they were both perspicacious and providential. Nobody knows everything, not even the Spurs, not even West. Because the Warriors stunk in 2010–11, they drafted high enough in 2011 to get Klay Thompson—the perfect complement to Curry, bigger and stronger than Ellis and a much better defender—at number eleven. (Everybody's favorite soda-shop guard of that draft, Jimmer Fredette, went one pick in front of Thompson. Think about that.) When Curry and Thompson started clicking, Pat Riley was reminded of a guard combo from long ago—Jerry West and Gail Goodrich.

With the seventh pick in 2012, the Warriors got Harrison Barnes, a valuable player in the revival until he suddenly and shockingly forgot how to make jump shots under pressure during the 2016 Finals and was allowed to escape to the Mavericks. But the 2012 draft wasn't about Barnes; it turned out to be about snagging Draymond Green with the thirty-fifth pick. Green has become the contemporary version of Manu Ginobili (the fifty-seventh pick in the 1999 draft) and Tony Parker (number twenty-eight in 2001), desired by so few, subsequently wrathful to so many. There was at least an excuse for San Antonio's Ginobili and Parker, both of whom played overseas; Green was hiding in plain sight at Michigan State.

In the summer of 2013 Andre Iguodala saw what was happening

at Golden State and said, *I want in*. He got there when Denver completed a sign-and-trade deal. At that same time, the Warriors stayed away from Dwight Howard, a self-centered stud/dud who would've been a terrible cultural piece, not to mention a terrible center for what the Warriors wanted to accomplish.

The Iguodala signing seemed as much symbolic as anything—a legit NBA starter picking a franchise that hadn't won a championship since the mid-seventies. But Iggy turned into the kind of player who epitomizes the Golden State ethos—unselfish, resourceful, a little arrogant, and damn smart, the guy who almost always gets, as Ray Ratto puts it, "the hockey assist, the assist that leads to the assist."

Iguodala was also the first player to acknowledge the advantages of signing on for the Silicon Valley synergy, being a savvy investor who proselytizes to his teammates about outside-the-box opportunities. "I'm just trying to get my colleagues to understand that there is a space for us outside of our normal investing," Iguodala told a tech magazine, sounding like, say, Joe Lacob. "You normally see players investing in the barbershop. You see the music companies. You see a lot of real estate. You don't see many go outside of their comfort zones. We want to change that."

So just a few years into the Lacob-Guber ownership, a once unthinkable Bay Area turnaround had happened: The Warriors had begun transmogrifying into the Bill Walsh–era San Francisco 49ers. Plus, Golden State's rise had coincided with hard times for what had once been the model NFL team. "Golden State's owners went out and hired the very best talent they could find and let them do their job," wrote *Chronicle* columnist Al Saracevic in December 2015. "Lacob openly admits that his primary attribute is the ability to hire talented people. And so it should be for the 49ers."

But we would be having none of this conversation about culture had the Warriors not hired, in the spring of 2014, a guy with no bench experience as a coach. Getting Steve Kerr not only gave Golden State its heart, its soul, and to a large extent its voice, it also ended a nasty little behind-the-scenes soap opera that was threatening the utopia the new owners were trying so desperately to create.

*"The Good Lord and four disciples couldn't
beat the Lakers tonight."*
—CHICK HEARN

CHAPTER 12

The Immortal Streak

Winning streaks are magical things, mysterious, dark amazements, inexplicable at root, rare above all, melting away like a late snow before anyone figures out how they happened. True, the Los Angeles Lakers of 1971–72 had great personnel, and it's sometimes difficult for the uninitiated to grasp why the team with superior talent would ever lose. Cooke once mused to his general manager, Fred Schaus, why a pro team could not win every game. It carried a message: *Since I bought you the best players, Fred, when the hell are we going to win every game?*

But sports operate under a harsh calculus. A .500 record generally puts you in the playoffs in basketball and hockey; .600 will usually get you there in football and baseball. A basketball player who makes half his shots might be rewarded with a max contract, a baseball player who gets a hit on one-third of his trips to the plate is compared to Ty Cobb.

To fully grasp what the Lakers accomplished—and what the Warriors would do decades later—it's instructive to look at the 1995–96 Chicago Bulls, a team that went 72-10, the best single-season record until Curry's Warriors eclipsed it with a 73-9 mark in 2015–16. Those Bulls had Jordan on the floor, Phil Jackson on the bench, a sharpshooting reserve guard named Steve Kerr at the ready, and a guiding philosophy that went like this: We come to kick your ass *every single night*. Yet Chicago's longest winning streak during their seventy-two-win season was only fourteen games. (In fairness, streaking was more difficult back then because of the skill of the power players. The Bulls had to contend with big men like Shaquille O'Neal, Patrick Ewing, Hakeem Olajuwon, Charles Barkley, and even a player like Rik Smits, little-remembered but highly skilled in the post. You got battered on a more nightly basis.)

In sports, it's simply too difficult to keep the plates spinning. There are too many variables. A dozen little things have to go right to win even one game, while one little thing going wrong results in a loss. One star's body clock out of sync, one bad meal on the road, one behind-the-scenes disagreement between teammates, one missed referee's call, one in-again-out-again free throw . . . all of those factor into a sport where the difference between winning and losing can be as thin as an eyelash.

Yes, streaks are rare and perfect things, like the petals on a lily or the opening five notes of REM's "Losing My Religion." They're fascinating because so much goes into them and they remain so elusive.

And here is the best one in pro sports history.

NOVEMBER 5, 1971

On the night of Baylor's retirement, the Lakers beat the Baltimore Bullets 110–106. Nobody thought much about the game. The main angle was that Baylor was gone and Chamberlain was now the captain of the Los Angeles Lakers.

Not Jerry West. Wilt Chamberlain.

"I didn't think it was important," West told this interviewer in 2017. "What I said back then was what I meant."

What West said then was: "I was asked to be a co-captain, but I wanted to concentrate on getting back from my injury, so I declined and Wilt was the sole captain."

Sharman knew that making Wilt a captain, whether or not he shared the job with West, would be an important move. And the fact that Wilt had the job alone was a *very* big deal for the big center, a sign that the Lakers were no longer a Baylor-West production, a sign that he was being taken seriously. It might've had a profound effect on the season; at several junctures Wilt went out of his way to show leadership and to remind everyone that he was the leader of the Lakers.

After that first game the reporters asked West about Baylor, who was not present and never did hold a retirement press conference. "You always hear a lot of talk about jealousy between us," answered West, "but that's not true. With him retiring I'm beginning to think that I'll be there, too, someday." West added that he was going to tell Elgin "when he saw him" what a pleasure and honor it had been to play with him.

As for McMillian in his first start, Sharman didn't exactly lead him gently into the fray. He played forty-one minutes, same as Wilt and West, and scored twenty-two points to go with thirteen rebounds. He fit smoothly into the lineup because that was McMillian's thing—he always fit smoothly. West would later call him the "easiest" teammate he ever had because he was always in the right place, and compared him to Bradley, thus subscribing to the standard cliché that Ivy Leaguers are perforce smart. In the case of McMillian and Bradley, it happened to be true.

"Of course it's an honor to take over for him," McMillian said after the game. "But I'm a different kind of player, and we're a different team without Elg."

McMillian was born in North Carolina but raised in New York City. He chose Columbia over basketball powers like UCLA and North Carolina because of its academic rep and its proximity to home. He will forever be mentioned among the Ivy greats, right up there with Bradley, Geoff Petrie, and his Columbia teammate Heyward Dotson, who became a Rhodes scholar. Sharman loved McMillian. He was a willing defender, a strong rebounder, a surprisingly swift player on the wing of a break, and a deadly shooter. Plus, it wasn't like he didn't know the score—the Lakers needed him.

One morning in 2016 Cleamons, who went on to become a successful assistant coach under Phil Jackson with both the Bulls and the Lakers, set up two saltshakers to explain what McMillian was able to do when he wasn't on the run. "Jimmy just kind of 'hid' behind Wilt," said Cleamons. "He played peekaboo, using Wilt as a brush screen, popping one way or the other. And Jerry always found him."

Princeton product Petrie played several classic Ivy League games against McMillian and said that the player Wilt called "Butter" turned into somewhat of a different player in the pros. "Jimmy really got into better shape," says Petrie, an NBA star until a devastating knee injury and later the GM of the Sacramento Kings. "He went from being a medium power player to being a wing guy. I knew he would be good in the pros but not *that* good. Think about it: He was a really, really good player on a team when West and Goodrich were almost unguardable and Wilt was on the court. McMillian made them special."

NOVEMBER 6, 1971

The Lakers beat the Warriors 105–83 in Oakland. Wilt had one of those bizarre stat lines that would come to characterize his season: four points, nineteen rebounds.

After the game he waxed about the differences between San Francisco (where he had played for two and a half seasons) and L.A. "What I like about it here," said Wilt, "is that it's so big that the tourists can't find you. When you go out in San Francisco the natives and tourists are all together."

Six years later a young L.A. broadcaster named Roy Firestone stumbled upon the now-retired Wilt at a restaurant and invited him on his show. Firestone gazes into the distance and conjures up the scene.

"He was driving a Rolls with the top down," says Firestone, "and a beautiful woman in the front seat and a giant dog in the back. Wraparound shades, headband, scarves, jewelry, no shoes, seven-foot-something, three hundred and fifty pounds. And Wilt says to me, 'Roy, I know who you are, and maybe I'd like to do the show. But you have to understand . . . I'm trying to keep a low profile.' "

Trust this: Wilt Chamberlain liked to be found.

NOVEMBER 7, 1971

The following night the Lakers beat the Knicks 103–96 back in the Forum. Wilt got credit for advancing out from his favored defensive position near the basket and defending long-shooting Jerry Lucas, a theme that would emerge in the NBA Finals six months later.

Speculation did continue about Baylor's abrupt exit, though it was nowhere near as rabid as it would've been today. Sharman offered another reason why the Lakers were better with McMillian than Baylor: His system required his forwards to "loop back out from under the basket" if the break didn't work, and that was simply too much running for Baylor.

STREAK: THREE GAMES
SEASON RECORD: 9-3

NOVEMBER 9, 1971

On the first game of a strange two-game road trip, one that would take them to Chicago, then to Philadelphia for one game before returning home—the schedule-makers back then were working without both a computer and a great deal of common sense—the Lakers beat the Bulls 122–100.

Chamberlain had another strange stat line—five points, twenty rebounds, eight assists. Bulls coach Dick Motta noted after the game that Wilt seemed to be looking for open cutters. Actually, Wilt had always done that, but many of his teammates over the years didn't do much cutting, preferring to stand around and watch him.

NOVEMBER 10, 1971

In Philadelphia, Wilt talked with one of his favorite writers, Jack Kiser of the *Daily News,* who had witnessed the one-hundred-point night nine years earlier. Wilt said several nice things about Sharman but also commented that the Lakers "overpracticed." One Los Angeles newspaper got ahold of the story and blew it up. Sharman wisely had almost no reaction. It was one of the few times that the shootaround emerged as a subject.

As for the game, the Lakers were starting to show their true power, winning 143–103, and that was with Chamberlain getting only six points. West had five steals in the third period alone, though that stat was not yet tabulated officially. More "hustle" money.

NOVEMBER 12, 1971

The Lakers won 115–107 at home against a Seattle SuperSonics team that was considered among their most serious rivals in the West. Seattle's roster included Zaid Abdul-Aziz, the former Don Smith who had joined Lew Alcindor in adopting a Muslim name, and an extraordinary talent named Spencer Haywood, who holds a central position in the revolution that was taking place in sports around this time. It was only a couple of weeks earlier that the Supreme Court had agreed to hear Curt Flood's argument that pro baseball "enslaves" its players. Flood lost the case, but the decision galvanized player unity and led to the advent of free agency.

Haywood played his role, too. He left the University of Detroit after one season as basketball's first "hardship" case, ignored the NBA, and joined the ABA's Denver Nuggets for one season, then gave his middle finger to both the ABA and most of the NBA by jumping to the Sonics in 1970. Among those most opposed to Haywood coming into the league was Cooke, not because he cared about labor issues but because L.A. wanted him and Seattle owner Sam Schulman got him.

This war between the two leagues was waged from 1967 to 1976, a much longer time period than anyone thought it would last. Imagine if this list of players who were in the ABA at the time had all been in the NBA: Haywood, Julius Erving, George Gervin, Artis Gilmore, George McGinnis, Connie Hawkins, Zelmo Beaty, Dan Issel, Charlie Scott, Mel Daniels, Darnell Hillman, Louie Dampier, Roger Brown, John Roche, on and on and on.

STREAK: SIX GAMES
SEASON RECORD: 12-3

NOVEMBER 13, 1971

The Lakers won easily in Portland, 130–108. The Trail Blazers were in just their second year as an expansion team. Sharman relied heavily upon LeRoy Ellis, Chamberlain's backup, in this game, both because he wanted to showcase the former Blazer and because the Celtics were coming in the following night and he wanted Wilt to get some rest. Ellis was an underrated factor during the streak season. He was fast and smart and always gave maximum effort. He just presented a less intimidating physical dimension than Chamberlain, to say the least. The line about the 6'10", two hundred-pound Ellis, thinner than a piano string, was that he needed only one belt loop for his trousers.

NOVEMBER 14, 1971

The Lakers easily defeated the Celtics, who were still in their post-Russell lull. Though the Celtics would pick it up as the year rolled on—wasn't it always so?—it was evident that they would not present the big challenge that season. It would come from Milwaukee in the West and New York in the East.

Fans didn't pay as much attention to stat lines in those days—newspaper reports were frequently incomplete—but Chamberlain had a doozy against the Celtics: three points, thirty-one rebounds, ten assists, and thirteen blocks, fourteen if you believe Chamberlain. "I counted them," he said.

The game was at the Forum, but Bill Russell was in attendance for some reason and was asked about Chamberlain's line. "Tell you the truth," he told reporters, "I wasn't paying much attention. I was trying to find out who was guarding Goodrich so I could introduce them."

It was vintage Russell, who could never quite bring himself to compliment Chamberlain. But he was correct—the Celtics couldn't guard Goodrich, who had thirty-six points. Boston coach Tommy Heinsohn tried stationing his guards down on the baseline so West and Goodrich would have to guard them deep and couldn't get out so easily on the break. It did limit L.A.'s fast break but it didn't matter—Goodrich scored almost at will in the half-court.

Goodrich was an unusual player, familiar and popular to local fans since he had starred at UCLA on Wooden's first two NCAA championship teams. It was hard to figure out exactly what he did well because he didn't look like much. But he was an outstanding all-around athlete with superb hand-eye coordination and quickness. Think of a former-day, chunkier version of Steve Nash. Goodrich excelled at volleyball and baseball (he played first base at UCLA) but basically grew up, as he says, "with a basketball in my hand." His father, also a Gail, had been captain of the team and an All–Pacific Coast player at USC. His mother, Jean, had been an outstanding athlete as well, a softball player who matched her height (5'8") in the high jump. One feature about Goodrich in the *Los Angeles Times* bore the headline "Softball-Playing Mother Helped Goodrich Reach the Top."

Goodrich grew up comfortably in the San Fernando Valley—his father was in business development for Consolidated Edison, the electric utility company. Goodrich had that look, too, the gifted SoCal brat. But Goodrich says he was "self-motivated and driven almost to a fault," probably because, as was the case with Nash, people couldn't believe what they were seeing, couldn't believe he was *that* good at *that* size, which is why he had few offers aside from Wooden's to play college ball. He was 5'11" and one hundred and thirty-five pounds when he headed for UCLA. One of his basketball heroes was Baylor, to whom he would never be compared.

The Lakers drafted Goodrich in 1965, basically ignored him, surrendered him to Phoenix in the '68 expansion draft, and got him back for Mel Counts. It remained for Sharman to pair him with West in what turned out to be one of the most effective backcourts in NBA history. He and West seemed made for each other, West the straight-ahead, you-may-know-what-I'm-going-to-do-but-I'm-going-to-do-it-anyway player, Goodrich the crafty and surprisingly long-armed southpaw, ducking in and out of screens, as McMillian did, getting himself open when West was double-teamed ("Gail was always so easy for me to read," says West today), hitting shots from all kinds of angles, "somehow squirreling it up there," as Cleamons put it. McMillian called Goodrich "the Killer."

"Gail just had a lot of . . . *stuff*," says Petrie. "He was great playing off Wilt and Hairston. Great handle, great shooter, deceivingly athletic. You might think he wasn't quick and then he was by you."

In coming up with a comparison for Goodrich, Pat Riley went modern: "He didn't have the three-point shot because it wasn't in the game. But, I'll tell you, Gail was a little bit like Steph. He was great without the ball, and he had a hundred little things he did when he had the ball."

NOVEMBER 16, 1971

Bill Fitch was already previewing the postseason after the Lakers disposed of his Cavaliers 108–90 behind twenty-five points by West. The reality that there exists an extremely small set of teams that can win the NBA championship is not new. "I think the Lakers can do it if Wilt goes to the hoop a little more," Fitch said. "He's going to have to score a little more to keep Kareem occupied. Otherwise, he'll be all over the place blocking shots."

It is impossible to overstate the degree to which the Lakers, whose streak had not yet garnered much attention, were considered the underdogs to the Abdul-Jabbar/Robertson Bucks. Fitch was also previewing the Lakers' upcoming game in L.A. with the Bucks five days hence. Then, as now, the regular season was a blur;

everyone looked forward to those rare red-letter showdown games on the calendar.

STREAK: NINE GAMES
SEASON RECORD: 15-3

NOVEMBER 19, 1971

The Lakers almost lost to the Houston Rockets at home, squeaking by 106–99. Sharman was alone on the bench because he had dispatched K.C. to scout the Bucks-Sonics game in Seattle, which Abdul-Jabbar won with two late free throws.

By this time the papers were starting to talk about "the Jerry Streak" more than the team streak. West had played in the first four games of the season, all wins. Then he got hurt and missed the next five games, three of them losses. Then he returned for the Bullets game that began the current streak. So West was 13-0.

NOVEMBER 21, 1971

If you're looking for a sign that these were different times, consider this one: The Lakers-Bucks game was shown on closed-circuit TV because it was not a nationally televised game. That's how pathetic the NBA television contract was at the time. West vs. Robertson and Wilt vs. Kareem . . . and no TV of any kind. The closed-circuit show cost five bucks, no reserved seating. Come early. (TV deals are the most accessible way to understand what a lowly position the NBA occupied in the sports hierarchy of America even into the eighties. The Lakers-76ers decisive Game 6 championship final in 1980, when rookie Magic Johnson had forty-two points and fifteen rebounds, was shown on tape delay. In the 1984–85 season, when Jordan was a rookie, only five NBA games had prime-time slots.)

The Lakers were in control most of the way, even though Abdul-Jabbar had thirty-nine points. The Bucks were unable to contain the scoring of West, Goodrich, and McMillian. That had become the pattern. Offensively, it was no longer about Wilt's scoring.

More and more, Chamberlain had started to concentrate on defense, rebounding, and outlet-passing. Yes, Abdul-Jabbar scored big, but he needed thirty-three shots to do it; no other Milwaukee player was able to establish a rhythm. Sharman tried something a little different with Kareem, too, having L.A.'s guards "dig" at him when he got the ball in the pivot—that is, come at the center and try to steal the ball when he put it on the floor. That speaks to the lack of sophisticated defenses that were being played back then. These days a player as formidable as Abdul-Jabbar, particularly one who played with his back to the basket, would be subject to double-teaming and digging on almost every play.

On this night the Lakers finally honored Baylor and retired his number. It was the first time he had been around since he walked away sixteen days earlier. He received a warm ovation from the fans, but the next day's story had a curious lack of warmth and a dearth of quotes from Elegant Elg.

NOVEMBER 25, 1971

On November 24, Thanksgiving Eve, the Lakers were on a flight when, somewhere in the L.A.-to-Seattle air space, they likely passed Northwest Orient Airlines 303. That plane, a Boeing 727, had been hijacked by a soon-to-be folk hero named D. B. Cooper. He and approximately $200,000 leaped from the plane and parachuted over the Cascade Mountains near Ariel, Washington. About $5,000 of the $200,000 ransom money was eventually found nine years later near Vancouver, but there has never been a trace of D. B. Cooper or the rest of his stash.

The Sonics might as well have parachuted out of the Seattle Coliseum for all the resistance they put up against the Lakers. Chamberlain had seven points, fifteen rebounds, and ten blocked shots; West had ten assists in the third quarter alone; and seven Lakers scored in double figures, including Riley, who had eighteen points in his first substantive action of the season. The final was 139–115.

Riley was a desperate man at this point. He had been a major college star—he played in the famous 1966 NCAA final when

Texas Western, starting an all-black team, beat Riley's all-white Kentucky, a contest credited with opening up the college game to black players—who was the seventh pick in the 1967 draft. But injuries and an inability to find the right position—at 6'4" he was a bit of a tweener—had limited him, and he had played on a San Diego Rockets team that at the tail end of the 1967–68 season lost thirty-three of thirty-four games. The Lakers had plucked him off the waiver wire for a hundred bucks the year before, largely because Chick Hearn had noticed his hustle. Riley was about to get axed from the Portland Trail Blazers after a preseason game against the Lakers when he heard Hearn's voice. "Don't worry, kid," Hearn told him. "In a couple days you'll get a call." And he did. Such was the power of Chick Hearn.

"Getting to the Lakers changed my life," says Riley today.

But Riley had played sparingly under Mullaney and wasn't happy scratching for minutes under Sharman. His logical mind told him that he wouldn't be playing at all except for an injury to Erickson, while his competitive mind told him that he should be on the court. He earned his minutes with hard-nosed defense, diving for loose balls, and driving West to distraction during practices. Sharman had saved him.

"Joe Mullaney didn't like me at all," Riley says today, "but I met Bill right after he was hired. He liked me. He told me I was 'Celtic-like.' I never forgot that." Riley lights up when he says it. "And he was very frank. He told me: 'Pat, the only way you're going to make this team is to get in the best shape of your life, and be the best practice player on this team. I'm going to use you against West, McMillian, and Goodrich, and I want you to kick their ass.' You know, it was the first time a coach had ever put a demand on me.

"So that's what I did. I ran the beach, miles and miles and miles. I lifted weights, I did things that I had never done, and I did them on my own aside from jogging with Jerry once in a while. So when we went to training camp I won every sprint, blew everybody away in the mile run, and was in better shape than anybody. That's the only reason I was a part of this team.

"Every day I played against my teammates hard, and every day they got pissed off at me. Hey, I had just gotten married and I wanted, I *needed*, a job. My competitive life was on the line; Jerry West's life wasn't.

"Jerry would say to me, 'Damn, Pat, I played forty-four minutes and got forty points last night. I'm sore as hell. Go after Goody [Goodrich] today.' And then, of course, Jerry would kick my ass. But I came right back at him."

Riley, recounting this in his palatial office in Miami, gets a little emotional when he talks about Sharman.

"As the season went on, Bill gave us a sense of belonging," continues Riley. "I had just lost my dad [Lee Riley, a former minor-league catcher] the year before, and Bill took on kind of that presence in my life. If the Lakers hadn't picked me up for a hundred bucks and Bill hadn't become the coach . . ."

He stops and waves a hand around his office. "Who knows? Maybe none of this."

STREAK: TWELVE GAMES
SEASON RECORD: 18-3

NOVEMBER 26, 1971

It was around this time that Chamberlain made it clear that he was more than aware of what the Lakers were doing. He bought two Great Dane pups and said he was thinking of naming them "Win" and "Streak." He brought them to practice once in a while—if Sharman had a no-pet policy it wasn't enforced—and would sometimes yell "Kill!" around his dog-leery teammates. Flynn Robinson liked the dogs. "Wilt Chamberlain has outstanding cars and outstanding dogs," Flynn commented one day. Robinson's eye would certainly have been drawn to the cars; he himself drove a white Eldorado with fur-covered hubcaps that he called "the Batmobile."

Wilt had an outstanding night against the overmatched Pistons, getting twenty-one points and thirty-one rebounds in a 132–113 rout. Every once in a while Wilt decided to show everyone that he, too, could join the scoring parade. "Wilt Goes to the Basket" read the *Los Angeles Times* headline.

Wilt played most of that season with a kind of ease, as if he knew the Lakers couldn't be beaten. He was almost always in control, on the court and off. Phil Jackson says, "You never wanted to excite Wilt during the course of a game. I made the mistake of blocking his dipsy-do shot one night, and after that he just kind of *hunted* me the whole game." But that didn't happen in 1971–72. Wilt played it cool, lord and master of all he saw.

NOVEMBER 28, 1971

The Lakers massacred the Sonics 138–121, their second rout in four days over the team that was supposed to give them trouble in the West. McMillian was sidelined with the flu, which turned Riley into a starter. As always, the attention he received centered on the theme that he was only in the league because of his work ethic. "I jog two and a half miles every morning," Riley said. "And as for diving for loose balls, that's something I learned when I was play-ing for Baron Rupp at Kentucky."

The headline read "A Perfect November."

DECEMBER 1, 1971

The red-hot Lakers came into Boston Garden to face a Celtics team that would finish this season with a fine 56-26 record and make it to the Eastern Conference finals, where they would lose to the Knicks. They had Havlicek, Dave Cowens, Jo Jo White, and a great defensive guard named Don "Duck" Chaney.

Havlicek was incredible that season, leading the league in min-utes played at forty-five—he was the NBA's Iron Man now that Chamberlain was getting long in the tooth—and averaged 27.5 points, 8.2 rebounds, and 7.5 assists.

Yet the Lakers toyed with the Celtics on each of the three occa-sions they played them during the streak. This one was 124–111. West, guarded by both White and the long-armed Chaney, had forty-five points.

"I had forty-five points? In Boston Garden that season?" West said, incredulity in his voice, in 2017. "Really? I'm shocked." His visitor pointed to the box score. "Well, there it is. Honestly at that time? I felt a little over-the-hill offensively. Guess I wasn't."

It is entirely possible that West is being disingenuous. The best guess is, he remembers getting forty-five on the parquet.

STREAK: FIFTEEN GAMES
SEASON RECORD: 21-3

DECEMBER 3, 1971

It was mornings like this that Chamberlain rolled his eyes at shoot-around. For whatever reason, perhaps because they were channeling what used to happen at Boston Garden, officials at Philadelphia's Spectrum did not turn on the lights, so the morning shoot was conducted in semi-darkness.

The Lakers were tired, coming off the game in Boston, and the Lakers were pissed, coming off a dark morning practice, and the Sixers went ahead 82–65 three minutes into the third quarter.

Surely this was the end of the streak.

But L.A. reached back, as it so often did, and came up with extra effort, some of it supplied by Ellis, who was used as a second center, with Hairston going to the bench. McMillian, who had flown in that morning after his bout with the flu was over—those would be the only two games he missed all season—had forty-one points, while West and Goodrich had thirty-two and twenty-eight. Once the Lakers found their legs, the fast break just kept coming at the Sixers in waves.

In *The Pivotal Season* author Rosen quotes Kevin Loughery shouting over to his Philadelphia backcourt mate Fred Carter, "Fuck! Here they come again!"

Reflecting today on the difference between the Lakers' game and what the three-point-shot-loving Warriors do now, West says: "Our fast break was much more layup-oriented. If we had a man advantage, I don't think we ever stopped for a jump shot. We made a lot more bounce passes, too, taking advantage of angles. That's probably one of the lost arts of the game. LeBron is one of the few modern players with remarkable judgment on angles, when to throw that bounce pass around or through a defense."

The final in that 76ers game was 131–116.

DECEMBER 5, 1971

It was around this time that Sharman began having real trouble with his voice. As Hemingway wrote in *The Sun Also Rises* about a character's bankruptcy, "It happened gradually, then suddenly." Riley remembers him starting to cough in time-out huddles. Everything would go silent for a minute and then he would resume, hoarsely. Should he see a doctor? Nah, he used the old walk-it-off philosophy, in this case the old talk-it-off philosophy. Anyway, there wasn't enough time, not enough of a break in the schedule. Besides, it was just his voice. It would come back, right? Voices always do.

It was mentioned here and there in stories, always in kind of a light tone. *Ha-ha, the coach who lost his voice. All coaches do is talk.* Some people called him "Squeaky." The Lakers were a veteran team anyway and didn't need a lot of guidance.

"I do remember that Bill started to use this small megaphone from time to time at practice," says West. "But it wasn't like we talked about it much. Bill wasn't really a screamer anyway, so it's not like we missed something we had been hearing all season. Once he had put a system in place that he believed in, and we bought into it, all we needed was a kind of refresher course. But, yes, it was sadder later when we realized the extent of it."

At some point Dorothy Sharman finally got him to a doctor. Laryngitis was the diagnosis. The wrong one. He was told to rest his voice for a week.

"I'll try," he said. "But we're in the middle of a season."

On this night the Lakers crushed the Trail Blazers 123–107. Seven players scored between ten and twenty points. The headline the following day included the words "Uninspired Lakers." That is how good they had become.

DECEMBER 8, 1971

The Lakers didn't always cruise—they beat the Rockets on the road 125–120, mostly because the Houston guards—Calvin Murphy, John Vallely, former Laker Johnny Egan, and future Laker broadcaster Stu Lantz—couldn't do anything with Goodrich, who had forty-two points. West shot twenty-two free throws but missed seven of them. But that's how it goes when it's going good. You win anyway. Chamberlain took only one shot. *One.* He made it. He had three points.

Shackelford, Hearn's sidekick, remembers pulling out a little pocket schedule around this time and showing it to Riley and Goodrich. They started perusing it. *We've already crushed them twice, I don't see us getting beat here, we should win this one.* "I remember somebody saying, 'I don't see us being challenged until that game in Milwaukee on January ninth,' " says Shackelford.

Sharman didn't want to hear it. He came from that baseball tradition where it was verboten to talk to a pitcher about a no-hitter.

STREAK: EIGHTEEN GAMES
SEASON RECORD: 24-3

DECEMBER 9, 1971

The Lakers had trouble getting out of Houston, and a three-hour flight to Oakland to play the Warriors turned into a seven-hour flight. Nobody was talking about the *Sports Illustrated* jinx back in those days, but perhaps it had a hand in the plane problems—Goodrich was on the cover.

It didn't bother him, though: He had thirty-six points, two fewer than West, as the Lakers won 124–111.

DECEMBER 10, 1971

The merciless NBA schedule-makers had sent the Lakers to Houston, back to the West Coast for the game in Oakland, and then home the following night to play the tough Phoenix Suns. It was the game that almost ended the streak.

Connie Hawkins was the star player for the Suns, his journey to the NBA a battle against racism and blind justice chronicled in an excellent 1972 book by David Wolf, *Foul!: Connie Hawkins*.

A playground legend on the streets of New York City, Hawkins was unfairly targeted in a point-shaving investigation, barred from playing in college and barred from playing in the NBA by then-commissioner Walter Kennedy. Hawkins was an easy target. He was undereducated and not well-spoken, and his entreaties that he had nothing to do with point shaving went unheard. He starred in the ABA and finally made it to the NBA in 1969—the league had paid him about $1.3 million to settle a lawsuit—and became an immediate star. The Lakers knew all about him. In the 1970 Western Conference playoffs the Hawk had averaged twenty-five points, fourteen rebounds, and seven assists against the West-Baylor-Wilt team that just got by the Suns.

Hawkins finished this game with twenty-eight, the same total as West. But he missed a shot in regulation that would've ended the streak, and the Lakers dominated the overtime period in a 126–117 win. Goodrich, playing against the team that had let him go, had thirty-two points, and McMillian had thirty-one.

DECEMBER 12, 1971

For a few days before this game against the Atlanta Hawks, which took place on a Sunday afternoon at the Forum, there had been talk in the press of "twenty-one." That would break the all-time record of twenty straight victories that had been set by the champion Bucks in the previous season. It was a milestone, and so it became a turning point in the attention being paid to the Lakers' streak. Now there was a measuring stick.

The Lakers were losing to Atlanta 77–75 after three periods, but the West-Goodrich-McMillian scoring troika kept going, and, when Goodrich found Wilt for a wide-open dunk with a minute left, the 104–95 win was secured.

It was a strange, strange afternoon, orchestrated by Cooke. The owner loved nothing more than ceremony and decided that twenty-one straight was the time to hold one. Emceed, of course, by Hearn, the postgame festivities included speeches by a couple of local politicians and the presentation of a plaque to Cooke for no apparent reason. Neither the day nor the recipient seemed plaque-worthy. The owner then went into a rambling soliloquy in a manner that suggested a shipping magnate coming down to talk to the deck-hands.

"Yes, Chick, twenty-one victories tonight, and I feel younger than twenty-one years of age and I know you do, too. It was a nip-and-tuck battle, and I nearly had a couple heart attacks near the end, but it was all worth it, wasn't it? I'll tell you, Wilt Chamberlain is playing just about the best basketball I've ever seen any man play in my life. And take little Gail Goodrich. He has developed a touch for shooting that is absolutely unbelievable. It's almost like a feather when it leaves his hand . . . and all of them. And Pat. And LeRoy. The whole crew. This is the wonderful thing. And all under the aegis of that genius of guidance William Sharman."

Cooke had called upon Baylor, who hadn't been much in evidence, to introduce Sharman. Summoning his voice, Sharman said, "We're going to do our best to bring the championship here this year," and got the hell out of there.

One watches the ceremony on video and gets the sense that it was somehow . . . desperate? Perhaps that's the word. So many losses to the Celtics and then the failures against New York in 1970 and Milwaukee in '71 and it was almost like Cooke had to have *this,* because nothing else was certain. Small wonder he didn't release balloons.

STREAK: TWENTY-ONE GAMES
SEASON RECORD: 27-3

DECEMBER 14, 1971

As Charles Manson was installed as San Quentin's ninety-seventh Death Row inmate, more than two years after the bloody murders, the Lakers flew to Portland. Some wondered if the game would have a kind of anticlimactic feel after the Cooke fandango celebrating the twenty-first win. It didn't. The Lakers won easily, 129–114. All five starters scored between twenty and twenty-four points. It was getting to the point that the Lakers could almost pick a random number and say, "Okay, we'll do that."

Hairston was particularly effective with twenty-two points and twelve rebounds. Happy was keenly aware that he was the "unknown" starter, and his resentment at doing the dirty work came out once in a while. West was the Legend, Goodrich was the Scorer, McMillian was the Guy Who Replaced Elgin, Wilt was Wilt, and Happy was . . . what?

"What he was," says Phil Jackson, "was a very, very underrated part of that team. He could run like the wind, and he rebounded his ass off."

Indeed, Hairston's acquisition in the 1969–70 season was one of the franchise's all-time best deals—he was obtained straight up for a player named Bill Hewitt, who never did much of anything. In a nice touch of statistical symmetry, Hairston averaged 13.1 in both points and rebounds during the streak season.

Sharman recognized Hairston's ability right away, installing him as a starter from day one in Hawaii for several reasons. First, Hairston knew his limitations. "Happy never shot it from beyond fifteen feet," says Goodrich. Second, he could get out on the break—Sharman liked the fact that he had been a low hurdler at NYU. Third, he never tired of rebounding. "I go after everything," Hairston told a reporter, "even if Wilt knocks me down." He and Chamberlain formed a friendship. They were the Hard Knock Guys doing the dirty work. Hairston was famous for talking behind teammates' backs, but he rarely did it about Wilt. They sat together on planes and sometimes chafed about their roles. But Hairston had a point about the sacrifices he had made—Happy, whose real name that nobody used was Harold, had averaged over twenty points per game just two seasons earlier, so he could've been a scorer.

Though he was a relatively unknown Lakers star, Hairston is the one who maximized his Hollywood connections. Wilt would later appear as Bombaata in 1984's forgettable *Conan the Destroyer,* but Hairston had a role in a *real* movie. During the streak season, grown men around the country were weeping over *Brian's Song;* well, Hairston was *in* it, with a small role as "Veteran Player #1." In subsequent years Hairston also appeared in shows such as *Columbo, Police Story, Emergency!, Sanford and Son, CPO Sharkey, Knots Landing, Fame,* and *Happy Days,* where he played the father of an epileptic basketball player. Hairston even got credited as "James Hairston" in the Ron Howard movie *The Paper.*

DECEMBER 17, 1971

The Lakers crushed the Warriors, and Flynn Robinson, Sharman's first guard off the bench, had eighteen points. Hearn called Robinson "Instant Points," but the team nickname for him was better— "Electric Eye." West used to say that Robinson's shot went so high in the air that "the ball has icicles on it when it comes down."

The oldest of twelve children, Robinson had a kind of innocence about him. When he began talking, his friends would hold their breath, wondering if he would meander off into some unknown syntactical path from which there was no return. When asked about his notoriously weak defense, for example, Flynn reasonably agreed that, "Yes, I've gotten some bad publicity about my defense." His defense wasn't bad, merely the *publicity* about his defense. But it really didn't matter exactly what he was saying—his teammates loved him.

Flynn wore a toupee, but few people knew it. Once during a game he got hit in the head with the ball and Chamberlain kindly rearranged his hairpiece without fanfare. These days there would likely be an @flynntoupee Twitter feed. Like most conscienceless shooters, Robinson had a folk-hero aspect about him. He came off the bench to shoot, dammit, and that's what he was going to do. Nobody held it against him. "He was a basketball junkie," says West today, "and the part he was concerned about was offense." Playing about fifteen minutes a game, Flynn still squeezed off an average of nineteen shot attempts, and, remember, he was usually on the court with either West or Goodrich.

"If they would've had a three-point shot back then," says Shack-elford, "Flynn would've been one of the best players in the league."

DECEMBER 18, 1971

Chamberlain was taking his responsibilities as captain seriously. It didn't inspire him to tidy up his gym bag at all—Big Musty was still Big Musty—but he was for the most part a mature and steady presence in the locker room. Remembering the overtime game from eight days earlier in the Forum, Wilt told the team that they had to take care of business early and efficiently in Phoenix. Then, right before tipoff, he asked the referees to measure and straighten the rim. Everything was copacetic, as were the Lakers, who won 132–106.

STREAK: TWENTY-FOUR GAMES
SEASON RECORD: 30-3
JERRY WEST SEASON RECORD: 28-0

DECEMBER 19, 1971

With seven minutes left in this game in the Forum—another back-to-back-to-back for Los Angeles—the Lakers were ahead of the Philadelphia 76ers 119–118. Over the next three minutes they out-scored the Sixers 18–1. Somebody pushed a button and the levee broke. That's how it happened, particularly to Wilt's old team, the 76ers, first in the conga line of stooges who fell before the Lakers over these two extraordinary months. In three games during the streak, Philadelphia surrendered an extraordinary 428 points.

DECEMBER 21 AND 22, 1971

The schedule-makers gave the Lakers one of those weird Eastern trips, back-to-back games in Buffalo and Baltimore before a flight back home. Against the Braves, Chamberlain had thirty-one points and twenty-two rebounds, dominating highly touted rookie Elmore Smith in a 117–103 victory. He also had fourteen blocked shots, though Wilt disagreed. "I had fifteen," he said, still counting. There is little doubt that Wilt considered himself to be, among many other things, the best statistician in the league, perhaps in the world, certainly better than weak-ass Lucille Ball. The next night Wilt had only six points in a 127–120 win over the Bullets. "I've criticized Wilt in the past, but I want to commend him and the entire Laker team," said Bullets coach Gene Shue after the game. "He's doing the things necessary to win, and that's a tribute to Coach Sharman."

That was typical thinking back then, and it used to drive African-American players nuts: Congratulations on the way you're playing, fellas, and it's all because of the coach.

The point about Wilt's scoring was this: He could have zero points or forty points and it didn't matter to the result. The Lakers had become not just virtually unbeatable but virtually unscoutable. Go ahead and take your notes, but L.A. just didn't have a verifiable weakness. Catch two or three of them on a very bad night, and, sure, you could beat them. Otherwise, the way they were playing now? It was nearly impossible.

They presented like Scylla and Charybdis, the mythical sea monsters imagined by Homer. You sailed too close to the former and you hit the rocks, too close to the latter and you got sucked into a whirlpool. Take your choice. Run or set up? With the possible exception of Milwaukee with Kareem in the post, they were better both ways than any other team. Challenge Wilt or try to win from the perimeter? They defended either way superbly. Double up West and leave—who?—Goodrich or McMillian open? Double up your box-outs on Wilt, and then Hairston gets every rebound; do it to Hairston, and Wilt gets every rebound. Put your guards on the baseline to stop West and Goodrich from getting out on the break? McMillian and Hairston will run the lanes.

The win over the Bullets enabled the Lakers to break what was then the all-time winning streak in American pro sports—the twenty-six straight in Major League Baseball by the 1916 New York Giants. The Lakers and everyone else around the team were aware of it. The newspapers did a story about the widow and daughter of Giants shortstop Art Fletcher watching the game on television. And a *Los Angeles Times* writer overheard a Laker shouting after the game, "Let's hear it for the 1916 Giants."

Beating the Giants' record was particularly delightful for Sharman because he had been sitting on the bench twenty years earlier when his Dodgers lost that dramatic game.

The only one who pooh-poohed the achievement, typically, was Wilt, who with characteristic bravado said: "I was on a Globetrotter team that won 445 straight games or something." It was a familiar Chamberlain line. At other times during the streak, he'd say: "Let me know when we reach forty-four. That's how many straight my volleyball team won this summer."

STREAK: TWENTY-SEVEN GAMES
SEASON RECORD: 33-3
JERRY WEST SEASON RECORD: 31-0

DECEMBER 26, 1971

Chamberlain later wrote in his autobiography that everyone was anticipating the elaborate Christmas gifts they would receive from Cooke and were disappointed when they opened pen-and-pencil sets. Cooke's tone deafness knew no bounds. As Flynn Robinson later remembered it, Wilt instructed everyone to put the pens and pencils on the floor and step on them. But even Cooke couldn't completely poison the broth. It was Christmas, a feeling of invincibility was in the air, and the Rockets went down placidly, 137–115. West had the flu. He also had thirty-four points and seventeen assists.

The only negative about the holiday season was Sharman's voice. It had gotten worse. Cleamons told me in 2016 that, as the Lakers players grew more and more concerned, sometimes they even played cautiously, at least early in the game, so that Sharman would not get up and yell instructions. Suddenly, it wasn't such a joke.

DECEMBER 28, 1971

As the Buffalo Braves were joining, for the second time, the March of the Condemned—the final in the Forum was 105–87—it had become obvious that the Forum was the basketball capital of the world, and its premier spokesman was Chick Hearn.

It is astonishing the degree to which anyone associated with the streak team speaks in awe of Hearn. "In terms of popularity for the Lakers," says West today, "it really started to turn in our favor when we hired Chick." That was in 1961, right after the Lakers arrived in L.A.

Bill Walton speaks of Hearn in worshipful terms. "One of the things about great leaders," begins Walton, "whether it's Bob Dylan or Jerry Garcia or Springsteen or John Wooden, is that they allow you to see a bigger world. That was Chick in the world of basketball. He wove these phenomenal stories about Elgin and Jerry, and he could talk faster than he could think. That was the antithesis of me back then. I couldn't say a word without stuttering. I'd read in bed until my mom and dad said, 'Lights out,' and then I'd have Chick under the pillow. It was wonderful. It was magical."

As with many announcers, Hearn fit the ethos of his team and his city, became the talking embodiment of franchise essence. Up in the Bay Area, Bill King, the Warriors TV and radio broadcast voice from 1962 until 1983, was a man with a Vandyke beard, mile-long sideburns, and a sinister, almost satanic countenance. He flaunted his intellectual bona fides, befitting the old San Francisco Warriors, whose original uniforms displayed images of the Golden Gate Bridge and cable cars and a simple "The City," as if there were only one city. Even New York never tried to pull that off. King loved ballet, opera, and Russian history, which he discussed with Meschery. King was urbane and eccentric, quintessentially Bay Area. (King is also believed to be the only announcer to ever be tagged with a technical foul, which happened in a 1968 game when he was caught "motherfucking" a referee after what he perceived was a bad call.)

In Boston, by contrast, Johnny Most, a four-pack-a-day man

who looked for much of his life like an under-rested truck driver, was the raspy radio voice of the Celtics from 1953 to 1990. He was rude, even crude, and saw nothing but green, an avenging Celtics hatchet man when he got behind the mic.

Opera? Russian history? Johnny Most? Don't think so.

Hearn was L.A., a showman, fond of offering what he called his "unbiased opinion." Even most visiting teams liked him. Hearn is generally given credit for several words and phrases that are such a part of the basketball argot that they seem to have thundered down from the gods. *Slam dunk, air ball,* and *ticky-tack foul* are a few of them. He was also able to go deep and come up with phrases on the fly. "The Hawk holds it like a peach." "Wilt holds it so high it might get wet up there." "Well, the mustard came off that hot dog." "The Good Lord and four disciples couldn't beat the Lakers tonight." He said that often during the 1971–72 season.

Only Shackelford, who had to fit in a "You got that right, Chick" somewhere in Hearn's avalanche of words, will offer a slightly more nuanced opinion of Chick. Commenting on Hearn's voice being on both TV and radio, as it was for many years, Shackelford said: "You got more words from Chick for two reasons—it was a simulcast and Chick liked to hear himself talk." But Shackelford said it gently. He, too, respected Hearn's talents immensely, as well as his knowledge of the game. Chick had done some officiating earlier in his life, and often during commercial breaks he would share his opinion about a call with fans. "Chick had an incredibly quick mind and a gift for painting a poem with words," says Shack-elford. Hearn's ego was directed toward the franchise rather than himself, his essence yoked to the responsibility of being the Voice of the Lakers. Though Hearn was undeniably a homer, he was not, unlike his counterpart in Boston, an insufferable one.

Hearn also did his job through two unspeakable tragedies, one of which followed this incredible season. We'll get into that later.

DECEMBER 30, 1971

Already there were starting to be stories written about the looming date with the Bucks, the one that Shackelford, Goodrich, and Riley had circled long ago. January 9, 1972. Milwaukee. There really wasn't much else to talk about. The Lakers were on automatic pilot. "It got so we didn't believe we could lose," West said in 2017. "I know that sounds crazy, but it was true."

Whatever the team needed, it just seemed that they could order it up, like they were gazing at a room-service menu. On this night against Seattle, Spencer Haywood was dominating Hairston. The Lakers needed Wilt to be a force, so he got twenty-four rebounds, wiping the boards clean whenever there was a miss. Both Lenny Wilkens, the only-go-left southpaw point, and Dick Snyder, a big 6'5" shooting guard, were tough defensive matchups for Goodrich, so the Lakers needed a lot from West. He gave them twenty points, eleven assists, and six rebounds, despite suffering a gash on his elbow in a battle for a loose ball. Press 1 and place your order.

STREAK: THIRTY GAMES
SEASON RECORD: 36-3
JERRY WEST SEASON RECORD: 34-0

JANUARY 2, 1972

Before this game against the Celtics at the Forum, Sharman's wife, Dorothy, was taken ill with the flu. It had spread through the team; small miracle that her husband hadn't gotten it and made his voice even worse. But the Lakers had yet to lose with Dorothy in attendance, so her husband said, nicely, "Suck it up and get over there." (He did not make her attend shootaround.)

So Dorothy did. The Lakers won 122–113, partly because they shot thirty-seven free throws to Boston's fifteen. "It's unreal," said Boston coach Heinsohn. "It's like giving them fifteen points. We should've won the game. Havlicek didn't shoot a free throw until the end of the third quarter." It was a good warm-up for Heinsohn, who in future years as a Boston broadcaster would never witness a single Celtics personal foul.

Heinsohn also said: "Wilt can play another ten years the way he's going."

JANUARY 5, 1972

As the Lakers boarded a plane for an eleven-day, six-game road trip, they could read a story about a CompuSport calculation that the odds of a team winning thirty-one games in a row were 15,000 to 1. That's where the Lakers stood. They made it thirty-two in a row with a routine 113–103 victory over the Cavaliers in Cleveland. Wilt blocked five shots in the fourth period as the Lakers went on a 15–0 run that clinched it.

Russell, working as a color commentator, said that teams were letting Wilt get into position and they should challenge him more. Cavaliers coach Bill Fitch was asked about it. He just laughed.

JANUARY 7, 1972

In Atlanta, West met another haunted soul, this one more boy than man, just twenty-four, a kid in his second year in the league facing pressures on the court that never confronted West or almost anyone else. West came into a league that was little noticed, onto a team dominated by Baylor. Pete Maravich came into a league in turmoil, at a time of war, and onto a team laden with veterans who were alternately seduced and repulsed by the fame that Maravich brought with him. "Watch the Milwaukee Bucks Play Pete Maravich in his Pro Debut" trumpeted ABC before Maravich's first game. The network had signed a contract to televise the game only if Maravich played.

While West endures, connecting the eras of basketball one to another like so much latticework, Fate conspired to lock Maravich in time. As Mark Kriegel wrote in his superb biography *Pistol: The Life of Pete Maravich,* Pete "is another relic of the seventies, not unlike bongs or Bruce Lee flicks."

In the history of basketball, Maravich is the player who comes closest to "Chamberlain numbers." In four years at LSU he averaged 43.6, 43.8, 44.2, and 44.5 points per game. He scored 3,667 points when no other player in Div-1 history had scored 3,000. That is just silly. Yes, he shot a lot and, playing for his father, got the greenest green light in the history of the game, greener than the light given Wilt, Abdul-Jabbar, Jordan, or Kobe. But Maravich also made a decent 44 percent of his shots and is still—without one sliver of doubt—the most entertaining college player ever, every game a piece of performance art, with no-look passes, behind-the-back-behind-the-legs dribbles, and a bewildering assortment of spin shots. He wasn't the best player. He was the most *entertaining.* And there is something to that.

It would've been a psychoanalyst's dream to schedule weeks of intense father-son therapy with the West and Maravich families—Howard and Jerry on one couch, Press and Pete on the other. Whereas Howard mostly stayed away from Jerry's games, inflicting most of his emotional blows with a lack of interest (though sometimes with a belt), Press was way, *way* too much in Pete's life, a smothering stage father who paraded his son around like a show dog, ordering him to dribble in front of Press's friends, in front of Press's teams, in front of the Harlem Globetrotters, for God's sake. Press wanted Pete to play "interesting basketball." Jerry West wanted only to play "effective basketball." Says West today: "I felt sorry for Pete for what his dad did to him."

Maravich was a thin wire of nerves when he arrived in Atlanta as the third pick of the 1970 draft, not just another Great White Hope but the basketball apotheosis of the "White Negro," a term coined by writer Norman Mailer to describe Caucasian hipsters who adopted black culture. He was free-form, an expressionistic genius, his failures merely evidence of artistic overreach. If West was Rembrandt, keeping it mostly between the lines in a play of light and shadow, Maravich was van Gogh, color and neurosis spreading all over the canvas. Yet Maravich, like seemingly everyone else, admired West. Kriegel writes that Maravich wanted to attend West Virginia because West went there and that he chose number 44 with the Hawks partly because it was his college scoring average but partly because West wore it. (Maravich wore 23 in college; he wanted it with the Hawks but Lou Hudson already had it. Because of Jordan and now LeBron *that* number has become the most famous in basketball history.)

Even with West having a mediocre game, the Hawks were no match for the rampaging Lakers. Maravich outscored West 17–12, but Chamberlain's defense was smothering and the Lakers put one of their Old Testament beatings on Atlanta, 134–90. "The result of that game was surprising," West remembers now. "They had a really, really good team."

After the game, Hawks coach Richie Guerin, who a decade earlier as a Knicks player was so angry that he would've bitten the head off a chicken during Wilt's one-hundred-point game, said: "I like L.A. over Milwaukee now because they have better balance. They also have great quickness and team speed. The Bucks like to set it up for Kareem."

Remember: Even at this point, after thirty-three straight wins, the defending champion Bucks were still the measuring stick.

And so it was on to Milwaukee, where Abdul-Jabbar and Robertson would be waiting.

STREAK: THIRTY-THREE GAMES
SEASON RECORD: 39-3
JERRY WEST SEASON RECORD: 37-0

"Fat, drunk, and stupid is no way to go through life."
—Steve Kerr, channeling Dean Wormer

CHAPTER 13

Kerr: Light Touch, Heavy Influence

In the summer of 1983, just weeks before he was to take his sweet high school jump shot to the University of Arizona, a leap that many thought he would never be able to make, Steve Kerr visited his parents in Beirut, where his father, Malcolm, was president of the American University of Beirut (A.U.B.). Steve had been born in Beirut, where Malcolm was a grad student, though Steve was raised mostly in Southern California after his father became a professor at UCLA. The era of the early eighties was an impossibly complicated time in Lebanon—hasn't it always been so?—and Malcolm had taken the job just one month after the acting president of the A.U.B. had been kidnapped. Still, as he thought about the transition that lay ahead in basketball, the young Kerr had a pleasant vacation in Beirut with his father, mother Ann, and brother Andrew.

But as Kerr waited to board his flight back to the States to begin his college experience, there was an explosion on a runway. Panic set in, and the airport was closed. How to get home? As detailed by writer John Branch in a memorable December 2016 feature in the *New York Times,* Kerr spent time talking to a group of Marines as he waited to see if he could board a U.S.-bound flight filled with diplomats, which he ultimately was not able to get on. Two months after Kerr's casual conversation with the Marines, a car bomb killed two hundred and twenty of them. Relating the story to Branch thirty-three years later, Kerr glanced at the photos of the dead and recognized several he had talked to. He began to cry.

At the airport, other Kerr exit options were discussed before a university driver volunteered to take Kerr over the mountains, through Syria, to Jordan, from where he could get a flight home. Two years after Kerr took that ride through the mountains, the driver, who was a family friend, was killed by a sniper in Beirut.

In January 1984, just as Kerr had started to find playing time at Arizona, he got a call in the middle of the night in his dormitory. His father had been shot twice in the back of the head outside his office. Malcolm Kerr was dead at fifty-two. Two gunmen had surprised him. They were never apprehended. Later in the day a group calling itself Islamic Holy War took responsibility for the killing.

Kerr never got to say a proper goodbye to his father. He couldn't make the funeral. It was just too risky to fly back to Beirut. The death hung with him. He had learned to play ball in his parents' driveway in Southern California. Malcolm was a tall man with, as Steve says, "a pretty good lefty hook." By the time he was a senior, Kerr was an Arizona star and a target for taunts. One night during a game at Arizona State they turned particularly ugly.

"P.L.O.! P.L.O.!" Arizona State students shouted, along with "Why don't you join the Marines and go back to Beirut?"

Kerr related this to Branch: "When I heard it, I just dropped the ball and started shaking. I sat down for a minute. I'll admit they got to me. I had tears in my eyes. For one thing, it brought back memories of my dad. But, for another thing, it was just sad that people would do something like that."

So by the time the Phoenix Suns made Kerr the fiftieth pick of the 1988 draft, the last selection of the second round and sixteen picks behind Wildcats teammate Tom Tolbert, he had seen a lot, been through a lot, learned a lot. Most of all, he learned this: The world went well beyond wins and losses and X's and O's. It's a big and complicated place, short on black and white, full of gray.

Mark Jackson wasn't much for gray. He was a cagey player, a street-smart New York kid who maximized his potential over a seventeen-year career with seven teams. You might win a bar bet asking buddies to name the top five all-time in assists: John Stockton, Jason Kidd, Steve Nash, Mark Jackson, and Magic Johnson. That's right—Mark Jackson finished with more assists than, among many others, Magic, Oscar, Isiah Thomas, and Gary Payton.

He also had the reputation for being a locker-room lawyer, which is possibly why he was traded so often, his seven teams including two different stints with the Knicks. But, look, someone's "lawyering" is someone else's "motivating." The point is, Jackson had an edge. Jackson had fire. Jackson had confidence. And when he decided to get into coaching, he made it clear that he was not going to begin his career as an assistant. Danny Ainge hadn't been an assistant before he became coach of the Phoenix Suns, Jackson always pointed out, never mind the superstars who had gone directly to the head position—Russell, West, Cousy, Magic, and Bird. Even as Jackson flourished as a broadcaster, he wanted a top job, dammit, and he was going to wait for it, getting passed over, most painfully for a Brooklyn kid, by the Knicks when D'Antoni was hired in 2008.

Jackson always stayed in the "possible hire" mix, and after Keith Smart (who had been Don Nelson's top assistant) failed to strike a match in his trial season with the Warriors, attention turned to Jackson. Lacob and Myer knew exactly what they were getting— a fiery newcomer, not a retread. That was exactly what the franchise needed, they concluded.

Jackson started slowly, with a 23-43 record in 2011–12. But stressing defense and effort more than jump shots and fast breaks, Jackson started to find his way, attaining a 47-35 record the following season that propelled the Warriors into the playoffs for the first time since 2007 and only the second time since 1994. Curry loved

Jackson and his preaching-to-the-congregation ways, which had a literal root: Jackson was an evangelical, hellfire-and-brimstone pastor at the True Love Worship Center International in Van Nuys, a neighborhood in the central San Fernando Valley of Los Angeles. In fact, Jackson had continued to keep his residence in L.A. so he could be near his church and preach whenever possible.

The team kept getting better, but not everyone was happy. The wins started to come but not the sangfroid. Lacob and Guber, particularly the former, envisioned a Silicon Valley openness to the franchise, but Jackson was a closed-door kind of coach. He loved individual battles, setting one player against another, one coach against another. He thrived on discord, an us-against-them mentality. Tension to muster victories. That's how he was as a player. There were some reports that he kept West from attending a practice, which would've been a moment of Jacksonesque déjà vu for the Logo, who during his Lakers general manager days had once been tossed out of Phil's locker room. For the record, West says that the Mark Jackson toss-out never happened, and he thinks, in fact, that Jackson should get another chance at a head job. That doesn't sound like the whole story. *Chronicle* columnist Scott Ostler reported that West was among those who lobbied with Lacob and Myers for Jackson to be fired. Even Jackson's supporters cannot dispute the fact that he was territorial. ESPN's Zach Lowe, then writing for *Grantland,* had Jackson nailed when he described his personality as "a strange brew of braggadocio, inspiration, and insecurity."

Other breadcrumbs started to drop along the path to Jackson's firing. When NBA player Jason Collins famously came out as gay in May 2013, Jackson said this: "We live in a country that allows you to be whoever you want to be. As a Christian man, I serve a God that gives you free will to be who you want to be. As a Christian man, I have beliefs of what's right and what's wrong. That being said, I know Jason Collins, I know his family and am certainly praying for them at this time."

So how do you interpret that? As a man staying true to his religious ideals? Or as a masterpiece of Christian condescension? It did not play well in the Bay Area generally and in the halls of Warrior

World specifically, where one of the sports world's best-known gay men, Rick Welts, was a high executive. (Collins's twin brother, Jarron, also a former NBA player, is now a Golden State assistant.) Plus, there was the issue of hypocrisy with Pastor Jackson. After his first season with the Warriors, Jackson admitted to an affair with a stripper that had led to an extortion plot against him, one that he helped the FBI squelch.

Jackson didn't routinely proselytize at press conferences. Ask him about his faith and ye shall be told, but he didn't get in your face with it. Still, he never hid his penchant for preaching. In April 2014, about a month before the Warriors would be eliminated in the first round of the Western Conference playoffs, Jackson preached a sermon on the same Oracle floor where he had coached a game (a 103–94 loss to Cleveland) an hour earlier. Over the years a lot of coaches have done a lot of postgame testifying but usually at saloons.

During the sermon Jackson evoked Curry and the healing powers of his own wife, Desiree Coleman-Jackson. "God told me to tell you this," Jackson began. "How can three years ago Steph Curry be an injury-prone basketball player, with ankle surgery after ankle surgery after ankle surgery, then decide to stop into our Worship Center International?" At that point Jackson introduced his wife and continued: "So Steph Curry comes to church, and she calls him to the altar, and she gets the holy oil, and she lays hands on his ankle. Now some folks don't believe this."

Then Jackson told the crowd that, ever since the holy oil application, Curry had avoided injuries. In other words, it wasn't the off-season ankle surgery during which debris was excised from Curry's injured ankle, or his dutiful rehab, or the conscientiousness of the Golden State training staff, or Curry's own work ethic that made him better. It was the oil.

In Marcus Thompson II's biography of Curry, *Golden,* the author describes the visit that Curry had indeed made to Jackson's church in the preseason of 2012. He was called to the altar, anointed with oil, and, after returning to his seat, was called back again by Desiree. "You don't get a blessing from the Lord and just walk off!" Jackson's wife shouted. "Show us you believe in the power of God." So Curry, remembering his old Bible stories, started shimmying and hopping on his injured right foot. "I didn't know what else to do," he told Thompson.

It should be noted here that Curry is deeply religious. He and Ayesha met in a church youth group in Charlotte when both were kids. Curry's first tattoo was a biblical phrase from First Corinthians that says, "Love never failed to be," which he has written in Hebrew. With Curry and Draymond Green along with now-gone players such as David Lee and Jarrett Jack, the Warriors were an openly religious team under Jackson. And when Curry writes "I can do all things" on his sneakers, it is not chest-pounding bravado but, rather, a condensed version of Philippians 4:13, which reads, "I can do all things through Christ who strengthens me." So while Curry was surprised and a little embarrassed by the oil rubbing, he did not seem offended.

However, Jackson's role with the church, as well as his living in L.A., began to be an issue with management. And that was before a civil war within the coaching staff became public. Jackson abruptly fired Brian Scalabrine, who had been a favorite of the owners, and another assistant, Darren Erman, who, fearing for his job under Jackson, was found to have been secretly recording team conversations between players and coaches. According to sources, Erman was trying to protect himself from what he believed were the efforts of Jackson and the other assistants to bad-mouth him to the players.

It was a mess of a soap opera, the very thing that could despoil a healthy culture. And after the first-round loss to the Clippers, soon after his Oracle sermon, Jackson was fired. His record in his final season had been 51-31. Told four years earlier that their team would've won fifty-one games by 2014, Lacob and Myers themselves would've hopped, shimmied, and done a great deal of righteous testifying.

After he was fired, Jackson described to his congregation what happened as he left his final Golden State meeting. He shook Lacob's hand and said, "I'm praying for you."

There have been subsequent awkward moments when Jackson and his ABC/ESPN broadcasting companions Mike Breen and Jeff Van Gundy have had to comment on Kerr's coaching, usually positively. Jackson asks only that his contributions to the Warriors not be forgotten. "You cannot disrespect the caterpillar," said Jackson, "and rave about the butterfly."

Whether you're preaching on the floor of the Oracle or sitting at the table with Mike and Jeff, that's a damn good line.

Much later, long after Jackson was gone, Kerr was asked how he turned Golden State into a great defensive team.

"I didn't," he answered. "Mark Jackson did."

Were he not so sports-obsessed as a boy, a pitcher of baseballs as well as a shooter of basketballs, Kerr might've become a preacher. His grandparents were missionaries, and obviously Steve's father had a bit of a pastorly bent, risking his life to teach in a battle-ravaged capital. And if Lacob, Guber, and Myers weren't seeking a literal man of the cloth for their coaching job after the Jackson firing, they were at least looking for a man who evokes a kind of personal peace. *Evokes* is the key word, for Steve Kerr is not always peaceful, as his shattered wipeboards over the years attest.

In those respects, one can find a line running from Bill Sharman through Steve Kerr. They were both hellacious competitors who were able to evoke a kind of harmony. Sharman was more of a star player than was Kerr, but they both checked all the boxes for being successful as a coach.

Consider Kerr:

Winning? Kerr played on five championship teams. Coaching models? Three of those championships were earned playing for Phil Jackson in Chicago and the other two for Gregg Popovich in San Antonio. Understanding all kinds of players? Kerr was a favored teammate of both Jordan and Tim Duncan, but he should also be considered a patron saint of hoop reserves—he played in nine hundred and ten NBA games and started only thirty of them, twenty coming in one season early in his career with Cleveland.

The man was more comfortable with the feel of pine than with the heat of the spotlight. Requisite broadcasting stop? Kerr spent several seasons as a TNT analyst, earning points for both substance and snark.

Kerr even checked two additional boxes. For three seasons he was general manager of the Suns. And Kerr was also an owner for a while, having bought in with Phoenix's Sarver group in 2003. (Kerr, obviously, divested his one percent share when he joined the Warriors.)

Beyond that, there is an undeniable It Factor about Kerr. The leading three-point percentage shooter in history is not Reggie Miller or Nash or, for that matter, Curry. It's Kerr, at .454. It's unclear how many of his players know that, or realize that he won the three-point contest at the 1997 All-Star Game. What they do know is that Kerr had enough old-school stroke to occasionally beat Curry in post-practice shooting games. A fifteen-second video of Kerr and Curry shooting free throws together shortly after Kerr got the job got two million views. Kerr didn't shoot much after the onset of his back problems but finally felt well enough to hoist a few free throws with Curry before Game 4 of the 2017 Finals, which turned out to be Golden State's only defeat in the playoffs. So . . . perhaps no more shooting. But Kerr's rep endures. After former Lakers guard Nick Young signed a free-agent deal with Golden State in the 2017 offseason, he was asked who was the best shooter on the Golden State team. "Kerr" was his answer.

Kerr also has his Seminal Moment. It's all over YouTube and in all those specials about the Chicago Bulls. He's sitting on the bench next to Jordan in Game 6 of the 1997 NBA Finals, Bulls against the Utah Jazz, score tied 86–86, Chicago needing one more win to capture its second straight championship. Kerr, blond and boyish (which he still is to a large extent), listens as His Airness, in his distinctive basso profundo, notes that Stockton is probably going to double-team him, a reasonable expectation.

"If he comes off, I'll be ready," says Kerr, who then vigorously rubs his face with a towel, perhaps thinking, *Wait, did I just make a promise to Michael Freakin' Jordan?* Then again, Kerr was a

player who wrote *FI* on his sneakers—short for "Fuck It," meaning
that shooters should just shoot and damn the consequences. Jordan
nods and stares straight ahead, sipping liquid from a Gatorade cup.

Play resumes. Sure enough, Stockton comes for the double-team,
leaving Kerr open in the middle of the floor, just beyond the foul
line, about seventeen feet from the basket. Jordan knifes between
Byron Russell and the doubling Stockton, and gets the ball to Kerr.
A catch-and-shoot player if there ever was one—the opposite of
Jerry West—Kerr wastes no time: the shot goes up, the shot goes in,
and the Bulls win. Another championship follows in 1998.

If a man needs more bona fides, Kerr has this going for him, too:
In the 1995–96 season, his first with the Bulls, he refused to back
down from Jordan in a scrimmage after Jordan, deep in his alpha-
male phase (one that has lasted his entire life), hit him with a fore-
arm shiver. Kerr hit him back. A few other glancing blows were
thrown. Order was restored. The Bulls went on to win a championship, and, for Jordan, Kerr became the second coming of John Pax-
son, his that's-my-boy bailout option.

All things considered, if Kerr didn't exist, Lacob would've had to
invent him.

To get Kerr, the owners had to purloin him from the clutches of
Phil Jackson, whose first goal, after he had become president of the
Knicks (a job he no longer has), was to land his former spot-up
shooter. Kerr was tempted by New York but took a long look at
ownership and immediate prospects—a quick one would've
sufficed—and signed a five-year, $25 million contract with the
Dubs in May 2014.

Shortly after Kerr was hired, the Warriors added to their coaching staff basketball lifer and defensive specialist Ron Adams, who
had been with seven other NBA teams (including the culture-
healthy Spurs) to play the designated role of Obi-Wan Kenobi,
which he has done superbly. Adams, seventy, sometimes looked
upon the Silicon Valley new-waveness with, if not a Jerry West
jaundiced eye, at least a skeptical eye. But since he had never been
with a championship team before Golden State, who was he to
argue with success?

Deep in his soul, Adams believes—as do an overwhelming majority of other lifetime assistants—that he could've been a head coach years ago. Though he's become a defensive guru, Adams also likes to work out shooters and big men. He would've seemed to be in many respects the logical person to take over the reins when Kerr's back problems kept him from coaching at the beginning of the 2015–16 season, and there was discussion among Lacob, Myers, and Kerr about Adams stepping in. But it was never going to happen. Luke Walton, thirty-three years younger and infinitely less experienced, more fit the Warriors' paradigm. When Kerr went down again in the 2017 playoffs, there was no discussion about it; Mike Brown had been brought in as the first assistant when Walton went to the Lakers. With two championship rings and a secure reputation, Adams has settled comfortably into the role of Bench Guy Who Has Seen It All, the man with the Philosopher's Stone in his back pocket.

Adams has been enormously important to the Warriors' success, beyond the fact that he is an outstanding defensive coach. First, Adams sent the message that, amid all the new-school stuff going on, the basketball operation had an old-school feel to it. When Phil Jackson was winning six championships in Chicago, he may have tromped through the New Age forest in Zen moccasins, but he had at his side Tex Winter, who had written a book about the triangle offense way back in 1962, and Johnny Bach, a smart, tough World War II vet.

Second, though no one could see this coming when he was hired, Adams had been extremely close to Durant during their two seasons together in Oklahoma City. Adams had always played up Durant's often overlooked abilities as a defender, particularly his willingness to listen. K.D. actually said this at his introductory Golden State press conference: "Ron Adams is the only reason I came here."

That was a little strong. But get Durant started on the subject of Adams, and he'll keep going. "I just love that man," Durant told me in 2017. "His spirit, his knowledge. It's no accident that everyone wants him, right? He's taught me so much."

Adams sometimes seems to be rowing his own boat through Warrior Waters, but that's often the way it is with defensive coaches.

They are the closest things to football-type coordinators in the NBA. But Adams also fits the Warriors' paradigm: a guy who works like crazy—even minutes before the game he's liable to be on his laptop figuring out alternative ways to play the pick-and-roll—but doesn't necessarily see the world as just X's and O's.

"I was just talking to our young guys here," Adams said to me one night before a game as he warmed up Warrior reserves, "and they never heard of the word *androgynous*. What kind of world are we living in?" Then he returned to the warm-ups.

After Kerr took the job, he walked into an immediate personnel dilemma: Should the team trade Klay Thompson for Minnesota's Kevin Love? (Thompson and Love, incidentally, had been teammates on the 2001 Lake Oswego [Oregon] Lakers all-star team that just missed a berth in the Little League World Series, Love an overpowering pitcher, Thompson a lithe shortstop.) At this point, remember that while Curry and Thompson had shown promise, they had not yet blossomed into a championship backcourt, while Love, a scorer and rebounder at 6'10", was a consensus top-ten player.

Everyone within the Warriors organization has his own story about what happened. West and Travis Schlenk were both firmly against the deal, the former even threatening to quit if it went through. West loved Thompson. Chris Mullin, then with ESPN, was at a Thompson predraft workout and remembers West walking onto the floor after it was done. "I said to everybody, 'The Warriors are going to take him,'" said Mullin. "'Jerry just loves him.'" Plus, though this probably shouldn't figure into draft decisions, West owed the Thompson family a debt. "We won a championship in L.A. [in 1987]," West says, "because Kevin McHale couldn't score much against Klay's father."

But the most reliable account has Kerr unwilling to make a big personnel change just weeks into his tenure, and Myers, though an early favorite of the trade, thought it best to fall in with Kerr. So Myers made the final call that the deal would not be done.

Sometimes what you *don't* do is more important than what you *do* do, and that was a big moment in the evolution of the Warriors' culture, the message being: *We've started something here, so let's not give up on it.*

Look, who's to say that the butterfly would not have emerged under Mark Jackson, that he would not have gotten the Warriors to a title. Another Jackson, Phil, took over two teams seemingly on the cusp of becoming champions, the Jordan Bulls and the Kobe-Shaq Lakers, and did indeed get them to the finish line. Was a coaching change the number one factor? There's little doubt that Doug Collins (Bulls) and Del Harris (Lakers) believed they would've pushed their respective teams across the line, too.

But the vibe did change under Kerr. Nothing works in an organization unless the head coach is behind it. Raymond Ridder can do all the hustling he wants for positive PR, but if the coach creates an anti-media template, the organization is going to be perceived as anti-media.

Kerr didn't open practices to the press—almost every team these days operates as if it is handling state secrets instead of a basketball—but post-practice, pregame, and postgame interview sessions were loose, friendly, and frequent. Warriors staffers no longer felt as if they were intruding. Lacob wanted to knock down the walls between church and state—in the corporate office, where cubicles now reign, he did so literally—and Kerr was all for it. Families of players started to attend practice and take to the court when it was over. Kids with special needs, charitable groups, and representatives from Bay Area and Silicon Valley businesses became part of the scene. Myers and Kerr invited back old franchise heroes like Rick Barry, Al Attles, and Tom Meschery.

The idea of a Golden State Past and Present began to take hold. Even a minor ex-Warrior like Jason Richardson was recognized one night by the franchise during a game, and he couldn't believe it himself. "I didn't win a championship," said an overwhelmed Richardson. "I didn't go to an All-Star Game. I wasn't All-NBA, All-Defense, or All-Anything. Yet this organization has a love for me, despite all of that." Larry Riley, the displaced general manager who drafted Curry, gets frequent invitations to come to games at Golden State's expense, from Myers himself. " 'Hey, when you coming to a game?' Bob still asks me," says Riley. "Sure, I'd rather still be there in the front office, but this is pretty good." There he was at the 2017 Finals in the Oracle, getting a few thanks-for-drafting-Steph handshakes from fans.

Together, Kerr and Myers crafted a user-friendly franchise. Sometimes they seem like versions of the same guy, Myers slightly more serious, Kerr slightly more, for want of a better word, mischievous, more a one-of-the-guys guy, mordant where Myers is sincere. After Myers read *Between the World and Me* by Ta-Nehisi Coates, he and Kerr turned it over at morning meetings. After the devastating Game 7 loss to the Cavs in the 2016 Finals, Myers became the first GM in history to quote Maya Angelou: " 'People will forget what you said, people will forget what you did, but people will never forget how you made them *feel*.' That's what I'll remember about this team." Myers and Kerr are extremely close, bound not just by common Warriors interest but also by family tragedy, Kerr through his father's assassination, Myers through the death of his brother-in-law, Scott Dinsmore, who was the victim of a rockslide during an attempted ascent of Kilimanjaro in September 2015.

But the more important part of the culture equation, at least to these eyes, is Kerr. He brought to the Warriors what Sharman brought to those West-and-Wilt Lakers—a steady hand on the controls, a mind and a voice that corralled abundant talent into a cohesive whole. Kerr is not above reaching a hand into the Old Coaching Trope bag. He coined "Strength in Numbers" as the slogan for the 2014–15 team that ended up winning the championship. On a board at the Warriors' practice facility in downtown Oakland are listed the team's "core values": "Competition, Compassion, Mindfulness, Joy."

Pointing to Kerr, the journal *Education Week* ran a story during the season that carried the following headline: "How the Golden State Warriors Can Help Explain Social-Emotional Learning."

But Kerr can also be a hoot. (Mark Jackson has many qualities but hootishness is not one of them.) During a road trip to Chicago, Kerr got onstage with Second City, the vaunted improv group. After a loss Kerr might turn philosophical or he may conjure up Dean Wormer from *Animal House:* "Fat, drunk, and stupid is no way to go through life." After he smashed a wipeboard in anger during Game 1 of last year's Finals—it came after a careless turnover, a Warrior specialty—Kerr quipped: "I coached on heart the rest of the way." He deals easily with the press, which he does not consider an enemy. He wakes up every morning and reads actual papers. As a student at Palisades High School in Los Angeles County he co-wrote a weekly column for the school newspaper with Mike Silver, who has gone on to become a celebrated football journalist. "If Steve wanted to be a satirist," says Silver, "he would've been really, really good." Kerr was also known for making prank calls to radio stations. To see him as a kind of high-IQ Dennis the Menace would not be far wrong.

The coach talked about books, including his reliance on an old sports psychology work, Tim Gallwey's *The Inner Game of Tennis,* which he has given to Andre Iguodala and a couple of other players. (But not Curry and Thompson. "They don't need to think," says Kerr. "They just need to shoot.") There is a Kerr Whisperer on the team—assistant coach/Curry shooting guru Bruce Fraser, to whom Kerr has been close since their days together at Arizona. Fraser will let Kerr know little details about the emotional state of the team, maybe suggest a few adjustments to the practice regimen (nothing during games), calming Kerr with his surfer-dude manner. Fraser's nickname is "Q," which came from his habit of asking so many questions. That's a very Warriors thing.

Kerr gave coaching a human side. He owns up to having bouts of anxiety and fear. (And certainly the world saw what pain is doing to him.) He practices yoga and prescribed it for his team. There is something of the nuts-and-berries-early-Phil-Jackson about him, except that Kerr, unlike Phil, never acts like he has it all figured out. He is a searcher, a self-examiner.

Kerr talks racial politics, gun control, bullying, Black Lives Matter, Colin Kaepernick, police shootings, medical marijuana (he'll discuss recreational marijuana if you want to), just about anything. He seems to fit in an area where Ganja Yoga classes are a real thing. Exchanging ideas, looking at the outside world, contemplating mysteries—the Warriors became known as a kind of think tank in sneakers.

Kerr isn't a preacher à la Jackson but more like the thoughtful guy sitting on a barstool talking while he sips a beer. (Okay, it's the Bay Area—maybe a dry but nonaggressive Pinot.) Yet he never jams his life story down anyone's throat. When people tell Kerr to shut up about gun violence—and they do—he never counters with the story about his father, letting someone know that maybe he's given a little thought to the subject. But he also never stops giving his opinion.

"On the hierarchy of building a team," says Myers, "your coach is very, very, very important. He drives the car. He touches the players more than anyone, and they have to have an enormous amount of trust in that individual. The thing about Steve is that he's a much better person than he is a coach. And he's a great coach."

Backup swingman Shaun Livingston, who came to Golden State as a free agent before the 2015–16 season, has much perspective on the culture, having played for eight teams before signing with the Warriors, including Riley's Heat.

"Every team has its own formula, but I can tell you that in Miami they run a lot tighter ship," says Livingston. "There's one chef in the kitchen, and everybody knows who that is. Pat Riley.

"Here it's kind of like a big panel. Everybody has their own opinions and we have a big box of ideas, and from that box we take the best one. And you don't necessarily have the best idea because you've been around the longest or you're in charge. That feeling starts with Bob Myers and Steve Kerr. Steve drives the ship, and Bob is behind him as the navigator."

Man, you certainly have the metaphors going, Livingston is told.

"I try," he says.

Now, Kerr was extremely lucky in terms of the personnel he inherited when he got to Golden State. Many new coaches have every intention to set a democratic tone only to discover that they are living in a monarchy with a superstar sitting on the throne. The Cavaliers in LeBron's first few seasons are one example; there simply was no franchise beyond LeBron. It was the Cleveland LeBrons. Every coaching decision, every personnel decision, every marketing decision was made to satisfy, mollify, justify LeBron. That's not his fault. It's just the way it was.

"There is no doubt that a superstar can swallow up a franchise," Kerr says. "Obviously I saw it firsthand in Chicago. But Jordan was different from almost anybody. Look, *we* were scared of him. Yes, it was all about Michael. But he was so freaking good that we knew we were going to win. It wasn't like he was going to damage the team. He was just going to beat the other guys. And in a sense he didn't just swallow up the Bulls, he swallowed up the whole league.

"The similarity here is more like Tim Duncan and Steph. Those guys set the tone for the entire team. Tim set a tone of inclusiveness. Everybody matters. Everybody gets a voice. Steph is the same way, and when we got K.D. he was the same way. Guys like Tim and Steph are skilled but also so modest that it makes for a really fun atmosphere and makes it easier on the coach. You come in and you know guys are going to follow their lead. Some of the ego stuff that goes on with other teams we just don't have."

No one knows that better than Kerr's top assistant, Brown, who spent five seasons in the Land of LeBron and a little more than one season in the Kingdom of Kobe (late in Mamba's career). Both players were franchise swallowers, though in different ways. Kobe was the prototypical lone wolf, on and off the floor. *Give me the damn ball, get away, and don't bother calling me for dinner 'cause I got other plans.* Over the years LeBron has sometimes waved off his power with an I'm-just-another-player disingenuousness, while never hesitant to exercise that power. Brown, a soft-spoken congenial type with the aspect of an accountant, did indeed get swallowed up by the early LeBron and the late Kobe. (Trust this: The latter is worse. LeBron has learned to at least pay lip service to the concept of teamwork on the floor and friendship off it.) Brown would prefer to bring the conversation back to San Antonio—does anyone not?—where he spent three years as Pop's assistant before getting his two head positions.

"The culture here is similar to what we had in San Antonio," says Brown in a familiar refrain. "Bob Myers and [Spurs GM] R. C. Buford are in similar positions, totally aligned with the head coach. But here it starts with Steve, just as it starts with Pop in San Antonio. And if the two at the top of the game food chain—

superstar and coach—aren't in line, you're screwed. But we had alignment in San Antonio with Duncan and Pop, and we have that here with Steve and Steph and now Kevin. When you have an abundance of talent, maybe you can get away with the isolated superstar for a while. But in the end, bad relationships will kill you."

So, chemistry? Check. But after Kerr got the job there was still the major matter of *how* his team was going to play. Curry had become an All-Star in the 2013–14 season, averaging 23.8 points per game, Thompson following at 21.7.

Even with a defensive-minded coach like Jackson, it was obvious that something was happening on the offensive side of the ball. The question was: Could it become something really special?

"It wasn't like we thought, Oh, this is inevitable. Had to happen. *No, we wanted to win every game."*

—JERRY WEST, AFTER THE STREAK-ENDER

CHAPTER 14

A Loss at Last; Wilt Throws a Bash for the Ages

West's Lakers knew that victory number thirty-four, on January 9, 1972, would not be easy, to say the least. Trying desperately to find some chink in L.A.'s armor, Bucks coach Larry Costello had been in Atlanta's Alexander Memorial Coliseum to scout. He departed with ten minutes remaining in the blowout to catch a late flight back to Milwaukee after telling reporters that the key to L.A.'s success was its long outlet passes. Costello already had a trick up his sleeve: After Wilt or Hairston got a defensive rebound, either Abdul-Jabbar or Curtis Perry was to stay home and wave his hand in front of the rebounder's face, thus slowing the fast break.

(West, incidentally, was no Costello fan. As Shackelford remembers it, as a player the scrappy 6'1" guard, who played against West for seven seasons, had more than once mentioned how he reveled in defending West and once stated: "I'm a veteran. I'm going to dedicate my life to stopping him." West took that personally and made sure that Costello rarely did stop him.)

The Milwaukee-L.A. game was played in the old Milwaukee Arena, where the Beatles had played a show during their 1964 world tour. This showdown was fraught and edgy, contested between two teams that had clearly been recognized as the best in the league. The Bucks were tired of hearing about the Lakers' streak, and the Lakers were tired of hearing that the defending champion Bucks were still *the* team.

If there is one play that crystallizes the difference between the NBA of the early seventies and the NBA of now, it happened with 7:47 left in the second quarter. Abdul-Jabbar gathered up a loose ball in the lane and went up for a dunk. Happy Hairston, coming over to contest him, tripped and fell awkwardly into Abdul-Jabbar, in effect undercutting him. Abdul-Jabbar made the dunk, came down on Hairston, then suddenly wound up and punched him, landing contact on Hairston's face. Hairston went down.

The play happened suddenly, so suddenly that it caught the broadcasting team of Keith Jackson and Bill Russell off guard. The two veteran refs on duty, Richie Powers and Mendy Rudolph, conferred for a moment—these days the conference would've lasted longer than an agricultural hearing on C-SPAN—and Abdul-Jabbar was assessed with what was variously called "a punching foul," a "deliberate personal foul," or a "punching technical." But it wasn't a technical, because Hairston, not West or Goodrich, took the attempt.

He missed. Abdul-Jabbar stayed in the game. After the game, Hairston showed reporters the lump on his jaw, yet it was still not a headline-making play. These days the image of Abdul-Jabbar winding up and landing would've gone viral, and the league office would've gone ballistic.

Asked about it in 2017, Abdul-Jabbar waved it off. "Oh, it was nothing," he said. "Happy was always getting away with stuff." Ah, simpler times.

Strangely, five years later, Hairston would figure prominently in Abdul-Jabbar's personal life. Abdul-Jabbar had an office in the same L.A. building as Hairston (by now retired but still a thespian), and one day Abdul-Jabbar noticed a woman talking to Hairston. He asked Happy about her and found out that she was Hairston's secretary. Kareem was interested but Hairston wouldn't help him. Recently divorced from a Muslim woman who was chosen for him,

Kareem stayed on the case, and eventually the woman, Cheryl Pistono, became his companion and the mother of his fourth child. They never married and broke up in 1984, but Kareem's relationship with Pistono was one of the most meaningful of his life.

When the surviving Lakers recap the streak-ender, they invariably remember it as being one-sided from the beginning. "They beat us like we stole something," says Cleamons. West, Goodrich, Erickson, and Riley all remember it being a blowout from the beginning. But in reality the game wasn't that one-sided, their collective recollection probably based on the fact that Milwaukee outplayed them so badly in the final six minutes. The score was tied at 71–71 in the third period before the Bucks reserves led a rally that made it 84–77 going into the fourth period. But Flynn Robinson came off the L.A. bench to lead a Lakers rally, and a Chamberlain tip-in midway through the fourth cut Milwaukee's lead to 94–92.

It was then that Sharman faced one of those age-old-not-one-good-answer-to-it coaching dilemmas: Reinsert a starter who has been cold? Or stay with a reserve who has been hot? Sharman chose the former, putting Goodrich back into the game for Robinson. The move seemed to put the brakes on the Lakers, and the Bucks dominated the rest of the way for a 120–104 win.

"Kareem Jabbar," as Keith Jackson kept calling him, had thirty-nine points and twenty rebounds. Chamberlain couldn't begin to match him, with fifteen points. Strangely, West, Goodrich, McMillian, and Hairston all had eighteen points. None was all that effective, though West clearly won his battle with the Big O, who had only seven points.

The Lakers were to a man gloomy after the game, none of this *Well, it was a good run* rationalization. Winning every game had become expected.

"I'm still disappointed about it," says West. "True, the Milwaukee game might've been one of the ones on our checklist as a possible loss. But it still hurt. We just never got any runs going. I was whor-a-bull. It was the rare game when I felt fatigue. My legs had no pop; I had almost no energy. And there wasn't an excuse for it. We had had a day off. We shouldn't have been tired.

"We went into the locker room after the game and you could

hear a pin drop. We were really, *really* disappointed. It wasn't like we thought, *Oh, this is inevitable. Had to happen.* No, we wanted to win every game."

Perhaps the Lakers were doomed from the beginning. They had to lose sometime, after all, and the Bucks at home, in a national TV game, with the opponents already on record as saying that they wanted to be the ones to end the streak . . . well, a thirty-fourth straight victory would've been asking a lot. Sharman might've contributed to a karmic inevitability: He had prewritten a speech in the event of a loss. He didn't read it, though, choosing to go with spontaneity. The speech remained in his pocket, dog-eared.

A couple of postscripts from the streak-ender:

First, NBA commissioner Walter Kennedy announced, after reviewing the Abdul-Jabbar punch, that the NBA's "one-punch rule" may not have enough, well, punch. He didn't do anything immediately, but over the course of several years, more stringent rules about fighting were put in place.

Second, the day after the game, backup center LeRoy Ellis sauntered up to Sharman and said, "Bill, I didn't play in that thirty-fourth game. Just wanted to let you know." Sharman got the message. It had been a miscalculation not to use Ellis on a day when Wilt had clearly been outplayed by Abdul-Jabbar.

Hearn pronounced, with his customary lapidary finality, "It was one of the most phenomenal records in the annals of sport. They accomplished what no other team in history has ever done and, probably, what no other team will ever do again. But as a wise man once said, 'Nothing lasts forever.' "

Asked forty-five years ago on that fateful Sunday afternoon how he felt about the streak ending, West said: "What with travel conditions as they are now, it'll be an awfully long time before somebody breaks the streak."

The following morning, Sharman caught the *Times*'s beat reporter, Mal Florence, a man with a quick and caustic wit, climbing into a cab.

"Where are you going?" Sharman asked him.

"Home," said Florence without missing a beat. "I don't cover losers."

STREAK: THIRTY-THREE GAMES AND OVER
SEASON RECORD: 39-4
JERRY WEST SEASON RECORD: 37-1

Forty-three years later, another winning streak would come to die in Milwaukee (although no one pulled a Mal Florence and stopped covering the team). As they sped as if on a downhill toboggan toward twenty-seven straight victories and seventy-three total for the season, West had a flashback. "It was just like with us," he told me. "Yes, we had won all those games in a row. Yes, we were trying to set the all-time record for wins in a season. Yes, we became the team to beat. But what if we didn't win a championship? What if the streak and the win record went to waste?"

The thought haunted West from the moment the Lakers lost to the Bucks. The reason was obvious: He had fallen short so many times before. After the Milwaukee defeat, the Lakers won thirty of their last thirty-nine games and beat Milwaukee three times before the season ended. But it didn't matter to West. The thought of failing on the big stage siphoned much of the joy out of a great season.

He was MVP of the All-Star Game, beating Walt Frazier off the dribble and converting a twenty-foot jump shot in the final seconds to give the West a 112–110 victory. Fittingly, in what seemed to be an L.A. season, the game was at the Forum, though that wasn't enough inducement for Wilt to attend the VIP reception hosted by Cooke. Abdul-Jabbar didn't make it either, presaging a time in the future when Jordan accepted a large fine to play golf in lieu of showing up at a "mandatory" media session. "It would've been better if they'd made it to the dinner and not shown up for the game," said Commissioner Kennedy, who, nevertheless, in these pre-Stern days, either did not have, or did not choose to exercise, fining power.

All-Star Weekend 1972 serves as an interesting time capsule. Cooke had arranged several events for the wives, and the coverage came across as more like something out of 1872 than 1972. Buddy Hackett laid down tired one-liners at "the Jack Kent Cooke VIP reception," and, at another event, the wives of the players were described in a *Los Angeles Times* article "as American and whole-some looking as apple pie." The story also noted wryly that "thirty-five-year-old bachelor Wilt Chamberlain had no representative."

That's clearly how Wilt wanted it. Indeed, the one person who seemed to be having a good time throughout that 1971–72 season was Wilt. Though he, too, was known as much for playoff failure as success, it's almost as if he knew a championship, which would be only his second, was preordained.

About three weeks after the streak-breaking loss to the Bucks, during a 153–131 rout of Portland, Wilt broke the all-time rebound-ing record, surpassing Russell. (With 23,934, he is still number one, more than two thousand ahead of his Celtics rival.) "Why, the record came as a complete surprise to me," said Wilt, deadpanning. The game was stopped, and Wilt was presented with a full-size back-board emblazoned with "Rebounding King."

On February 16, during a 110–109 loss to the Phoenix Suns, Wilt became the first NBA player to score 30,000 points. He retired with 31,419, still fifth behind Abdul-Jabbar, Karl Malone, Kobe, and Jordan, though he will almost certainly be passed by Dirk Nowitzki of the Dallas Mavericks as well.

By that time Wilt had launched the NBA's first collectible. Wilt had long worn a headband and wristbands during games, not for style but to help with his excessive sweating. "I guarantee you that no one ever sweated as much as Wilt," says West. Wilt began wear-ing them in Lakers gold, two sets per game to accommodate his perspiration flow, and the nascent NBA marketing arm knew enough to make a licensing agreement with a marketing company. Headbands and wristbands became a smash hit at the concession stands in the Forum. Headbands are commonplace now, but they were rare back then, and Wilt, to the best of anyone's memory, not only began the trend but also rocked it better than anyone, with the possible exception of Donald "Slick" Watts, a SuperSonics guard in the mid-1970s. (Bill Walton had a headband phase that is best forgotten.)

What really moved Wilt during that 1971–72 season, what really made him feel like this was a special year, was the completion of his $1.5 million home in the Santa Monica Hills. (Those were the days, weren't they, when cracking that $1 million figure meant something?) He found a hole in the Lakers' schedule—it was on March 11, between home games against expansion teams Buffalo and Cleveland—to host an open house for 350 of his closest friends, including a football legend named O. J. Simpson. "I only live a few miles away from Wilt," proclaimed the Juice, two decades before he found infamy, "but now I'm finding out I'm farther than I thought."

Details about Wiltapalooza drifted out by word of mouth and newspaper stories. They would include breathy reports about his purple-painted guest room that included a water bed sheathed in black rabbit fur, the bathtub constructed of gold mosaic tile, the fourteen-foot-high front door, and of course the enormous bed upon which presumably unfolded world-class sexual gymnastics. Wilt called his home—invariably referred to as a "pad" or a "pleasure palace"—"Ursa Major," the constellation that contains the stars that make up the Big Dipper, his preferred nickname. The picture that comes most vividly to mind is of Wilt himself. He proudly showed his guests around while wearing what the *Los Angeles Times* described as a "pale-gold antelope suit." Not everyone can pull off gold, and far fewer can make antelope work. There was no sign of the small cast that Wilt had worn in the 132–98 rout of Cleveland the night before, the result of a fracture at the base of his right index finger. Wilt said that the injury was most difficult when he was catching a pass. He could still dunk or hold the ball aloft, so high that it might get wet, as Hearn had put it.

"Wilt always had two parties when he had a party," remembers West. "An early one for the married couples, the later one for the singles." Wilt claimed in his book that West had held a housewarming party a year earlier—a much more pedestrian affair, no gold or antelope—and hadn't invited him. West says today that was nonsense. At any rate, West showed up at Wilt's for the earlier married slot, though he perhaps longed for the second shift, which ended sometime after dawn. Wilt allowed that he didn't get to bed until seven a.m., though that was sometimes his M.O. even on normal days.

It's hard to imagine a more seventies scene than that day in Wilt's pad, afternoon rolling into evening, evening rolling into morning, the big man moving through the crowd like a magnum-sized Hefner, pointing out features made from slaughtered animals, hugging the fine ladies, music, food, laughter, groove, and sex wafting through the home to the San Fernando Valley on the other side of the mountain, no talk of Vietnam, the plague of AIDS still a decade away. Only Wilt could've been lord and master of this scene. Only Wilt, who would die in Ursa Major, alone, twenty-seven years later, on his seventy-two-square-foot bed.

On the night of March 24, 1972, West had the ball in his hands with about three seconds left. The game with the Phoenix Suns, who had been a particularly feisty opponent throughout the season, was tied at 110–110. He went up for a jump shot from just beyond the foul line, a familiar spot for West, and connected. That gave the Lakers their sixty-eighth season victory, tying them with Milwaukee for the all-time record. Two nights later a much more commonplace 124–98 rout of Seattle gave L.A. the all-time mark.

The Lakers had finished a full six games ahead of the Bucks, who had the second best record, and it was a big deal, representing a windfall of $2,300 for each player. That wasn't chump change back then. There was additional scratch for having the best records in the division and conference. But the big prize was the championship—each man on a title team would earn about $17,270.

Perhaps because reporters had tired of West's straightforwardness, Wilt's evasiveness, and Sharman's raspiness—the coach used to joke that it "cuts down on my technicals because the officials can't hear me yelling at them"—John Q. Trapp emerged as an unlikely team spokesman heading into the playoffs. He described the regular season thusly: "Fantastic, marvelous, extraordinary. The personnel here is beautiful, and it's like a complete, little family. There are no bad feelings on this team." Which wasn't quite the case, as we shall see.

Yet in several publications the Lakers were labeled variously as "professional sports' most renowned second-place team" and "eternal runners-up." Vegas felt so, too, installing the Abdul-Jabbar–Robertson Bucks as the favorites to win the championship.

The Lakers had to take care of the Chicago Bulls first, which they did in four games.

So it would be, inevitably, Wilt vs. Abdul-Jabbar and West vs. Robertson. The former matchup, a cross-generational battle, might well decide the series, but the latter matchup? That was one for the ages, one that helped define the formative years of the NBA, the backcourt version of Russell-Wilt.

West and Robertson marched lockstep into the history books, much as Magic and Bird would do two decades later. They entered the NBA in the same year (1960), as did Magic and Bird (1979), and were bound together by a seminal event (the 1960 Rome Olympics in which they co-captained the U.S. to the gold medal), as were Magic and Bird (the 1979 NCAA championship game in which Johnson's Michigan State team beat Bird's Indiana State team). They had a similar college pedigree. Both were outstanding scorers but also bruising rebounders who were always—*always*—around the ball.

Hard as it is to believe since they came to define the guard position in the 1960s, both West and Robertson were considered forwards in college. (Official statistics are hard to come by, but West says he was third in the nation in rebounding as a senior.) They were supposed to be on a collision course for a showdown in college, one that would've predated the Magic-Bird epic, but the Big O's Cincinnati team was beaten in the semis by Pete Newell's Cal team, which went on to nip West Virginia and West 71–70 in the final.

So who was better, West or Robertson? Is that a foolish question? Can it be answered? Are there objective standards by which to judge this? Can we not just agree that both were phenomenal in their own way and leave it at that? We can and probably should. But this is sports, and sports demands an eternal measuring stick, a judgment, a *decision,* dammit.

There is little doubt that Robertson was the more *influential* player. Soured by the racism he felt throughout his life, Robertson was a political being. He was among the leaders of that 1964 threatened boycott of the All-Star Game, and, later, when president of the NBA Players Association, it was his name that went on the antitrust lawsuit—*Robertson v. National Basketball Association.* West stayed silent; Robertson lashed out.

They shared championship frustration. As great as they were, each won only one title, and that came only after they teamed up with a big man, Oscar with Kareem, Jerry with Wilt. They were both tortured by the Russell Celtics, though West usually got a step further. Robertson's Cincinnati Royals teams lost three Eastern Conference playoff series to Boston and two to Philadelphia.

As team leaders, they were entirely different. Robertson was demanding and even demeaning, always willing to put the blame on someone else, publicly and privately. West was the opposite, too quick to put the blame on himself, place the burden on his back and carry it around. They responded to authority in completely different ways. West rarely said anything to the refs—the Garretson double-technical incident notwithstanding—while Robertson never heard a whistle he agreed with. (In Terry Pluto's *Tall Tales,* referee Joe Gushue says he referred to Robertson, Barry, and Heinsohn as "the Debating Team.")

By the numbers, Robertson has the edge over West. He scored more than 1,500 more points, grabbed about 2,300 more rebounds, and collected about 3,500 more assists. He was also more durable—they played the same number of seasons (fourteen), but Robertson played 108 more games (1,040 to West's 932) and almost 5,000 more career minutes. Like Wilt, Robertson almost never came out of the game, and, like Wilt, Robertson is a statistical outlier. His numbers are eye-poppingly outsized, and they came into clearer focus during the 2016–17 season when Westbrook finally matched the Big O's triple-double-for-a-season average.

Indisputably, Oscar was better than West for the first half dozen or so years of their respective careers. If Magic and Bird came in as relative equals, this tandem from the sixties did not. West has always strongly made the point that "Oscar was ready not just to play but to be a star from the beginning. I was not."

But West stresses that, one suspects, partly to advance the notion, however subtly, that he became the superior player as time went on. Neither one would be caught dead proclaiming his superiority in this little pas de deux, much as Magic and Bird will deflect, almost genuflect, to the other. There is little doubt that West's scoring numbers would be considerably higher had he not played eleven seasons with Baylor, a prodigious scorer. Oscar played with several terrific players, Jerry Lucas and Jack Twyman among them, but nobody remotely like Baylor. On the other hand, West's assist totals probably were augmented by the fact that he had Baylor as a finisher, much as, say, Stockton had Malone two decades later. On the *other* other hand, Robertson had the ball in his hands twice as much as West, owing to the fact that he didn't have a teammate like Baylor.

In his West bio, author Lazenby collects this comment from Kevin Loughery, who played against both West and Robertson in their prime. "I hated to guard [West]. I really did, because of his quickness. I'd rather guard Oscar Robertson, because Oscar just backed you down and beat you with strength. But Jerry embarrassed you. He was just so quick, one of the quickest guys that size who ever played the game." Geoff Petrie adds this: "Certainly in their early years Oscar was more difficult. But then it was Jerry for sure."

What about defense, which rarely comes into the comparison game unless the subject is Russell? Defensively, West was infinitely better than Robertson—as a lockdown defender, as a steals opportunist, and as a shot-blocker. West made five all-defensive teams—he would've probably made ten had the category been around before 1968—and Robertson made zero. That means that over a forty-eight-minute game West would've probably have had as much effect on the outcome as Robertson, no matter how full the latter's box score happened to be on a particular night.

So, look, take your pick. This observer would love the ball in either one of their hands with the clock running down. But the choice here, all-around, is West.

One of the dominant story lines coming into the series was that West didn't play particularly well against the Bucks. (Nor did Robertson play well against the Lakers, for that matter.) In six games over the previous two seasons against Milwaukee, West had only a 17-point average and a 32.3 shooting percentage, numbers that paled against his marks of 27.8 points and 43.7 percent against the rest of the league. Then again, none of the Lakers shot particularly well against Milwaukee—the percentages of Goodrich, McMillian, and the team in general were below 40 percent, because of both the presence of Abdul-Jabbar and the coaching of Costello, known for using help defense with zone principles, something that only grew the following season when he brought in Hubie Brown as an assistant.

Still, West had dominated Robertson during the season, outscoring him in five games 133–62, though Oscar missed one of those games. But a head-to-head matchup didn't always tell the true story, much as it didn't with Magic and Bird. West and Robertson guarded each other sparingly, mostly because Robertson didn't want any part of chasing West around.

If West and Robertson were a matched set, Chamberlain and Abdul-Jabbar, upon whose shoulders the series might well rest, had only their height, their center position, their skin color, and the complicated way the world looked upon them in common. (Okay, that's a lot.) They were ten years apart in age, but that gap seemed even wider, like they were representatives of two entirely different generations. Think of it this way: A fourth-grade Lew Alcindor, already two heads bigger than anyone else, wrote Wilt a note when Chamberlain was at the University of Kansas.

But it was more that they were coming from two entirely different spheres of existence. They had met years earlier in New York City when Wilt reached out to Alcindor, a confused teenager who was stared at like he was a zoo animal. Alcindor found solace, music, and female companionship at Wilt's club, Big Wilt's Smalls Paradise, a Harlem jazz staple that Wilt had purchased in 1961, his second year in the league. In his bio about Wilt, author Cherry describes a late-night game of hearts that involved the seventeen-year-old Kareem, Wilt, and a few other players. The rules, strangely, called for the loser to drink a quart of water, and after three straight losses the young Alcindor couldn't drink any more. "So we poured it on him," one of the players told Cherry.

But now Kareem was older and trying to find his own way, hardened by what he saw as America's resistance to outspoken black athletes. Wilt was still the carefree bon vivant, while Abdul-Jabbar had the fervor of the convert, having changed his name the day after his Bucks won the championship in 1971. Kareem was adamant that both "Abdul" and "Jabbar" be used but probably knew it was a losing battle since, as he said back then, the Bucks' home announcer "sounds like he works at a carnival." Over the years Kareem came to accept that people simply didn't seem to consider that "Jabbar" is only half his name, but he never liked it.

Members of Wilt's family despaired that he never settled down and married; by this point in his life Abdul-Jabbar had already agreed to a marriage arranged by his Muslim teacher, Hamaas Abdul Khaalis. Years later in his autobiography *Giant Steps,* Abdul-Jabbar would describe his disconnect with Wilt thusly: "He was a high-profile, jet-set, trickle-down Republican, and I was a private, community-oriented, share-the-wealth Muslim."

Wilt talked about their differences in a newspaper story right before the series: "Jabbar's mode of life is just a little different than mine," he told a reporter. "I just don't particularly like some of the things he believes in." Wilt also noted that he had "shown Kareem the ropes" years ago in New York City, "but I think some people forget quickly." It's a tutor-tyro story that plays out endlessly, not just in sports: *I showed you the way, then you went and grew up on me.*

Wilt and Kareem went back and forth as frenemies over the years, but this reporter was with Abdul-Jabbar at a gathering in 2017 when he spoke affectionately of Wilt. "He took me and showed me around," Kareem said. "You know, I still have people come up to me and say, 'Hey, you're Wilt!' It's okay. I can live with that."

If Sharman was looking for a bad sign, he got it before Game 1 when he learned that his wife had shown up at the Forum with the wrong set of playoff tickets. They let her in anyway.

If West was looking for a sign that his playoff frustrations would continue, he got it in Game 1, which the Bucks won 93–72. Forum fans were booing by the third period, when the Lakers made only four of twenty shots. Here was a team that had failed to score in triple digits only once in eighty-two games—eighty-six including the Bulls series—and it scored exactly eight points in the third period. Costello had decided on a strategy that left Hairston absolutely alone, let Kareem play Wilt by himself, and put the other four defenders on West, Goodrich, and McMillian. It worked. That trio made only seventeen field goals, and Hairston led L.A. with sixteen points.

As Rosen notes in *The Pivotal Season,* the result seemed to make a prophet out of New York's Walt Frazier, who, gearing up for what he saw as a championship series against the Bucks, had said: "Bet your bucks on the Bucks because the Lakers always lose big games."

West remembers the obvious sense of desperation about Game 2. Lose the first two at home and the series was all but over. Between Games 1 and 2, the NBA draft was held, the Lakers selecting Travis "the Machine" Grant from little-known NAIA Kentucky State— believe it or not, he is still college basketball's all-time scoring leader. The newspapers had themselves a joke: Maybe the Lakers could use him for Game 2. (Grant played sparingly the following season for the Lakers, was waived, then had a few unexceptional seasons in the ABA.)

As befitting his Ivy League background, McMillian spent the off day between Games 1 and 2 reading. His choice was Leon Uris's *QB VII,* which was not a book about John Elway but, rather, a tautly told courtroom drama. He also watched *The Godfather.* He was also busy on a correspondence course on photography. Those Ivy Leaguers. Then McMillian scored forty-two points, of which the Lakers needed every single one, in a 135–134 victory that tied the series. "There may not be a better sophomore in the league," pronounced Hearn.

The Lakers were enormously lucky in that game. They had a 44–23 advantage in free throws attempted—"I'd like to see a movie of this game," said Oscar, who said little else—and a loose ball that was bouncing toward a backcourt violation that would've given

Milwaukee possession and a chance for a final shot instead bounced off a referee and enabled West to retain possession. "That's the first time Manny Sokol has been in the right place at the right time," offered West in a rare quip.

Inside, though, West wasn't feeling very quippy. His shooting was poor—he had been 10-of-30 in Game 2—and would continue to be so throughout the series. He couldn't seem to stop talking about the doubt and the dread roiling within him, alternately blaming himself ("I'm turning my hand too much on my shot") and the burden of expectation put on him. "In the past—when we've always lost in the playoffs and I scored so many points—they always talked about why we lost and not about all the points I scored," West told Peter Carry of *Sports Illustrated*. "Now we're winning and they don't talk about that. All anyone seems to be concerned about are the points I'm not scoring." It was atypical West, looking outside for blame, adopting a kind of woe-is-me posture. In Lazenby's bio, he has quotes from West during the Milwaukee series that run along the same lines. "I'm tired of doing everything," said West. "I'm supposed to score, and then I'm supposed to defend against the other team's high-scoring guard. I played too many minutes again this year. When there are seventeen thousand people in the Forum, for example, I have to play forty minutes whether the game is close or not." West was no doubt correct, but the words didn't sound like they came from a confident man. Neither did his actions—West kicked over a press table in pique after missing an open shot in a practice.

The Lakers won Game 3 108–105 in Milwaukee—notable because of a bomb scare that was phoned in but not acted upon—then lost Game 4 in a blowout, 114–88. But L.A. won Game 5 at the Forum in dominant fashion, 115–90, despite West's continued shooting struggles, and went back to Milwaukee with a chance to put away the Bucks.

That game would belong to Wilt. Once he had dispensed with his memorable open house at Ursa Major, the Dipper had become unusually focused. Shackelford remembers that late in the season Sharman had questioned the team about whether they should hold an off-day practice, and Wilt, who a decade earlier would've rather surrendered a kidney than attend an extra practice, said, "Let's do it." Despite his advanced age, Wilt had been third in minutes played that season, meaning that he played the second-most minutes of any human being. Abdul-Jabbar was second and John Havlicek was first, but Hondo didn't count—he was bionic. Wilt also led the league in shooting percentage (.649) and rebounding average (19.2).

As even Abdul-Jabbar, his young nemesis, noted at the time, Wilt played him alone, without defensive assistance. If Kareem scored prodigiously against the Lakers—and he did—at least the other Bucks were kept in check. "Wilt had lost his agility a little bit," West said in 2016, "but he was never going to lose his ability to block shots and get rebounds. It was harder for him to score, so his focus became defense and rebounding."

The only time Wilt griped the entire season was when the Lakers missed two or three quick pull-up jumpers in a row, usually in transition. Like most centers, Wilt hated to be placed in that cartoon-character dilemma, getting caught going one way while everybody's heading back the other. "If you don't have something, stop and set it up," Wilt would say.

Before Game 6, Chamberlain called a team meeting. His message was clear: "Let's not fuck with another seventh game." (West was undoubtedly nodding in assent.) Forty-five years later, Cleamons, then the bench-sitting rookie, had clear memories of what Chamberlain said.

"He used the example of him and Russell," Cleamons remembered. "He said something like, 'I've always been the best center in the league, but I never had as good of teammates and therefore Russell won. Now, this kid, Jabbar, is the best center in the league. But I have the better supporting cast. Let's get this over with *now*.' "

Hard to imagine that a pivotal game involving three NBA legends (West, Wilt, and Oscar) and a legend-to-be (Abdul-Jabbar) would be a second-class TV event, but that was the case: ABC showed the final moments of a three-week-old auto race, the 12 Hours of Sebring, instead of the first quarter of Game 6. Such was the hold that the NBA had on America back then.

With ten minutes left the Bucks led 85–75, but Wilt played like a man possessed for the rest of the game. He even sunk two free throws with just under a minute left to give the Lakers a comfortable lead. He finished with twenty-four rebounds, ten points, and, most important, ten blocked shots, five of them against Abdul-Jabbar, in the 104–100 victory, which sent the Lakers into their eighth championship series since they moved to Los Angeles, none of them having resulted in a championship.

The Lakers came home to find ten thousand fans waiting for them at Los Angeles International Airport. Wilt raised his arms in triumph, signed a few autographs, then went to his car to discover that he had a parking ticket.

CHAPTER 15

Gaining a Record but Losing a Title

The Golden State Warriors strode, tired but confident, into the BMO Harris Bradley Center on the night of December 12, 2015. It was the same town where the Lakers' streak had ended forty-three years earlier but a different venue. The place was packed, as every place always was to see the Warriors. Milwaukee was in the process of trying to rebrand itself, as Golden State had done, as a franchise for the new millennium, flush with capital from hedge-fund titans. But the Bucks, coached by Jason Kidd, a future Hall of Famer who had himself grown up in the Bay Area, were one of the NBA's many *meh* franchises, capable of winning on any given night but probably no match for the high-flying Dubs. To fans who don't care about ownership metrics, the Warriors were in one league, the Bucks in another, right along with Atlanta, Detroit, Memphis, Philadelphia, and Sacramento, other teams with new money but little resonance.

So the attention paid to the 2015 game—and it was considerable—was generated almost entirely by the Warriors, who on the night of their visit had won their first twenty-four games of the 2015–16 season. Added to the three in a row they had won to capture the 2015 championship against LeBron's Cavaliers, Golden State now shared, with the 2012–13 Heat, the second-longest winning streak in NBA history behind West's Lakers. But there was a further way to deconstruct this. The Warriors had won the final four games of the 2014–15 season, meaning that they had won twenty-eight straight regular-season games.

Many Bucks rooters wore T-shirts that read "24-1," a solid bit of fan fun. Steph Curry noticed the shirts as they called out to him during his pregame shooting ritual, which had become de rigueur entertainment for early-arriving fans. It made him smile. A lot of things made Curry smile, sometimes even in the heat of the action.

The Bucks sent out a starting lineup of Giannis Antetokounmpo, aka "the Greek Freak," Khris Middleton, Greg Monroe, O. J. Mayo, and Jabari Parker. The point is not to contrast how weak that was compared with the Warriors' starting five of Curry, Klay Thompson, Draymond Green, Andrew Bogut, and Brandon Rush, a starter-in-name-only who was subbing for the injured Harrison Barnes. The point is that the Milwaukee lineup was pretty good. All of those starters are legitimate pros, and the Freak might turn out to be a superstar. But the Bucks were only 9-15 at the time, which speaks to how difficult it is to coalesce a group of individuals into an entity that plays together as a team, as the Warriors had done.

What made the Warriors' winning streak even more amazing was that they were doing it without the masterful hand of Kerr, "the guy who made the soup," as assistant coach Adams put it. Kerr was still trying to recover from the spinal fluid leakage that occurred in the aftermath of surgery in the summer of 2015, an agonizing condition that had sent him to the sidelines at the beginning of training camp, and would continue to furnish a subplot for the 2016–17 season. Luke Walton, son of Bill, the deep-voiced, effortlessly handsome young man who could still pass for the easygoing jock in any B sports film, was in charge.

To get this out of the way, since you already know the result, the Bucks beat the Warriors 108–95. It wasn't much of a game and certainly had none of that clash-of-the-titans feel like that day decades earlier when the West-Wilt Lakers fell to the Kareem-Robertson Bucks.

What was most interesting had already happened, hours before tip-off.

The Warriors had touched down in Milwaukee at two-thirty that morning, feeling 'bout half-past dead, to steal a line from The Band. They had left thirteen days earlier on a seven-game road trip, and everyone was tired. But happy. Hours earlier the Warriors had outlasted the Boston Celtics 124–119 in a double-overtime victory that showed their toughness and tenacity, qualities not always ascribed to the Warriors, even though they were the defending NBA champions. Klay Thompson hadn't even played, due to a tender ankle, yet the Warriors had beaten a very good Boston team in a very difficult place to win.

By the time the team arrived at their Milwaukee hotel it was three a.m. and the temperature hovered around zero. Nevertheless, a couple of hundred fans lingered outside the hotel, holding basketballs and Sharpies, wearing heavy parkas and looks of hope. Arriving amid a sea of autograph-seekers was not new to the Warriors, but *this*? It was three hours past midnight, for God's sake, and frigid even for Milwaukee.

"I think it was at that moment," says Raymond Ridder, "I knew we had become America's team."

The reasons that teams attain this kind of freeze-your-ass-off-for-an-autograph popularity—it's rare even today, when team arrival times can be instantly heralded through social media—are at once simple and complex. The team must be a winner, of course, which the Warriors had become. A popular star player is another prerequisite, which in the Warriors' case was Curry, a hero for the social-media age, his life an open-book reality show. There he is playing golf with Barack Obama, there is he doing the Carlton with Justin Timberlake at a celebrity golf tournament, there he is calling for an end to the bathroom bill in North Carolina, there he is cranking out Disney tunes on James Corden's "Carpool Karaoke," there he is eating eggs with Drake, there he is playing Ping-Pong with Serena Williams in a commercial for Chase Bank. Curry seemed to revel in being a public personality along the (less annoying) lines of a Kardashian, and a multi-platformed Silicon Valleyite who contemplates a future with robot referees and comfortably addresses tech geeks at conferences around the Bay Area.

But you don't get just one Curry. You get wife Ayesha, who has morphed into a kind of It Girl version of Martha Stewart, with her own cooking show on the Food Network (Steph and pals die for her bacon popcorn), a line of tableware for kids, a cookbook, assorted videos during which she'll show you things like a DIY eucalyptus-and-peppermint chest rub that is "crazy easy" to make, and details about how she lost her baby weight (boxing, kettlebell workouts, and SoulCycle).

You get adorable daughter Riley, who became an almost daily staple on social media, the phrase "Riley Curry's Playhouse" even trending on Twitter for a while. The Internet can be a dark place, and Ayesha had expressed fears about Riley and younger sister Ryan getting too much attention. But the Currys had to share part of the blame for the social-media exposure—much of the family publicity was self-generated through Twitter, Snapchat, and Instagram.

Whatever you thought about his here-there-everywhere presence, the chapel-attending Curry had become a cultural crossover sensation, in a different kind of way, a *nicer* way, than, say, Michael Jordan and certainly Kobe Bryant. If you melded a little Jay Z with a little Beaver Cleaver, you'd come up with something like Steph Curry.

There are dozens of ways that Curry's popularity could have been measured on that December day, and here is but one: Rover .com, a network of dog sitters and walkers, measured a 143 percent increase in owners naming their dogs "Steph Curry."

But as much as anything, it was the *way* the Warriors played that had grabbed hold of America and turned them into must-see entertainment. Kobe Bryant called them "the Suns on steroids," for they had taken the D'Antoni-Nash offense and upped the ante, running whenever possible, yes, but also hurling up three-pointers from East Jesus, sometimes in the middle of a fast break, their attack seemingly a few bubbles off plumb but almost always devastating. And when the first line of their break was stopped, they had a terrific secondary break that operated as kind of a hybrid, complete with set-offense features like weakside cuts and pick-and-rolls. "They just *flow* right into it," says Pat Riley admiringly. "You can't get organized quickly enough to scheme them."

The offense had turned Curry into a sensation, Thompson into an all-star, Green into an unlikely all-around playmaker, and Kerr into a genius. The funny thing is, Kerr didn't come from a get-up-and-go background. His Bulls—okay, Jordan's Bulls—played the sacred triangle favored by Phil Jackson. They most assuredly capitalized on their athleticism but not so much to get up and down the floor as to dominate in the half-court. *We'll slow it down, and even if you're ready for us Jordan and Pippen will kill you.* Two or three times per game, Chicago would invariably get a triangle backdoor cut and a dunk from Jordan or Pippen off a pass from the elbow, even though other teams were geared to stop it. Gregg Popovich's San Antonio teams, for which Kerr played, also had an extremely efficient offense predicated on teamwork and motion—a running, heaving-it-up team is bound to make mistakes—and didn't rely so much on speed as on indefatigability.

But when Kerr got to Golden State and took a quick look, he realized what he had in Curry. Adams was already in place as a defensive coach, so Kerr hired Alvin Gentry, who had worked with Mike D'Antoni in Phoenix's offense.

"There's no doubt that's why Steve wanted me," said Gentry, now the head coach of the New Orleans Pelicans. "He wanted some of Mike's ideas. I thought what the team needed to do was to really open up the floor. They didn't play slow, but they also played a lot of isolation with Harrison Barnes. I said, 'Steve, let's push the ball to get into the open court but also get guys into some special situations.' The main thing was to keep the ball moving.

"We saw we had something special in Steph, who was not only a shooter but also a penetrator. He is truly one of the great finishers at the basket. Steve Nash wasn't quite as good at creating as Steph is because of how well Steph can finish."

The Warriors, or the Suns for that matter, can't take all the credit for the increase in three-pointers. Tim Bontemps of the *Washington Post* tracked the numbers from the 2002–03 season to 2016–17 and found, incredibly, a *90.2* percent increase in three-ball attempts, from 34,913 to 66,421. Now, Curry was a major reason, his 2012–13 campaign being his coming-out party as the three-point king. In an injury-plagued season the year before, he had taken only 121 treys; the next year he took 600. As for makes, Curry took another jump between 2014–15 and 2015–16, when he went from 286 to 402.

All those threes have fundamentally changed the game, particularly on defense. Teams used to stress the art of careful closeouts— that is, getting out on a perimeter shooter but not getting too close to him, for fear he would go around you. Now teams charge pell-mell toward a shooter because, chances are, he's going to take it. "We teach that if you run by a shooter, that's okay, but you just have to pivot and get back in the play," says Adams. Plus, defenders have to be increasingly wary of getting too close to a shooter, lest he throw up his shooting arm and draw a foul, a tactic that Warriors assistant coach and Curry shooting guru Bruce Fraser calls "cheating the game." Curry and Thompson don't do that much.

In his first year Kerr was still a little reluctant to just open the tap. He couldn't quite get his Chicago and San Antonio experiences out of his head, and who could blame him? Those teams had so much success and such beautiful offenses.

"I knew I didn't want to run the triangle per se, but I wanted elements of it," Kerr told this reporter in 2017. "You'll see us throw the ball into the post, do a lot of split cuts, guards screening for each other, real traditional stuff from the triangle. I also incorporated from Pop what he calls 'weak' and 'strong.' The guard throws the ball ahead immediately, and there's a sequence of cutting as the ball swings from side to side.

"The biggest change was getting Steph off the ball. Before I got here there was a lot of screen-roll with Steph, and obviously that can be effective. But I wanted more passing from our forwards and less ballhandling from our guards. The main thing I told them is we are *not going to hold the ball.* We are going to move. Alvin brought some of D'Antoni's concepts about spacing the floor and running dummy actions into high screens like he did with Nash. I told the team: You can shoot any shot you want, but you have to move it first. We gave them a lot of rope with some structure."

Kerr realizes he's just sent out a decent helping of basketball gobbledygook. "What I just told you," he says, "is more than you'd get from Pop in a year. But we had to remember something else. We were inheriting a pretty good team. The last thing we wanted to do was announce, 'Okay, we're the guys with all the answers.'"

As it turned out, there was something about to happen that almost nobody saw coming, something that changed the geometry of the game and the physics of shooting. It had a touch of magic, it was beyond the pale, and it's what made Golden State something that no one had ever seen before.

After the Bucks stopped the Warriors' winning streak—it was, remember, early in the season—over the next few months another Golden State drama unfolded that obscured the twenty-seven straight, as hard as that is to believe: The Warriors set their sights on the all-time season win-loss record.

And so rather than coast into the playoffs, maybe rest a starter or two down the stretch, the Warriors pressed down hard on the accelerator. They won twenty-three of their final twenty-seven games, grinding out three of those wins in overtime, to finish the season with a 73-9 record, one victory better than Jordan's (and Kerr's) Chicago Bulls in the 1996–97 season, considered one of the most dominant teams of all time.

Their quest became the topic of conversation around the league. "I thought it was great," said Lacob. "I wanted to go for it." That was classic Lacob.

Others weren't so sure. Kerr was caught in the middle. He understood that rest and keeping the big picture (i.e., a championship) front of mind was the prudent course. But who could think about *prudent* when history presented itself? So the Warriors played all out and got the record. But then they had to go all out *again* to rally from a 3–1 deficit to beat the Durant-Westbrook Thunder in the Western Conference finals to make their second straight championship series against Cleveland.

Rick Barry, the iconoclastic underhand free-throw shooter, was one of Golden State's few bright spots until the current team.

Like so many players through the ages—and up through Steph Curry—Chris Mullin did not want to become a Warrior.

When Curry was a collegian, there were concerns about his size and his ability to become a pure point guard.

Curry manages to muster a smile on Draft Day 2009, but general manager Larry Riley, who never wavered in his decision to take Curry, is overjoyed.

Things started to turn around for the Warriors after Joe Lacob and Peter Guber bought the team in 2010.

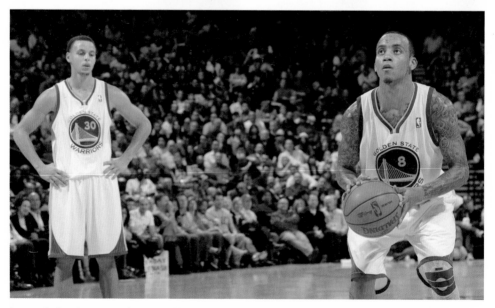

It wasn't that long ago that most Warriors fans would've selected Monta Ellis (shooting) over Curry. But it turned out that the front office knew what it was doing when it traded Ellis.

Bob Myers made a successful transition from player agent to general manager and has now won NBA Executive of the Year twice.

One of the new ownership's smartest moves was hiring veteran NBA hand Rick Welts as president and chief of business operations.

"I'll be ready," Steve Kerr had told Michael Jordan during a time-out. And he was. He took a pass from Jordan and hit this shot that helped the Bulls win the 1997 NBA championship.

The dynamic duo of Russell Westbrook and Kevin Durant lifted Oklahoma City to the NBA elite. But less than two months after this photo from the 2016 playoffs was taken, Durant was paid a fateful visit by the "Hamptons 5."

Curry's long-distance bombs changed the basic physics, architecture, and geometry of the NBA game.

Golden State's epic failure in the 2016 Finals, when LeBron James dominated them in the final three games, led to the pursuit of Durant.

West always liked Klay Thompson's game and felt he owed a debt to Klay's father, Mychal, for helping the Lakers beat the Celtics when West was GM.

There were some incohesive moments during the 2016–17 season, but when Durant and Curry put their heads together the Warriors started to roll.

One of West's favorite players on the Warriors was Draymond Green, who tried to talk West out of leaving the franchise.

No love was lost between former Thunder mates Durant and Westbrook in the four Golden State–OKC games during the season, all Warriors victories.

Even after Steve Kerr (head down, flanked by assistants Ron Adams and Mike Brown) returned for Game 2 of the Finals, he had to deal with agonizing pain.

Are the Warriors Curry's team or Durant's team? In the 2017 Finals, they were both. Durant's mother, Wanda, beams in the background.

Durant and LeBron hug it out after the 2017 Finals. Durant was the MVP.

The Currys have become rather the First Family of the NBA. Father Dell, a sharpshooter in his day, is in the background.

Of all the Warriors players, West most appreciated Durant, who has an old-school type of game.

A long winning streak and a record win-loss season would be diminished without a victory in the Finals, so the question had to be asked: Was the combination of the long winning streak and going after the season wins record too high a price to pay? Curry came into the Finals with a sore right knee that he had sprained early in the postseason. Bogut had a bad knee also. Iguodala had a bad back. And Draymond Green had a bad temper.

Warriors assistant Adams talks often about the "bubble" that floats above every contemporary professional sports team. "Guys are under such scrutiny these days," says Adams, who has been in the NBA since 1992 and a coach since 1969, "and it gets worse every year. Now you achieve something like we do with the winning streak, and the social-media bubble gets bigger and bigger. And if you jump into that other bubble as a player or coach? You're screwed. You better jump back. We did pretty well with it but . . ."

Adams's voice trailed off. The Warriors did *pretty* well with it. Until they didn't. All those wins in a row, all that mounting pressure, all those times when you just had to win proved to be too much.

It's not just players who enter the bubble. Though each individual Warrior—owner, exec, coach, player, support staff—stumbles over himself or herself to deflect credit onto others, a sufficient amount of all-knowingness has escaped from the mouth of Lacob to impart upon the Warriors a touch of the insufferable. Lacob's big gaffe, one from which he's still backpedaling, was telling the *New York Times Magazine* that the Warriors were "light-years ahead of probably every other team in structure, in planning, in how we're going to go about things. We're going to be a handful for the rest of the N.B.A. to deal with for a long time." Now, there is no cause-and-effect between a comment from the owner in a magazine story and the result of a championship series ten weeks later. But it surely didn't help the Warriors' mojo.

In the fourth quarter of Game 4 of the Finals, which would end in a 108–97 Golden State win and a 3–1 series lead, Draymond slapped at LeBron James's groin area, earning Green an automatic suspension for Game 5 because he had surpassed his point total in the NBA's cumulative flagrant-foul system. It was a brainless move and not his first. Though Draymond's disingenuous what-me? act is inspired, no one makes accidental contact with another player's groin as frequently as Green does. But Draymond plays a very distinctive role for the Warriors, and it's not an easy one. As Golden State's prime physical force, Green is asked, in the words of Kerr, "to walk up to the line without crossing it." Sometimes he crosses it. And when James dared to mention the incident after the game—What? He was supposed to ignore it?—the Warriors doubled down by poking the bear. Thompson, who generally keeps his mouth shut, said: "I'm surprised some guys take it so personal. It's a man's league. I guess his [LeBron's] feelings got hurt." And reserve forward Marreese Speights simply tweeted a photo of a baby bottle. Smart.

Without Green, the Warriors fell 112–97 in Game 5 at home, the game that was supposed to cement a second straight championship. James owned the Warriors in Game 6, which ended with Green still berating the refs, Kerr drawing a fine for doing the same, Curry being ejected for throwing his masticated mouthpiece, Ayesha tweeting about rigged games, and the Cavs winning 115–101. Welcome to the bubble, Golden State Warriors.

Game 7 ended when James, who had psyched himself up for the climactic game by watching *The Godfather,* made an all-world block of an Iguodala layup, and the Warriors suddenly couldn't make a three-point shot.

When the final buzzer sounded on the 93–89 Cleveland win, Thompson and Green headed straight to the locker room without acknowledging the Cavs. Green, to his credit, subsequently returned to the court, tearfully, and congratulated the winners.

Clearly, Golden State had beaten itself in two ways. It had expended an excessive amount of physical and mental energy by winning twenty-four games in a row and pursuing the seventy-three-win season. And it had acted too arrogantly, instead of taking care of business, during the Finals. Yes, that's probably too glib, and it will be a matter of eternal conjecture whether the Warriors should've been content to win, say, sixty-eight games and leave the record where it stood. It did not have a Jordan, as did the Bulls, to get through a record season *and* a first-class championship performance.

Still, there was something noble about the pursuit of the streak. "No one denies the legitimacy of the Warriors," *Chronicle* columnist Scott Ostler wrote after it had ended in Milwaukee. "This team is not a gimmick. The Warriors are the new truth in basketball, and their streak was not lucky or fluky. It was freaking glorious."

But that is a poet's truth. Jordan, owner of the Charlotte Hornets, delivered the hard truth to Lacob when he ran into him after the season: "Seventy-three wins don't mean shit." Meaning: You may have broken our record for wins in a season, but you failed to notarize it with a championship.

The shocking defeat did, however, make one thing clear—the Warriors would need help for the 2016–17 season.

Draymond was already on it.

"It took me two weeks, really, to even realize we had won."
—JERRY WEST

CHAPTER 16

Championship Brings West Only Muted Joy

The air of contentiousness that permeated the Lakers-Bucks rivalry did not exist between the Lakers and Knicks, who would be L.A.'s opponent in the 1972 Finals, which seemingly represented Jerry West's best—and perhaps his last—chance of winning an NBA championship. Still, the rivalry between him and Walt Frazier, while less obvious than the one between him and Oscar Robertson, was nevertheless intense. West knew that he had been outplayed by Frazier in Game 7 of the 1970 Finals. West and Frazier were more or less the same kind of player in that both could shoot jumpers and drive and also win games on defense. (Though Frazier, known as "Clyde," after the character played by Warren Beatty in *Bonnie and Clyde,* earned many more style points than West.) Frazier had said earlier in the season that he thought he was as good as any guard in the league. "But other people have to tell you," he added, "and the writers have to write it."

As with Robertson and West, Frazier and West didn't always guard each other. Before an early-season game against the Lakers, Frazier conceded that chasing around West might take too much out of him and said that his backcourt mate, Dick Barnett, was an underrated defender who often checked West. West confirmed that point. West was deeply stung the following year when Wilt, in his autobiography, made an offhand comment that Frazier always dominated West. "I just never knew why Wilt said stuff like that," West says today. "He knows it isn't true."

Game 1 at the Forum was delayed by President Richard Nixon's nationally televised speech about Vietnam. While proclaiming that the "Vietnamization" strategy that enabled the United States to begin withdrawing troops and reducing conscription was a success, he also said that the bombing of North Vietnam would continue.

The schedule was already a matter of concern, as it was so often in the NBA back then. Due to various other entertainment options at the Forum and Madison Square Garden—including the Myron "Mr. Accordion" Floren Extravaganza with Lawrence Welk (not making that up) at the Forum and the Ringling Bros. and Barnum & Bailey circus at the Garden—the schedule was just plain silly: April 26 and 30 in L.A., back to New York for May 3 and 5, all the way back to L.A. for May 7, and a bounce back from L.A. to New York and back to L.A., if necessary, for Games 6 and 7.

The Knicks—still basking in the warm glow of that 1970 win over the Lakers and undeniably the favorite of the cognoscenti— seemed to have struck a perfect basketball balance. Their black backcourt of Frazier, Barnett, and Earl "the Pearl" Monroe (aka Black Jesus), who had come over in an early-season trade, was hip, pure jazz, while the white frontcourt comprised of Dave DeBusschere, Jerry Lucas, and Bill Bradley was brainy, basic, almost classical. Those generalizations plug into the reigning stereotypes of the time, of course, and ignore the fact that Frazier, Barnett, and Monroe were all extremely smart players, too. But there was something out of the ordinary about those forwards. Bradley was a Rhodes scholar who would go on to be a U.S. senator and a presidential candidate. DeBusschere would become commissioner of the ABA and the Knicks GM who drafted Ewing. Lucas was odd but undeniably brainy, a man who would go on to write books about memory (he called himself Dr. M.) and was never shy about revealing how smart he was. In a 2013 story in the *New York Times,*

Lucas told writer Scott Cacciola that his doctor told him that he wanted to take a picture of Lucas's brain. " 'I think it's got to look different,' " Lucas said the doctor told him. " 'When people age, certain things happen.' So he took a couple shots of my brain, and he said, 'Your brain looks like you're eighteen years old.' That's because I've used it so much." Generally eighteen-year-old brains don't work that well.

Then, too, there was the Willis Factor. Few men in the game were as universally beloved as Knicks center Willis Reed, somewhat the African-American version of West for the affection and respect he engendered among teammates and rivals alike, a reputation that long outlasted a playing career that spanned only ten years. But Reed wouldn't have any effect on the series. Two years after his iconic limping walk from the dressing room onto the Garden floor, a moment that inspired the Knicks to a Game 7 victory over West, Chamberlain, and Baylor, Reed was injured and didn't play at all in the Finals.

That was a blessing for the Knicks in Game 1. They were not even tempted to go inside against Wilt. Lucas, the owner of a peculiar one-hander that he released like a shot-putter, stayed well outside and made thirteen of twenty-one shots. Bradley made eleven of twelve. The Knicks shot 72 percent in the first half. They could do no wrong. Even a backup forward named Phil Jackson, whom coach Red Holzman had put on a "one-dribble rule," had thirteen points. The final was 114–92, a strange reprise of the Lakers' futility in Game 1 of the previous series against Milwaukee.

"President Nixon said we will continue the bombing," said colorful Lakers trainer Frank O'Neill after the game, "but Jerry Lucas and Bill Bradley are carrying it a little too far."

West was beside himself, confused, anxious, wondering why the shooting slump that had begun against Milwaukee was apparently going to continue throughout this series. "I felt like a hitter in baseball standing at the plate with a pencil in my hand," he told reporters after a game in which he went 3-of-15 from the field and scored only twelve points. Between games he had studied himself on film and laid it all out for reporters. "When I look at those films and see myself it's just not the same person I've known," West said, angst dripping from every syllable. "I just hope I can snap out of it tomorrow," he said. Not I will. I *hope*.

West was off again in Game 2, with only six makes in twenty-one shots, but it didn't matter. DeBusschere pulled a muscle early and saw only limited action. Sharman changed the defensive strategy, forcing Bradley to go baseline, and Chamberlain was much more active on Lucas, outscoring the memory maven 23–16 and also grabbing twenty-four rebounds. The Lakers won 106–92.

As the Knicks flew to New York for Games 3 and 4, the City of Los Angeles celebrated Johnny Carson Day in the streets. The *Tonight Show* host had moved his wildly popular show from New York to L.A.—actually Burbank, as the unending fusillade of Carson jokes about the town continued through the next twenty years—further proof of L.A.'s cultural currency. West seemed in some way a version of Carson—handsome, well dressed, popular with women, but also secretive, tightly wound, almost neurotic in many ways, a private man in a very public profession. One wondered if they, two stars of La-La Land, had ever met and found kinship as reluctant kings.

"I never met Johnny Carson," said West in 2016. "But if he had asked me to be on his show, I would've probably said no. I would've doubted I would've been worthy for something like that." Worthy? Now that's a strange way to put it.

The series turned definitively the Lakers' way in Game 3. DeBusschere was still out, West began to find his stroke, Wilt continued to dominate, and Monroe, inserted for Barnett in an effort to generate more offense, couldn't contain Goodrich. Even a strange sideshow named Dancing Harry, who was making his Garden debut as a self-appointed lucky charm, couldn't stem the tide. Dancing Harry (real name Marvin Cooper) had been performing at Baltimore Bullets games but came north with Earl the Pearl. (He was not officially part of the deal.) Dancing Harry was active throughout the game, "flitting around" the Lakers bench, as one reporter put it, but it didn't make a difference. The Lakers won 107–96 to take a 2–1 lead.

The following day, between games, Sharman went to see Stephen Sondheim's *A Funny Thing Happened on the Way to the Forum*. Pity for writers seeking a setup lead sentence that Game 4 wasn't at the Forum.

At about the time that Chamberlain and Lucas were lining up at Madison Square Garden for the opening tip in Game 4, conductor Zubin Mehta was preparing for a concert three thousand miles away. Mehta had arranged for his Los Angeles Philharmonic to play at the California Institute for Men at Chino. The game was in the second quarter when Mehta tapped his baton to start the performance. The crowd wasn't bad—talk about your captive audience— but Mehta said during the show, "I hope even more will come after the game is over." Between movements, he provided game updates that came from a prison official.

Meanwhile, passengers on Western Airlines Flight 407, Salt Lake City to Los Angeles, were also getting updates. What made those unusual was that the flight was in the process of being hijacked by a University of Utah dropout named Michael Lynn Hansen, who had taken control with a pistol that he had brought on in a hollowed-out book. Hansen, a recent draftee who had just said no, announced that he wanted to fly to Hanoi and was acting on behalf of "the anti-Imperialist movement."

Quite possibly the world's most polite hijacker, Hansen agreed to let the pilot stop in Los Angeles for refueling, allowed eleven passengers to deplane, and responded to a request for a score. "Los Angeles losing 75–72," the pilot reported. The passengers groaned. Hansen then changed to a more realistic destination, Havana, by which time the final was announced: "Los Angeles 116, New York 111." The passengers cheered. When the plane landed in Havana, Hansen asked the soldiers who boarded the plane to arrest him, "Can you have someone get my luggage?" The story didn't end so nicely. Hansen, who was imprisoned in Cuba until 1975, became a neo-Nazi after he was transferred to a jail in the States.

Game 4 marked some semblance of the offense the Lakers had run during the streak—West, Goodrich, and McMillian scored 28,

27, and 23 points, respectively. The only downside was Chamberlain, who had fallen during the game and injured his right wrist. Chamberlain said later that he had broken a bone (some doubted that diagnosis) and that team doctor Robert Kerlan didn't see how he would be able to play. In his autobiography, released the next year, Wilt wrote that he was positively, absolutely not going to miss the next game, and found a way to throw shade on his two most prominent Laker teammates:

> The Lakers had never won a championship with Elgin Baylor and Jerry West and all those great teams they had, but no one had ever called them a "loser." They were tragic heroes; people felt sorry for them. I was the "loser"—the scapegoat—and I knew damn well that I'd be blamed again if we lost this championship even though I'd play well and Jerry should've been the goat for his rotten shooting.

Wilt said that he slept only two or three hours the night before Game 5, which just about matched West for z's. "I thought we would win the game," West told me in 2016. "We were just better. There was always this little doubt, of course, but I was fairly confident. But what would it feel like? What would it feel like to have at last gotten that monkey off your back?"

Wilt, his hand shot up with an anti-inflammatory and covered by a padded splint bandage, was ready to play. So were his teammates. The game was tied 53–53 at halftime, but the Lakers pulled away steadily in the second half. Be-splinted Wilt had twenty-four points and twenty-nine rebounds. Goodrich led the scoring with twenty-five. McMillian had twenty-three points and made all the clutch baskets down the stretch. And West, though still shooting poorly, got twenty-three points and nine assists. With 1:37 left, Sharman took out West and Wilt to cheers of "We're number one!" West had never heard that before.

Several fans made a halfhearted attempt to lift up Chamberlain, who had been named the series MVP after the 114–100 clincher, but made it only a few feet. He was a load, as van Breda Kolff had once said. Hearn looked around for Baylor, who had shown up only sparingly during the season, and finally found him. But Elegant Elg didn't have much to say. There were no balloons in the rafters, but "Happy Days Are Here Again" did play over the loudspeakers. There was something about that song that Cooke just loved.

West and Riley ran off the court together, Riley holding West in a semi-headlock, Riley looking "a lot more excited than I do," as West wrote in his autobiography, both of them unaware of how much future history they would share and how much they would continue to impact the NBA.

In the locker room, Sharman was close to whispering. He was going to Hawaii, he said, to rest and recuperate and say nary a word. His voice was all but gone. In a congratulatory letter he would receive a few days later, President Nixon wrote: "I think the only entry in the loss column will be your voice."

Baylor was in the locker room. He embraced West, but videos show him looking a little . . . wistful perhaps? That would be understandable. West felt that way, too. He and Coleman wrote later in *West by West* that for West the Finals were defined "by the sad, conspicuous absence of Elgin Baylor." The following night Baylor would not attend what turned out to be a disastrous team championship dinner (more on that soon). Then again, he had no reason to—Baylor was not granted a playoff share.

Russell stopped by to congratulate West, and Russell said, "I'm just glad to see this finally happen to him." It's unclear if he spoke to Wilt. Cooke approached and started to pull West's cheek toward his lips, thought the better of it, and gave him a bear hug. Lucas and DeBusschere also stopped by to congratulate West. On his way out of the locker room, Goodrich stuck in the needle. "You got to work on that jump shot tomorrow morning, Jerry," he said.

Years later, in a 2016 interview, West talked about his feelings back then. "It was the worst I ever played in a playoff. I was terrible."

Well, not terrible, it was suggested.

West jumped on it. "No, I was *turr-a-bull*. It took me two weeks, really, to even realize we had won. I had always played so well in the Finals, but this time I had played whor-a-bull and we won, so maybe that was the key to it.

"I do remember being physically exhausted. That's when I knew the ravages of a long season, and, of course, I wasn't young anymore. If Bill Sharman hadn't been there, I honestly wonder if I would've been able to make it through the season. Running made it easier, instead of fighting through screens and all that."

What Goodrich remembers seeing the day after the championship game was a sign at Inglewood High School that read "Wilt Chamberlain Volleyball."

"Wilt had set up a match for the night after our game against the Knicks," Goodrich said. "That's how confident he had been."

Jerry West, for his part, didn't go on a bender, or light candles, or sing hosannas that his prayers had at last been answered. No, he drank a little bit of champagne, accepted all the congratulations, made a few obligatory comments that he wished Baylor had been able to win it with him, returned home, and thought about a song by Peggy Lee called "Is That All There Is?" Winning one after he had already lost eight did not fill his heart with gladness. And little did he know at the time that all that Lakers success would start to unravel not months, not weeks, but only a *day* later.

CHAPTER 17

A Season Not on the Brink Exactly, But . . .

And so we return to the Oracle, June 12, 2017, Steph Curry speed-dribbling, maybe showing off a little, maybe a lot, his shot in the air, his shot good, the 129–120 victory secure; Kevin Durant and LeBron James hugging at midcourt; Durant, redeemed, receiving his Finals MVP trophy; Jerry West waiting in the tunnel to shake hands, champagne in the locker room; Counting Crows lead singer Adam Duritz at the victory party; Steve Kerr looking (but not necessarily feeling) healthier than he had looked in months; Joe Lacob and Peter Guber looking on like proud fathers.

Was it that simple? Did it move at the pace of a Michael Mann spectacle, no Wes Anderson nuance? Was the 2016–17 NBA season a fait accompli, the suspense power-vacced out of it on July 4, the moment that Durant signed on? Were the Warriors indeed *bad for basketball*, as so many were saying? Should we break them up?

Well, if you celebrate mystery above mastery, perhaps the Warriors were not the team for you, nor its dominance the theme you were looking for. But nothing in our games is guaranteed, and the

Golden State season, if you looked close enough, had subplots and twists and turns and ins and outs and high drama. What you saw with the Warriors was not a clear-cut favorite cruising to the championship; what you saw was a favorite winning it all but one that had to make considerable adjustments and overcome major obstacles to grab the brass ring. No team, no matter how strong on paper, autopilots its way to fifteen straight wins in the postseason. This one didn't. Here are some of those subplots.

OF CUPCAKES, K.D., AND RUSS

About a month after Durant signed with Golden State, one fan started a petition to change the name of Durant, Oklahoma, to Westbrook, Oklahoma, never mind that this Durant has nothing to do with Kevin and is in fact the capital of the Choctaw Nation of Oklahoma. It remains so today, thank the Lord. But the petition was at least a more original anti-Durant offensive than, say, the epidemic of "Durant 35" jersey-burning that went on after he left.

L'affaire Durant-Westbrook unfolded with a kind of *Troilus and Cressida* aspect, being both a broad comedy and a dark tragedy. (At least tragedy was the way it played in Oklahoma City.) Each side had its reliable instigators. Tony Durant was as aggressive with a tweet as his brother was going to the rack. Ray Westbrook played the brother role for Russell with an occasional weigh-in from Nina, Russell's wife, and a major assist from OKC center Enes Kanter, who seemed to have made it his season's goal to get under Durant's skin.

The squabble was always harder on Durant than on Westbrook, and the newest Warriors star spent much of the season balancing on a verbal tightrope, watching what he said while dodging the slings and arrows being flung at him from every direction. At the Warriors' first exhibition game in Vancouver's Rogers Arena against Toronto, Durant received a substantial number of boos. Really? They care about Durant leaving OKC in Vancouver? When Michael Jordan served as Westbrook's presenter into the Oklahoma Hall of Fame and praised Westbrook's "sense of loyalty to the state of Oklahoma," Durant served as the red-meat subtext. "I'm not here to try to bash anyone that's not here," said His Airness, as the pro-Westbrook audience conjured up thoughts of Durant. "Everybody has a choice. And when I saw that he [Westbrook] chose to stay here in Oklahoma, I was so proud." Kendrick Lamar even took rap-aim at Durant with these bars in a song that otherwise skewered Donald Trump:

> *Tables turned, lessons learned, my best look*
> *You jumped sides on me, now you 'bout to meet Westbrook*
> *Go celebrate with your team and let victory vouch you*
> *Just know the next game played, I might slap the shit out you*
> *Technical foul, I'm flagrant, I'm foul*
> *They throwin' me out, you throw in the towel*

Late in the season, when this reporter brought up Westbrook and what had transpired between them, Durant smiled and sighed heavily. "Man, does it make much of a difference now?" he said. "Russ is Russ and I'm me. I really think we wish each other well." Fair enough. But given what transpired during the season, it's hard to believe that Durant-Westbrook won't continue—particularly if Oklahoma City gets stronger with the addition of Paul George—and that everyone won't be watching.

Here's how the saga unfolded.

Durant might've lobbed the first grenade, albeit more of a passive-aggressive one: He texted Westbrook to say that he was leaving. Breaking up by text still ain't right. That's all Westbrook needed. Seeing himself as having the moral high ground—after all, he was the loyalist who stayed—Westbrook could afford to be the aggressor. Shortly after he learned that Independence Day had a double meaning for Durant, Westbrook Instagrammed a photo of a platter of cupcakes, that being the word that OKC players had used for a soft player. Kremlinologists deconstructed the Instagram and discovered that the three tiers of pictured cupcakes added up to thirty-five. Durant's number.

And so it was on.

Early in the preseason, Durant was asked about his adjustment in Golden State. "There's a lot I need to learn about the game of basketball," Durant said. (Lots of players these days seem to have adopted the Michael Jordan formality of saying *the game of basketball*.) "I'm not as smart as I thought I was about the game. It's played a different way here then I was used to playing." But just as quickly Durant practically stumbled over himself to add: "It's not a knock on Oklahoma City. It's not a knock on my past teammates or that organization. . . . I mean it's different here. It's fun here. It's fun playing where I was before, but that book is closed." Durant always faced this dilemma: While he didn't want to apologize for leaving Oklahoma City, he also wanted to avoid any signs that he thought life in Golden State was better than it had been in Oklahoma City. (Which, of course, it turned out to be.)

A short while after that, Durant was onstage at Stanford when the Warriors accepted the university's prestigious ENCORE Award, given to organizations that demonstrate entrepreneurial excellence, and said this about joining the Warriors:

> You hear *family* a lot. That's just a word sometimes, but this is really a lifestyle here. You can feel it when you walk in the door, in the practice facility, everybody is just together. That's something that I can appreciate as a basketball player and someone who values relationships. You can tell that that's what they stand on, that's what we stand on. I feel really grateful to play for a team like that and play with a bunch of players who are selfless and enjoy the game in its purest form. They make it about the players, they make it about the environment, so it was really an easy choice.

His comments did seem a bit overboard, particularly since they were offered at a setting where a franchise worth $2.6 billion (and perhaps as much as $4 billion) gets an award for entrepreneurship. (What, there wasn't some Bay Area mom-and-pop that started with a hundred bucks and is now worth $1 million?)

Westbrook, it seemed, was just waiting to hear something like that. "That's cute," he said when relayed Durant's comments. "My job is to worry about what's going on here; we're going to worry about all the selfish guys we've got over here, apparently."

Westbrook would've been even more exercised had he been able to plug into the early Durant-Warriors dynamic. To Durant's belief that *there's a lot I need to learn about the game of basketball,* the Warriors said amen. There was the feeling throughout the club that K.D. needed to be, for want of a better phrase, "de-Westbrooked"— that he brought bad habits from his years at OKC. (Durant probably wouldn't have put it that strongly.) Most of his mistakes involved standing instead of moving, and failing to set weakside screens or find imaginative cutting angles. No doubt true to an extent, but that feeling also speaks to the arrogance of the Warriors: *We are the only ones who can play the beautiful game.*

At times the pressure of succeeding with his new team, and showing his old team that he was worthy, seemed to overwhelm Durant. Early in the season a video taken at a Durant shooting session seemed to show a player almost neurotically desperate to prove . . . something.

"They say I ain't hungry!" Durant says. He takes a shot. "I'm out here!" he says. Durant shoots some more and, as he finishes, adds this flourish: "They told me I ain't have no drive! I'm out here! They called me a coward!"

Durant later explained his words to Ethan Sherwood Strauss, who covered the Warriors for ESPN. "That's what I say to myself when I'm working," says Durant. "I hear it all the time. You hear the noise. You hear what they say about you. Everybody hears it. So it's a little extra motivation when you hear it."

It was typical athlete psychology: Take whatever criticism you hear, massage the message, transform it into a behemothic whole, and use it for motivation. Durant does this all the time, this nobody-said-I'd-be-any-good trope. His Nike commercial that aired on ABC right after the Finals struck the same note. K.D., you were the second pick in the draft. You were the league's MVP when you were twenty-five. Stop with the nobody-said-I'd-make-it thing.

Westbrook kept the pressure on. For the first Warriors-Thunder game in Oakland early in the season, Westbrook strode in wearing an all-white outfit and a red photographer's bib, another jab at K.D., who dabbles in photography and had a sideline photo pass for Super Bowl 50. Then Westbrook mocked Curry's pregame shooting drills, making a long one, then sprinting for the locker room, the way Curry does. Hey, Durant and Curry are teammates now; might as well go after both of them. Westbrook and his teammates also pointedly ignored Durant as the teams stretched and warmed up before the game.

On February 11, Durant's first visit back to Chesapeake Energy Arena, he was greeted with loud shouts of "CUUUP-CAAAKE!" the sight of a young girl dressed as a cupcake, and the revolting tableau of an obese man wearing an image of a cupcake on his naked chest. Even in a free society some things should be banned.

All four meetings between the teams were confrontational to varying degrees. Durant traded insults with Westbrook directly and with the Thunder bench generally. Curry—allowing *some of the opposite to creep in*—got into a shoving match with backup point guard Semaj Christon, which Westbrook got into, too. But the games themselves weren't competitive. In the four meetings with the Thunder, Golden State prevailed by an average of almost twenty points; Durant didn't even play in one of them. Plus, the Warriors held this belief about Westbrook: *He is a great individual talent who will eventually sabotage the game with ill-timed three-pointers and what one Warrior called his "kamikaze" drives. We don't fear him. His stats, particularly on rebounding, are empty and bloated.* Nobody would say it aloud, but that's what the team as a whole believed.

But, see, Durant couldn't win. The Thunder jabbed at him while somehow seizing the moral high ground, and when the Warriors chewed up OKC, it only proved the point about the Warriors loading up.

It would be wrong, though, to turn Westbrook, who signed a three-year, $86 million extension to stay in OKC, into the bad guy. He is a supreme talent and a proud young man, and there is something honorable about him and his decision to stay in OKC, when all around him stars are fleeing in search of rings. "I don't know if Russ was hurt," Thunder center Steven Adams told Lee Jenkins in a *Sports Illustrated* profile of Westbrook, "because he'd never tell me, and he'd never tell you."

And if you want to see a great acceptance speech, dial up the night that Westbrook won his MVP. The man can turn soft, but he's no cupcake. For that matter, neither is Durant.

A CHRISTMAS CALAMITY, A CALMING CONFERENCE

Everything seemed to be rolling along for the Warriors as they approached the Christmas Day showdown with the Cavaliers in Cleveland. Their record was 27-4. Aside from a couple of occasions when Green hollered at Durant for what he perceived as a mistake—nothing speaks clearer to the peculiar leadership skills of Green than that he, the fourth-best player on the team, can get in the face of a superstar—all seemed well.

But there was only the patina of cohesion. "We were scratching out wins, but we weren't playing very well," Curry said in an interview weeks after the Christmas game. Neither Curry nor Durant felt entirely comfortable with the offense. Curry, in particular, was taking heat for not being the player that he was in previous seasons, not living up to his back-to-back MVPs. Against the Brooklyn Nets three days before the Cleveland showdown, for example, Curry's off shooting night (6-of-19, 3-of-13 from three-point range) was the topic of conversation, ignoring the fact that the Warriors won the game 117–101 and that Curry had a team-best +25 player rating, a metric that measures a player's overall contribution. The standards had been set so high that no one was satisfied.

With 8:14 left in the game against Cleveland, Golden State led 95–82. But from that point on the Warriors looked befuddled. Who should run the offense? Who should take the big shots? In the B.K. days—Before Kevin—Curry and Thompson would work something out, and Green or Iguodala would get them the ball. But now it was more complicated. What rotation was best? As the lead began to shrink, Kerr even took Durant out of the game for a couple of minutes to see if the Cavs' momentum could be stopped.

It couldn't. And when Irving hit a thirteen-foot jumper over Thompson, the Cavs had a 109–108 victory, and the basketball world had the sneaking suspicion that the Cavs still had Golden State's number, with or without Durant. For that final sequence,

Curry wasn't even on the floor, because Kerr had gone with Shaun Livingston for added length.

Having finished with just fifteen points on 4-of-11 shooting, Curry took most of the heat. That wasn't a new theme—he had taken most of the heat after the Cavs blew a 3–1 lead in the 2016 Finals, too, though some of the criticism was not without merit. The Warriors pushed back against the idea that this wasn't the same Curry as in previous years, but in truth he was confused and playing without his customary verve. It was Curry, remember, who made these new Warriors, it was Curry, as Spurs coach Popovich commented, who had "taken on the responsibility to be a star every night." It was Curry who had helped construct a championship team by accepting a relatively modest four-year, $44 million deal in 2012 after his rookie contract had expired.

But Curry wasn't playing like the leader he was; he was playing as if he had turned the team over to Durant. There comes a time even in the life of a superstar when he has to do some dead reckoning. For Curry, this was one of those times.

"Going into the season I was very aware of the transition process we would have to make to balance what K.D. brings to the fold," Curry told me late in the season, sounding a lot like a coach. "But I underestimated how much of a mental transition that would be."

Meaning?

"Meaning that I was very conscious of having to get K.D. into the game. That was on me. That was my responsibility. I had to become a more cerebral point guard. But I still thought it would be more . . . more . . ."

Organic?

"That's the word. Yeah, I knew we all had high basketball IQs, we all supported the system, and none of us are ball-dominant players. But we were adding a thirty-point scorer who is supremely efficient. That's what I kept thinking. You can't call it a *problem* because anyone would like to have that problem. But it's something you have to deal with because you also have Klay and Draymond and what I bring to the table. We have so many weapons that you can get kind of paralyzed by your own talent because you have so many options and you tend to overthink things.

"I used to run a lot of pick-and-rolls and have a lot of freedom to make plays. But then at some point there became—I'm not going to use the word *sacrifice*—but more of an *awareness* of other things I needed to do during the course of the game to make everything work smoother, whether that was laying off the ball a little more or setting more decoy screens.

"But then we started realizing we were getting too far away from who we were. The Cleveland game was a great moment for us to reflect on the things that had happened in the previous two and a half months, and what we decided was to simplify things and not get all caught up in the number of options."

So the Warriors cleared the air at a team meeting. It was about letting Curry go back to being Curry—though no one, it should be emphasized, had expressly told him *not* to be. "It spoke to our versatility and talent level that we could figure it out," said Curry.

After the meeting, the Warriors, and Curry in particular, started playing more cohesively. But that wasn't the end of the story. More adjustments would be needed when a frightening injury threatened the season.

YOU SAY YOU WANT A REVOLUTION? HERE'S STEPH AND THE LONG GAME

On the last day of February, less than a minute into a game against the Wizards in Washington, Golden State center Zaza Pachulia fell into Durant's left knee and Durant fell in a heap, not to return to the lineup until April 8. The Warriors lost that game (on a defensive mistake by Curry), lost the next game, won two, then lost three in a row. Durant later told Bill Simmons in a podcast that he "burst out crying" because he initially thought that it was a season-ending injury.

"It was a real checkpoint for us when K.D. went out," Curry said. "And it took a while for us to figure it out. Everybody might think we went through the season without any adversity, that we had all this good luck. Are you kidding? Losing K.D.? That's not good luck."

After Durant went down, it was put-up-or-shut-up for Curry, the time when the basketball world would see if it was still Curry's team or if it had become Durant's team. The early signs were not good. In the eight games after Durant went down, Curry made only twenty-five of his eighty-five three-point attempts. Factoring in his strange 0-of-11 trey shooting in the game before the Durant injury, the three-point king was only 26 percent over nine games. During one stretch he was 4-of-35. So maybe it *was* Durant's team. Curry was asked during that stretch if K.D.'s absence made a difference.

"Not really," Curry answered. "He obviously provides a huge magnet when he's on the floor, but for the most part, we've created really good shots. Shots that I normally take and make aren't falling. There's nothing mechanical that's wrong."

And Curry had the predictable shooter's remedy: "I'm going to keep shooting them until they fall."

By this point in the season, interestingly, the MVP race had gotten away from both Curry (back-to-back MVP nods in 2015 and '16) and Durant (the 2014 MVP). In fact, it was probably gone the moment that Durant decided to come to Golden State. The assumption was: They essentially canceled each other out. Expectations were so high for the Warriors, went the reasoning, that how could an MVP possibly come from that team? Curry and Durant understood that. In separate interviews both expressed the opinion that winning another MVP for each of them might be impossible as long as they stay together. (The prize of a Finals MVP, however, is even more possible.) A version of the same reasoning was going on in the East with LeBron, a four-time winner with a powerful team. So the MVP race early on centered on two guards with outsized stats and overachieving teams, Westbrook and James Harden, the latter of whom locked up early the MVB—Most Valuable Beard.

For the most part, the Warriors stayed away from making MVP predictions. Curry ventured out on a limb at one point and said that he believed Harden had the edge because the Rockets had the superior team, which prompted this response from Westbrook: "It don't matter what he say. Who's he?" Later in the season I asked Curry about his choice, and he backed into his answer. "Well, you have Kawhi Leonard," Curry told me. "Efficient at both ends of the floor. Doesn't do anything *historical*. But the way Russ finished? Hard to top that."

It was the analysis that made the most sense and the one that ultimately carried Westbrook to the award: Even if you weren't fully invested in his game, his triple-double season, only the second in NBA history, was impossible to ignore. The Warriors took great quiet joy, though, that neither MVP candidate (Harden finished a distant second) played particularly well against the Warriors, except during a fraught February 11 night in Oklahoma City when an angry and inspired Westbrook dropped forty-seven on them. And even that game ended in a 130–114 Warriors rout.

Eventually, Curry's shooting came around, and from mid-March until Durant's return on April 8, right before the playoffs began, he carried the Warriors to fourteen straight victories. He was so efficient that, had the MVP race been based on the last month of the season, Curry had his own candidate: "I think I played better over that time than I did during my MVP years."

When Durant was out and Curry was misfiring, a palpable sense of glee could be detected in some corners of the NBA. There was still an air of disbelief about the drop-from-the-sky suddenness with which Curry had ascended to the top of the NBA player hierarchy, the sense that he had risen much too quickly to be *that* good, that his back-to-back MVP awards in 2015 and '16 must've been some kind of fluke. There was his failure in the '16 Finals, and even when the Warriors won in '15, Iguodala had taken home the Finals MVP trophy. And there was in some quarters a general resistance to the Dubs, too, a team defined by grace, not power, less panzer division than swift-moving mobile force. The chorus of Warriors doubters was reliably led by Charles Barkley, who insisted that the Warriors play "girlie basketball." Then again, Charles says a lot of things.

Some of the anti-Curry sentiment was only tangentially related to his play, a sentiment comparable, in some respects, to that which Jordan went through in his early years. Marcus Thompson II, author of the Curry bio, has his pulse on it, and talked in a radio interview about it. "There's something that burns them"—he specifically mentioned James, Westbrook, and Chris Paul—"that Steph is the one that is exalted and because of that they want to go at him and demean his hype," Thompson said. "They want to take him down."

Green, as is his wont, took it a couple of steps further in a podcast with Thompson. It's worth looking at the whole of it because it says a lot not only about Curry but also about Green.

> Looking at Steph, he's not supposed to be what he does. [*Being what you do* makes a kind of profound Draymondian sense.] So that right there alone, it pisses people off. Also, he's way more than what everyone expected him to be or gave him a shot to be. I think most people looked at him, "Oh, man, this is a 'privileged kid' growing up. Like how did he become this? He ain't supposed to become this. This supposed to be the kid from the hood that never had nothing and had to grind for everything."
>
> But when you look at Steph's life, like they had money, but he wasn't treated like they had money. They [NBA father Dell and mother Sonya] didn't raise him like he was a privileged kid. People automatically think that this guy ain't from the hood, like he ain't cut from a different cloth, like he supposed to be soft. Like he's light skin so people make him out to be soft. People make him out to be a soft, jump-shooting guy. And he continued to get better and better. But the number one thing, whether it's former players or current players, all those that hate on Steph. Some of them will show you their hand that they're hating, and some secretly do it. It all boils down to the saying: "They want to see you do good, but never better than them." It's jealousy. But how much of this world is built on jealousy? It ain't never changing . . . and he's doing better than a lot of people.

That was some solid testifying from the Destroyer of Groins. But what is the essence of Curry as a player? Were the Golden

State Warriors once his and are now Durant's? Or are they still Curry's? Or were they *never* Curry's?

As we try to get at the answer, let us conjure up a player from the past—Isiah Thomas of the Detroit Pistons. Talented, versatile, and ballsy, Thomas was driven nuts by the fact that, no matter how well he played, he could never quite step into the mystical troika of Jordan, Magic, and Bird. Thomas's size, 6'1", prevented him from doing that. For the same reason, Allen Iverson was never going to be as influential on a game as two of his peers, Jordan and Bryant. (Though the night AI broke Jordan's ankles on a crossover remains a YouTube staple.)

Kerr got into this subject on a podcast with ESPN's Zach Lowe. Here's what he said:

> Steph is one of the great players in the world, a two-time MVP, incredibly dominant in terms of the way he impacts a game. But you're talking about Kevin Durant at six-foot-eleven protecting the rim, scoring thirty-five a game in the Finals and getting to the line, doing whatever he wants to do. There's a different level of impact that is actually possible for Steph and for K.D.
>
> Steph is my size. He's literally exactly my size, so what he's capable of is all based on his amazing skill. But he can't do anything about being six-foot-three and one seventy-five. In the playoffs especially, when you're having to protect the rim and do so many different things, there has to be a level of physicality that factors in when you're having these conversations about who's the best player in the league.
>
> That's why LeBron is there [at the top of players who dominate]. That's why Kawhi is there. That's why K.D. is there: that combination of skill and physical, sheer force.

So in clearest terms: Curry is not as good or as powerful a player as Durant. Durant is a better rebounder, a better shot-blocker, a better defender. He is also more effective as a one-on-one player, the Warriors' best pressure-release valve.

To this, by the way, Jerry West would add: *Duh, really?* Durant is West's guy. He loves his old-school game and his old-school ways. "I so admire Kevin for what kind of person he is," West said right before the Finals. "Perfect teammate. Most selfless guy I've ever seen. He shot the third most shots on our team this year. [Correct. Curry attempted 18.3 shots per game, Thompson took 17.6, and Durant took 16.5.] Think about that. Leading rebounder, leading shot-blocker. Never says a word. He'll look for Steph and Klay and Draymond like crazy, but when the game gets bogged down he will take over. With his skill, his size, and his knowledge of the game, he's unguardable."

Curry? West loves his soft touch, his ability to go from bounce to shot in a split-second, his work ethic, and his spirit. But West does not love Curry's sometimes casual defense and his careless flamboyance—such as the ridiculous behind-the-back pass he made at a crucial juncture in Game 7 of the 2016 Finals—that leads to turnovers. The modern-day Warriors are in many ways the perfect team, and Curry the perfect player, to drive West nuts. They often play "the beautiful game," unselfishly sharing the ball, knowledgeably spacing the floor, moving as one. But the Warriors are also subject to bewildering periods of carelessness, when they throw the ball around like kids in a playground dodgeball game. West is looking at *you*, Steph, and in no universe would West choose Curry over Durant.

Let us harken back, however, to the word Nash used to describe Curry: *revolution.*

Curry is a revolutionary player in a way that Isiah and Iverson were not, or even *today's* Isaiah Thomas is not. You have to go back to Cousy, who revolutionized the game with his dribbling, and from this perspective Curry is more revolutionary than Cousy, who was doing things that the Harlem Globetrotters could do better. Kerr went so far as to suggest that Curry is more "disruptive" to defenses than Jordan was. Not *better,* more *disruptive.* You can argue that all night, but remember this:

Because of the length of his outside shooting, Curry is the Warriors' special sauce. Throw in a healthy helping of Thompson, also a distance shooter, and you have the special *special* sauce.

Curry's Davidson team was playing St. Mary's in the second round of the 2009 NIT when he thought, *Hell with it.* "The coach [Bob McKillop] had given me a play to run, and I called it out as I was dribbling downcourt," Curry related in 2017. "But then I got to this spot on the court, right like where that logo might be"—he points to a spot on the Warriors' practice court—"and I just let it go. Twenty-five feet out? Twenty-seven? Not sure. It went in. It was just kind of like a rebellion thing. I looked over at the coach and gave him a smile. He wasn't smiling, but he was okay with it."

Curry stares out at the court, perhaps envisioning how far out he might be when he unleashes his next long-range missile. "It's funny what happened in the league," he continues. "A while ago there weren't many three-pointers. My dad played then. Then there were just regular three-pointers. Now there's long-distance three-pointers, like a whole new stat. It was never a conversation until maybe three years ago."

But it's a conversation, he was informed, largely because of you.

Curry shrugs. "During games I'm really not concentrating on how far out I am," he says. "Most of the long ones come when the defense is backpedaling and I'm in rhythm. I don't look down to see where I am. It's where I feel *comfortable* from. But it's fun to watch people break down something that seems so natural to me."

He pauses and smiles. "I guess it has gotten pretty far out there, hasn't it?"

It has. Keeping in mind that the three-point line is 23.75 feet from the basket behind the top of the key and 22 feet in the corners, the NBA now tracks shots from 24 feet to 30 feet and from 30 feet to 40 feet, with the stipulation that they are not desperation shots but, rather, shots taken within the flow of the offense with more than three seconds on the game clock. The numbers are startling, considering how recently taking a large volume of *normal* three-pointers was verboten in many quarters.

In the 2016–17 season, Houston's Harden attempted a league-leading 660 shots of between 24 and 30 feet, making 234 of them for a percentage of .354. Not bad. But Curry was just insanely accurate, making a league-leading 254 of them on 57 fewer attempts for an almost unbelievable percentage of .421, about what the league as a whole shot *before* the three-point line was part of the game.

And Curry can't be touched on the long, *long* ones either. He made 11 of 28 from 30 to 40 feet, a percentage of .393, which coaches would rate as acceptable for some players on two-point shots.

Even as Curry, Thompson, Harden, and Portland's Damian Lillard started connecting from way, way out, the predictable sclerotic criticism rolled in about too many threes, too many long threes in particular. "He's hurting the game," Mark Jackson said on-air of Curry. "And what I mean by that is that I go into these high school gyms, I watch these kids, and the first thing they do is they run to the three-point line. You are not Steph Curry. Work on the other aspects of the game."

We can't separate Jackson's comments from his getting fired, one supposes, but they seemed sincere, and not without support. Oscar Robertson has continually griped about how Curry wouldn't get those shots off in yesterday's game. "When I played years ago," Robertson said on a radio show, "if you shot a shot outside and hit it, the next time I'm going to be up on top of you. I'm going to pressure you with three-quarters, half-court defense. But now they don't do that. These coaches do not understand the game of basketball, as far as I'm concerned." (Hmm, did the Big O's *the game of basketball* come from himself or has he also been listening to Jordan?)

In contrast to his old rival Oscar, West professes not to worry about all the free-flying threes. "Steph and Klay both have beautiful shooting forms," says West. "It was probably inherited in Steph's case but not in Klay's. Mychal was a bricklayer and his son is Picasso." (When Curry played a round of golf with Barack Obama, the president opined that Thompson had the prettier shooting form.) West suddenly rises and raises his right arm. "Neither Steph nor Klay have a flying elbow, no shooting across the ball, which creates sidespin. Their rotation is beautiful. Form matters because form keeps you going even when you're tired or under stress. I've never talked shooting with them because what they do is always correct."

West is asked if he could estimate how many three-pointers he would've made had there been a line in his day. He says he has no idea but probably not all that many. West was a player who worked his way into a comfortable mid-range spot before squaring and firing. "I do know that I would've shot the corner three," West says. "That's an easy shot, almost like a free throw. But these guys make all of them look easy."

If West is okay with their threes, what about Steph's "fours"?

He thought for a moment before answering.

"It is a fine line, but I'm not sure Steph can take it out much further. But that's on him, not me and not his coaches. Players who are great shooters and who have great form will find a place where they're comfortable from. Everyone else may not be comfortable watching them from that distance. But *they're* comfortable. And when you're comfortable, great things happen."

It's difficult to say exactly what Curry's Lexington-Concord moment was in this longball thing. Early in the 2015–16 season against the Memphis Grizzlies, Curry stole the ball, spun away from a defender, and launched a forty-footer from near the half-court logo that banked in. That had a degree of luck to it, though, even for Curry, so the one that really resonated was his bomb that beat Oklahoma City in overtime on February 27, 2016. That seemed to awaken everyone to the Longball Era.

First of all, it won a dramatic overtime game 121–118. Second, it was his record-tying twelfth of the game and his 288th of the season, which broke his own record. But what made it notable was that Curry launched it from about thirty-eight feet with such insouciance, such ho-hum nonchalance, that it didn't have the feel of a desperation heave. It was like a normal shot taken in normal circumstances. A minute after it went in, a "No Way!" tweet showed up from Dirk Nowitzki, the greatest seven-foot distance shooter in history. It seemed like everyone around the NBA was watching that night.

One might reasonably ask: Okay, but so what? A nonchalant thirty-footer counts for three points just like a hard-earned twenty-two-footer from the corner. A few side points before we answer the so-what.

First, there is significant entertainment value to the longball. "I'm watching the Warriors and Curry is dribbling upcourt and he's at three-quarter court and I'm yelling, 'Shoot it! Shoot it from there!'" says Bill Walton. The vision of a shirtless Walton yelling at the TV, Grateful Dead sound track banging in the background, is irresistible. Offers an NBA superstar from a different age and a different style: "Nobody plays like that. Nobody has *ever* played like that." That came from the mouth of Iverson.

Then, too, there is the fact that the longball is deflating to the opposition, particularly when it comes accompanied with style points, as it often does with Curry. "What separates Steph from all shooters—and I think he's the greatest shooter in the history of the NBA—is that he can do it off the bounce, he can do it off a screen, he can cross you over," says former Warrior Tom Tolbert. "A lot of those guys who were great shooters had to have someone create a shot for them. Not Steph. He comes down, goes between his legs, crosses over, pulls up from twenty-eight feet, and makes a high percentage of them. You're talking about something that is insane."

When Kerr arrived in 2014 and got a gander at Curry's burgeoning long game, he did not sit down and sketch out special plays for it. Even the Warriors are not at the point when they *want* a thirty-footer. (Are they?) But neither did the coach raise an eyebrow. "I never had a moment when I said, 'We're shooting too far out,'" Kerr said. "I realized quickly that long makes are just such a devastating force. I can literally see teams hanging their heads. So it's almost like a four-pointer."

The subject of adding another category of scoring has come up for discussion around the NBA offices and will do so as long as shooters continue to "suburbanize," the Kirk Goldsberry term for moving out. (Goldsberry became so respected for his advanced analytics that the Spurs hired him as vice president of strategic research.) Among those who have expressed a favorable opinion about a four-point line are Larry Bird, Byron Scott, and two people with Golden State ties—Rick Barry and Mychal Thompson. "It would create even more excitement for the game," says Klay's dad. "They'd say that it's gimmicking up the game, but that's what they said about the three-point line once upon a time." Still, a four-point

line has never been put on an agenda and remains a far-off hypothetical.

The Curry three has also brought an interesting academic dimension to the game. An excellent 2014 article in the *Wall Street
Journal* by Ben Cohen highlighted the fact that Curry doesn't have
a classic jumper; he has more like a newfangled version of the one-
handed set shot. "His kinetic efficiency comes from Curry shooting
as he's jumping, rather than jumping and then shooting, which also
lets him release the ball in as little as 0.3 second," wrote Cohen. It
also allows Curry to release long shots with a normal form. "It's
not a heave," Curry says about his long shot, and he's correct.

More important, Curry releases his three-ball higher than do
most shooters—the average arc tops out at 15.77 feet as opposed
to Curry's 16.23 feet—a "mathematically optimal" height, wrote
Cohen, since the steeper a shot, the wider the opening into the basket. In other words, while everybody understands the inefficiency
of a line-drive foul shot, even proficient shooters might want to
consider higher trajectories as they move out farther from the basket.

After the OKC game-winner, Egghead Nation arrived en masse.
A retired professor named John Fontanella, author of a book called
The Physics of Basketball, was called upon to discuss the precise
"launch angle" at which Curry releases the ball. "I'm absolutely
certain Curry releases the ball at the angle of the softest shot," Fontanella told the *San Francisco Chronicle.* "What that means is, he
has mastered the technique of when the ball gets to the rim, it trav-
els as slowly as it possibly can."

"I did read one of those stories," Curry says. "But if I start thinking about things like launch angles and trajectory, it'll really mess
me up."

But the most important aspect of Curry's space shots happens
before he takes them. It has nothing to do with entertainment or
armchair academia. It has to do with offensive efficiency.

For years and years defenses could pretty much rely on the fact
that offenses were not going to emphasize threes. How many times
did you hear someone say—and you still hear it—"We're going to
pack it in"? You never heard anyone say, "We're going to pack it

out." But with Curry, Thompson, and now Durant on the floor, that's what you have to do. Defenses have to defend Curry almost as soon as he crosses the midcourt line, and, because the Warriors run a sophisticated system of off-the-ball screens and backdoor cuts, that distance-from-the-basket aspect creates immense difficulty for defenses, who now find themselves expending energy in what was once uncharted territory.

"Because the Warriors' pick-and-rolls are that much *higher* you have to be up there to defend them," says Spurs coach Popovich. "They set a pick and you don't come out, well, Steph or Klay will just shoot it, and they're making forty to forty-five percent and you're screwed. So you have to be up.

"Now you have your big guys far away from the basket. How are they going to be in a pick-and-roll, then go back and defend against a roller? You can't cover all of it. So it's hard to play with big guys, and Golden State forces teams to go small. But guess what? Their small team is better than your small team."

Detroit Pistons coach Stan Van Gundy agrees. "Steph is a major, major factor because of how far out the offense starts," says Van Gundy. "So you have to push out on him. But then he doesn't always shoot. He willingly gives it up, so you can't trap him. Like everybody else on the team, he's unselfish. So now your defense is spread all over the place, and Draymond makes a play. Or Klay makes a play. Or Iguodala makes a play. Never mind what Durant is going to do to you anyway. But it starts with Curry."

Which is also why Curry makes such a devastating decoy. The Warriors' offense is, to quote the Stones, practiced in the art of deception. Curry often runs away from the ball, either to set off-ball screens or simply to open up the court for his teammates. He screens away. Or he screens on the ball, then goes down and makes another screen. Or he uses those ballet-dancer feet to quickly slip his screen. Stockton used to be extremely successful as a screen-setter for a point guard, but his were more basic take-the-hit screens; Curry is an all-over-the-place screener, setting so many within, say, ten seconds, that it's hard to understand that he may eventually get the ball. Because of the way the Golden State offense functions, Curry is arguably the best guard screener in the history of the league. Doing a deep statistical dive—because that's what they do over there—FiveThirtyEight.com calculated that Curry led NBA guards in screens that led to baskets, with 108 during the 2016–17 season.

But it's not just Curry. All the Warriors screen and do it well. "One of the things I appreciate about them," says Hubie Brown, who, if you have a couple of hours, will deconstruct the Warriors' offense for you, "is that they brought back-screening back into the game."

The Warriors' greatest contribution to the aesthetics of basketball is that they have at least three players—Curry, Durant, and Thompson (and Green and Iguodala aren't bad)—who could easily get their own shots, but they don't play an unappetizing isolation style.

Still, in the final analysis it's Curry who makes the Warriors different, a new kind of lethal, the one who makes Golden State almost impossible to guard if they're reasonably in sync. If you ask the Cavaliers whether it is tougher to guard Curry or Durant, the guess here is that, to a man, they would say Durant. But if you ask them which player they have to *set their defense against* primarily, their honest answer would be Curry.

K.D. HAD SOME ADJUSTMENTS, TOO

By his second or third year in the league, Durant was a big deal. He doesn't have a Big Personality in the same sense that Jordan, Kobe, and LeBron do, but he has his ego, and, in reality, he answered to no one by the end of his tenure in Oklahoma City. It was his team more than Westbrook's, yet when the Thunder fell short it was usually perceived as the fault of Westbrook for taking too many shots and not getting Durant the ball.

So now Durant comes to Golden State, where they have carved out this seemingly perfect little utopia that hums along on charm, goodwill, and *joy,* except that from time to time Durant finds himself on the receiving end of an on-court tantrum from Draymond, who is—what?—maybe one-half the offensive player Durant is. During a loss in Sacramento on February 4, Durant, who had a terrible game (10 points, 0-of-6 from the three-point line), got *Dray-moned* during a time-out, both players trading f-bombs in a team huddle.

With a knowing wink, Green later said that it was all calculated, and Durant, the Superstar Who Aims to Please, took the fall.

"I didn't have any energy as far as pressuring the ball, boxing out, getting out in transition," said Durant. "He saw that. And as a teammate you can just let me be in the clouds or you can bring me back down, and I think he did a good job. We went back and forth there, and that kind of got me going. I had three or four blocks in the fourth quarter. I didn't score well, but I think defensively I was there for the team and made plays on the offensive end. . . . He [saw] me kind of drifting the other way and whatever that was we had, it helped. And it felt like it was planned [laughter]. . . . Sometimes you need that. It's a long season. . . . It was good for me."

The Draymond-Durant verbal dustups got a lot of attention, but much more important were their congenial conversations behind the scenes. It was Green who repeatedly reminded Durant of this fact: *We don't need you so much during the regular season; it's during the playoffs when you'll have to carry us.* It was solid reasoning; the game slows down in the postseason, and Durant, the best weapon in isolation on the rare occasions when the Warriors do have to play that way, was bound to become more important.

Durant's ongoing struggle to find his place on the team didn't get any easier when he went down in Washington with the knee injury. By the time he was ready to return to action after missing nineteen games, the Warriors had clinched home-court advantage throughout the playoffs. He had watched Curry, after his early troubles, return to MVP form, watched his team, after a few initial stumbles, figure out how to play without him, watched as Kerr artfully juggled spare pieces like Matt Barnes, Patrick McCaw, and Ian Clark in an effort to produce one Durant, a patchwork job of estimable proportions.

Durant also heard the whispers: *Maybe the Warriors are better without Durant. They didn't need him to win a championship in 2015, after all.*

"I don't think anyone on the team believes that," Durant said to me late in the season, "so it's not a concern."

Who knows if he was telling the truth about being concerned— a player can't shut out everything, especially one who freely confesses to hearing his doubters—but the idea that the Warriors thought they were better without Durant was just plain silly. "He brings something nobody else has," Curry had said. Which is? "A kind of automatic ability to score, an ease about scoring," he answered. "Not too many players have that."

It was evident right away on Durant's April 8 return against the New Orleans Pelicans. As if to test the premise that the Warriors *never* need everybody, Curry missed the game with a knee contusion, but Durant, despite playing limited minutes (everyone played limited minutes), scored an easy sixteen points, including back-to-back shots to open the second half that essentially told the Pelicans, Don't bother. "Kevin is Kevin," Kerr said after the game. "He could fall out of bed and get twenty points after a long nap, he's so talented."

More to the point, Durant had ten rebounds and six assists and played great defense, something that made Warriors assistant Adams, who had first worked with him in Oklahoma City, quite proud. Whether or not Durant truly needed to be "de-Westbrooked," he had become a transcendent all-around player, something that might've been overlooked when he was with the Thunder because he had to score so much.

A few days after his return, Durant talked about the adjustments he had to make when he came to the Warriors. He acknowledged that the onus to play differently was more on Curry, the point guard and incumbent leader of the offense, but said that he had his own changes to think about.

"I was coming from a place where they just gave me the ball," Durant told me. He continued:

I had to create for myself and create stuff for my teammates. Here we have so many ball handlers and people who want to handle the ball, I do more [he laughs] roaming around.

There was also a mental adjustment. Look, I understood that

they were adjusting to me. I was the new guy coming into a system where they've already had success. That can be tough. When do you go out and look for your own stuff, and when do you play a little more in the background? It's a balancing act.

We figured it out in the half-court eventually. I'm not saying it's better or worse, but you get more space to shoot the ball here. [Durant was still extremely careful about saying anything that could be construed as a knock on Westbrook and OKC.] But the big difference is actually in transition. Russ would usually just give me the ball unless he was taking it himself, and I would look ahead for guys like Andre Roberson and Dion Waiters. They liked to run out. It was simpler. But now I have to think about Klay and Steph. A lot of time on the break they would rather stop and shoot threes, and we go into a lot of offensive stuff off of transition. So you look at that aspect of the game differently.

And did Curry's penchant for shooting long threes make a difference?

"Look, players who are looked on as scorers and whose teams depend on them for points all take what some people consider to be crazy shots. Mine might be an off-balance shot, a shot off one foot. Some shots that I take another guy wouldn't take.

"Steph's so-called crazy shots happen to be from way out. I was taught that was an inefficient shot, so I wouldn't do that. I wasn't tempted to come in and start taking long shots just because Steph took them."

It's mentioned to Durant that he has a kind of old-fashioned game (in a new-fashioned sense, to be sure), a kind of no-frills economy.

"I would agree with that," he said. "I can't say I ever copied an old-time player, but you know what I like to see? I like to see the ball going through the rim. I don't have to do a hundred moves to get to where I want to go. Back in the day you could see the fundamentals, see some of the simplicity. That's missing from our game today. It's more about excitement right away.

"We have to wrap our mind around the fact that not every player is the same. Steph changed the game by shooting way-out threes, sometimes in transition. LeBron changed the game with being able to pass the ball for a wing player. Russ changed the game with his athleticism as a point guard. Me? I'm just trying to get the job done."

That was a natural transition to the subject of West. Durant was asked how much West's phone call to him the day after the Hamptons 5 visit had to do with his switching teams. Some initial reports put far too much weight on the West call, which West said himself. "I was not the damn reason that Kevin Durant came to Golden State," he snaps. Lacob, always prickly about a perceived slight, was not happy either that his role was diminished and West's amplified.

Durant sighed heavily because he didn't want to embarrass anyone. "I never said I came here because of Jerry West, and Jerry never said it either," said Durant. "But it was part of the package. It was nice to hear. He talked a lot about how my game was a classic, old-school game, how I would've fit into any era. It meant a lot that a guy like him thought I could be a part of this."

"Things fall apart; the centre cannot hold."
—WILLIAM BUTLER YEATS
(THE CENTER CANNOT HOLD EITHER.)

CHAPTER 18

Cooke Stirs the Wrong Pot

The Lakers' 1971–72 season had been glorious, with the longest winning streak in history and a redemptive championship for West. But it had also been in its own way torturous. With all the travel, every NBA season since the league began had been a protracted war of attrition. More than one champion has asked: Can we possibly go through this again?

Once Russell and his iron will departed after the 1969 season, dynasties were a thing of the past. No NBA team would win back-to-back titles until the Lakers of Coach Riley and GM West did it in 1987 and '88. It became one of the prevailing leitmotifs of that time period, something that journalists chronicled year after year, right along with the sartorial misdemeanors committed by coaches in the Bee Gees era. Nobody could repeat in the NBA, while over the same time frame the Miami Dolphins and Pittsburgh Steelers both went back-to-back in the NFL and, in baseball, the Oakland A's won three straight and the Cincinnati Reds and New York Yankees each won two in a row.

It was, one supposes, an example of the much-sought-after par-

236 · JACK McCALLUM

ity that league officials claim to want. But it didn't come across like
that. It came across as an absence of excellence.

"The seventies was the fall of the Roman Empire, or the last
vestiges of the Gilded Age," says Pat Riley, reaching deep into his
metaphorical bag. "You had your four historical teams that were
coming to an end—the Lakers, the Celtics, the Knicks, and the Sixers. Wilt was gone, Jerry was gone, the great Knick players were
gone. Drugs were in, anti-establishment was in, and, starting with
the Warriors in 1975, you had a bunch of one-hit wonders."

As were the Lakers, a masterful mix that won thirty-three straight
but became themselves a one-hit wonder, unraveling in spectacularly rapid fashion. *Sic transit imperium.*

As the Lakers (minus Riley, who was sick, and McMillian, who
had already headed back east) gathered at the Forum Club to celebrate their 1972 championship, there was a significant fatigue factor in place. They were tired of one another, and private agendas
had come to the surface. West was never one for overt complaining
but did internalize the slights he felt. He believed, not without
merit, that he had carried the Lakers through much of the sixties,
after Baylor had become less effective, and so he deserved to be the
highest-paid member of the team. When Wilt came, West accepted
the promise that they would be paid equally, but he began to
suspect—accurately, as it turned out—that Wilt was getting more
money after making a secret deal with Cooke.

Then, too, West had long chafed under the general managership
of Fred Schaus, his old coach at West Virginia and in the pros. Athletes tend to have long memories, and West never did forgive Schaus
for not playing him much as a rookie and even starting him slowly
way back when he was a sophomore at West Virginia. West valued
some of the things Schaus had done as coach, such as mixing white
and black players as roommates. But like many of the Lakers, he
didn't see Schaus as having much value as a GM.

There were other tensions. Hairston had mumbled all year about
not getting enough credit for his rebounding. Goodrich had already
been let go by the Lakers once and wondered about his future. The

southpaw shooting guard had been undeniably splendid during the streak, but he and Chamberlain were never on the best of terms. Wilt wrote in his bio that Goodrich had "a well-deserved reputation as a spoiled kid, a selfish gunner who dribbled too much and shot too much and sulked when things didn't go his way." For the record, no one else said that, at least publicly.

Now that the season was over, Ellis and Riley and the other reserves wondered if they could've played more and what their future was. As for Wilt, well, he had his house and his championship and his Finals MVP award, but he was always looking for something else, even if he sometimes never quite knew what that was. The little minuet he danced with Jack Kent Cooke—the mysterious "Mr. Norman," during their semi-secret seduction period, was in the past. At one point Cooke had introduced his great and good friend Sam Yorty to Wilt and told him that Hizzoner would love to see Wilt's house. As author Rosen reports in *The Pivotal Season,* Wilt said that he would put Yorty's name on a waiting list like everyone else. Cooke was deeply offended.

And so, as the celebrants chomped down on roast beef, "there was another beef in a private meeting room," as Mal Florence wrote in the next day's *Los Angeles Times*. The row was over a playoff share for Sharman, which Cooke—quite remarkably though not surprisingly—wanted to be extracted from the players' share of the record $224,500 pie, which came to $17,269 per man, a sizable chunk of change in those days. (Trainer Frank O'Neill was also granted a full share.) "We asked Jack Kent Cooke to pay Bill a playoff share and he wouldn't do it," West remembers today. "So we said, 'Okay, take it out of ours.' What made everyone so furious was that Cooke made it out like we wouldn't give the money to Bill. It came out in the papers that way. First of all, Cooke should've done it, and, second of all, we *were* willing to do it. We were made out to be the bad guys and *they* were the good guys." Sharman did get his full share, from the players' pool. West was so furious that he stormed out of the dinner and went to watch a boxing match that happened to be going on that night at the Forum.

Cooke later complained that none of the players would talk to him during the dinner and singled out the one Laker who rarely came in for criticism. "I was just appalled by their behavior and very hurt," Cooke was quoted in Lazenby's bio of West. "It was just an air of sullenness. It was Jerry West again. He went up and down the hall sulking."

The party simply didn't conform to Cooke's notions of decorum, which pretty much started with deference to him and certainly did not include complaints about something as pedestrian as money. The way Cooke saw it, everyone should be happy. The players got paid. We won a championship. And, hey, remember those Christmas presents? They're not *giving* away pen-and-pencil sets, for God's sake.

The saying around pro sports is that when an athlete declares "it's not about the money," it's about the money. That's not always true these days when top players can get maximum deals anywhere, never mind what can be reaped in endorsement deals even in small markets. When Durant signed his two-year deal worth about $54.2 million with the Warriors, it was honestly not about the money because he would've commanded that anywhere; it was about trying to win a championship. And when he took about $9 million less on his contract extension than he could've gotten after the 2016–17 season, it was about enabling Golden State to re-sign other players in an effort to win *another* championship.

In the days of West, however, it *was* almost always about the money because there was rarely enough of it. Playoff shares meant a lot, and they were both symbolic and literal, evidence of a job seen to completion. Kerr remembers when he was the player rep for the Chicago Bulls during the championship 1996–97 season and told reserve forward Brian Williams (who later changed his name to Bison Dele) that he had been voted a full playoff share even though he had joined the team late in the season. "I was a little surprised when Brian told me, 'Thanks, Steve, but [general manager] Jerry Krause told me I would get two full shares,'" remembers Kerr. "I told him I would talk to Michael and Scottie, and of course their response was, 'That's fucking bullshit.'" Krause always swore that he had cleared the request with Jordan and Pippen beforehand, but at any rate, Williams (who died in 2002 in the waters of the South Pacific in an incident still cloaked in mystery) got only one share.

Cooke's banquet was but a small window into what happened after the streak season. But it set a tone, established a paradigm. Things weren't the same. The magic was gone. And the Lakers soon became a condensed version of themselves.

Schaus left as GM to become coach of Purdue. "I am thrilled to take a fifty percent cut in salary," he said, subtly indicating that it would be a pleasure to distance himself from both Cooke and egotistical players. Though Schaus wasn't a favorite of anyone's, he had in fact put together the streak team—stealing Chamberlain from the 76ers; getting Goodrich, Hairston, Erickson, Robinson, and Ellis in trades; and snagging Riley and Trapp from the waiver wire. Pete Newell took over for him.

K. C. Jones, Sharman's right-hand man and defensive coach, left to become head coach of the San Diego Conquistadors in the ABA. (K.C. would take over the head job with the Capital Bullets in 1973 and was replaced in San Diego by none other than Chamberlain. Wilt was not, shall we say, exactly a Sharman in the way he approached coaching; he missed a couple of games during the season to attend his own book signings.) The Lakers public relations man, Stu Zanville, left to take a job with the Harlem Globetrotters, another sign of the relatively low place the NBA had in the sports culture—flacking the Globies was a better gig than working for the NBA champions.

Right before training camp, Cleamons was traded to Cleveland. "I cried and cried," says Cleamons today. "All season I heard, 'Rook, next year you get your chance.' And I never got one." A couple of weeks into the season, Ellis and Trapp would be traded to the Philadelphia 76ers, who would subsequently lose a record seventy-three games, four more than the Lakers had *won* the year before. And three months into the season Flynn Robinson would be sent to the Baltimore Bullets.

Also, there was a minor outcry from the fans because ticket prices for the 1972–73 season had been raised. By fifty cents.

The worst news came on June 1, about three weeks after the Finals win: Gary Hearn, Chick's twenty-nine-year-old son, died of a drug overdose. Years later, in a story written by Steve Springer of the *Los Angeles Times,* Hearn remembered what happened when the final buzzer went off: His son "shot up out of his seat, raced up to where I was broadcasting, leaned up, and squeezed my hand."

Sports is unrelenting, every accomplishment shadowed by expectation, the mandate to do it again. After his Cleveland Cavaliers won the 2016 championship, general manager Dave Griffin was intercepted by one of the team's minority owners as he hurried across the floor to celebrate. "We're going to do it again next year, right, Dave?" the man said.

(And when they didn't do it again, losing in five games to the Warriors, Griffin was let go by owner Dan Gilbert.)

West says now that he doesn't look back all that much upon the 1971–72 season. But when he does? "Frankly, I'm just amazed at what we accomplished, the way we played, and how easily we beat almost everybody," West said. "And I wonder: What would our record have been, and how many games might we have won in a row, if we had started the season with the lineup that finished it?" Meaning: What would our record have been if McMillian had been a starter from the beginning and West hadn't missed those early five games?

Consider what this team accomplished in that magical season:

- The Lakers scored over one hundred points in eighty-one of eighty-two games. There was no three-point line.
- They were behind at halftime only four times during the season.
- Their average margin of victory was sixteen points.
- In one game, against the Warriors, they scored forty-nine points in a quarter and ninety-one in a half. They won 162–99.
- As a backcourt, Goodrich and West averaged 51.7 points, divided almost evenly, Goodrich at 25.9, West at 25.8. At this writing no other backcourt combo has scored so prolifically.

- Wilt made almost 65 percent of his field-goal attempts, far ahead of the second-best mark in the league, which was Abdul-Jabbar's .574.
- At age thirty-five, Chamberlain also led the league in rebounding average with 19.2.
- At age thirty-three, West, having been converted by Sharman to pure point guard, led in assists with 9.7.
- West and Wilt made the all-NBA first team along with Boston's Havlicek, New York's DeBusschere, and a tie for the final guard spot between Chicago's Jerry Sloan and New York's Frazier. Still, Abdul-Jabbar was voted MVP even though he was the second-team center. West was second in the voting for the third straight year and the fourth time overall in his career. Over the years he also had a third and three fifths. He was even sixth in 1973, his penultimate season. Jerry West may be the Logo, but he was never the MVP.

A *Sports Illustrated* writer named Richard Hoffer once wrote the immortal line: "It never ends pretty." He was talking about boxing, but it's true of so many other sports. This Lakers story didn't end pretty.

West had a good 1972–73 season (22.8 points and 8.8 assists), but he was hampered by injuries. Wilt was still a force but clearly running on fumes; he was far from the good-natured, everybody-gotta-get-together-gotta-love-one-another Captain Wiltie he had been the year before. On December 13, 1972, as the impatient Lakers stewed aboard a delayed TWA flight that would take them from Chicago to a game in Philadelphia that night, Wilt was overheard by airline personnel saying, "I may take over the plane. I'm so mad I may shoot somebody." It was the hijacking era and echoes of the massacre at the Munich Summer Olympics were still in the air, so officials took it seriously.

It was decided that Wilt would not be thrown off the plane, but TWA did ask Chamberlain and "Coach Shermen" (as the FBI report says) to step into the jetway for a conference to remind the player of how serious his comments had been. Wilt didn't take well to scolding. "I am tired of this bullshit," he told airline officials. "I got this kind of bullshit all through my life." That was Wilt at his Wiltiest, making a life generalization over a specific incident for which he was at fault. He went back on board, grabbed his luggage, and stormed off—in effect deplaning himself—and caught a later United flight that got him there right before the game, which turned out to be a 128–90 L.A. laugher.

The 1972–73 Lakers needed seven games to beat the Bulls in the first round, and in the Finals they went down meekly to the Knicks in four straight after winning Game 1.

Then it got rockier. The Lakers knew that they were still a good team but probably not of championship caliber. They were on edge, testy among themselves, fed up with Cooke and his penny-pinching ways. West, Chamberlain, McMillian, and Erickson made a pact to stay out of training camp in the fall of 1973. West wanted his contract renegotiated. Goodrich and Hairston had gotten raises; hell, Chick Hearn had his deal renegotiated after the championship season.

GM Newell, who was acting under instructions from Cooke, didn't blink. So Chamberlain retired and took the Conquistadors job, McMillian was traded to Buffalo (for center Elmore Smith since the pivot was now open), and team rep Erickson was shipped to Phoenix for Connie Hawkins.

As for West, well, he came back to camp and ended his holdout. Because that's what he always did. (And he and Newell remained the closest of friends; West still tears up at the memory that he was on his way for a visit when Newell died in 2008.) West played well when he could but suffered a series of injuries (groin and pulled stomach muscles), and the Lakers finished with a 47-35 record. Predictably, they were blown out in five games in their first-round playoff series with Milwaukee.

Everyone thought West would quit. For a while, West thought West would quit. But something brought him back, be it love of the game, love of the money, the thought of an empty life without basketball, or all three. He negotiated a two-year playing deal with

Cooke, who also made a vague proviso that West would remain with the team, in some capacity, after his playing days were over.

But then West learned that Cooke and Wilt had, in fact, worked out a secret deal that paid Chamberlain about $400,000 a year, not the $250,000 he and West were supposed to be making. West still came to camp and played well in one preseason game before deciding, with the 1974–75 season just weeks away, that he was done. There was too much resentment, too much acrimony with Cooke, whom he would later sue for back wages. Oscar Robertson had already retired. It was only fitting.

And when West hung it up, this superb, once-in-an-era team, and all vestiges of it, was gone, gone like tears in the rain.

"If I ever got to the point mentally where I thought I was losing it, I would stop. But in many ways I feel sharper than I ever have in my life."

—JERRY WEST

CHAPTER 19

West and the Art of Talent Evaluation

As the Warriors advanced to the 2017 Finals, twelve straight wins behind them (bye-bye Portland, Utah, and San Antonio), West knew his days as a Golden State executive were numbered. He was feeling melancholy and reflective, two states of mind not unfamiliar to him. For the past six years he had prepared three personnel reports per year in which he gave his frank opinions about the players, and countless verbal opinions, solicited and unsolicited. The big picture is the big puzzle, yes, but the devil is always in the details, and West notices the little things, too. On one occasion this season, for example, he told Kerr that the Warriors didn't look prepared on jump balls. "You never know," he said. "One possession can mean a ballgame." During the 2015–16 season he noticed that the Warriors almost never got an offensive rebound after a Harrison Barnes miss because "he has too much weird spin on his shot."

All in all, West felt he had made a difference, and this observer never heard anyone, on or off the record, belittle West's contributions. He brought personnel wisdom, gravitas, and, in the words of Guber, cover of darkness in the formative years.

But West had been asked by Lacob to take the pay cut. That hurt him. There is little doubt that West's counsel was needed less than it was in the beginning, before Curry was a proven superstar, before Thompson and Green became all-stars, and before Durant signed on. On the other hand, with the Warriors having a conservative net worth of $2.6 billion—and some say it could be $4 billion after they move into the Chase Center—they could obviously afford to continue West's services.

But West no longer felt like he was needed, not like before anyway. The man in the front office with whom West felt the most comfortable, Schlenk, had departed for the GM job in Atlanta. He and West talked the same no-nonsense language.

Something else was going on, too. West had begun having conversations with the Clippers about coming aboard as a consultant. The contact was made by Dennis Wong, who was formerly a minority owner of the Warriors and now had a small chunk of the Clippers under Steve Ballmer, the Microsoft billionaire who had famously paid $2 billion for the franchise that the miserable Donald Sterling had done his best to devalue. West sometimes flew on Wong's plane to Warriors games, and they had always gotten along.

West was torn. He still had a strong allegiance to the Warriors and close relationships with some of the players—Durant, Green, and Thompson in particular. But there was that matter of the pay cut, and the lure of having a team right in his hometown. Sure, the Clippers franchise was the one that treated Baylor so badly years earlier, but this was a different time and different people were in charge, basketball people, West kept saying, like team coach/president of basketball operations Doc Rivers, executive VP Lawrence Frank, and general manager Dave Wohl. (Rivers later lost the team president title.)

"I don't feel the same about things up in Golden State," West said. "It has changed. I'm just not sure I'm wanted anymore. What propels me is the competitive part. If I ever got to the point mentally where I thought I was losing it, I would stop. But in many ways I feel sharper than I ever have in my life. And I think over the years I've demonstrated that I seem to have a gift to identify players."

That's like saying Spielberg has a gift for storytelling.

West, who didn't officially become general manager until 1982, doesn't deserve credit for drafting Magic in 1979. New owner Jerry Buss insisted on that from the get-go, and Sharman was actually the man who was front and center with that pick. As the Lakers president at the time, Sharman reluctantly gave Chicago Bulls general manager Rod Thorn permission to stage a coin-flip promotion to settle who would get the number one pick. He did it because he thought it would help the league. The Bulls fans chose heads, it came up tails, the Lakers got Magic, the Bulls got David Greenwood.

But West put the pieces around Johnson that made it all go, players like James Worthy (whom he insisted on picking over the more spectacular Dominique Wilkins and later protected when Buss wanted to trade Worthy for Roy Tarpley, an eventual drug casualty), Byron Scott, Jamaal Wilkes, Kurt Rambis, A. C. Green, and Mychal Thompson. ("I was never so nervous as the first time I met Jerry after he signed me," says Thompson. "It was like I was having an audience with the Pope.") And since the Lakers were perennial winners, West rarely had the chance to get an obvious star. "He [West] once went 10 years in a row without picking earlier than 23rd," observed Scott Howard-Cooper on NBA.com, "and still unearthed players who not only had careers, accomplishment enough, but became starters on good clubs and even All-Stars."

After those Magic-Kareem-Riley Lakers made seven Finals and came away with four championships, it was time to rebuild. So West did it again. First, there were small moves that set the table, like the drafting of Nick Van Exel in 1993 and the trade for Cedric Ceballos a year later. The Lakers never fell apart or drifted into irrelevance, even during Jordan's reign. Then West went after big game. He lured Shaquille O'Neal from Orlando as a free agent. Then he drafted Kobe Bryant as a seventeen-year-old high school senior, the move that vaulted West into the realm of immortal GMs. It happened, first, because West had a strong relationship with Arn Tellem, who had just started to become a super-agent. Not only did West and Tellem share a mutual professional respect, but Arn's wife, Nancy, and their son Matty were Mommy and Me friends with Karen and Jonnie West. You can't get any stronger bond than Mommy and Me. Tellem, a University of Pennsylvania graduate, had Philadelphia roots, knew Kobe's father, Joe "Jellybean" Bryant, who had played with the 76ers, and was able to sign Kobe as a client.

Tellem kept Bryant from working out for other teams—"Once I sold Kobe on being a Laker, he was okay with the plan," Tellem said in 2017—and held a Lakers-only workout at Inglewood High School in Los Angeles. West enlisted one of his former favorites, defensive specialist Michael Cooper, to go at the kid hard. Yes, Cooper was forty years old and six seasons retired, but he was still in excellent shape and knew every trick. But Bryant owned him. It was no contest, even after Cooper went physical. That's not just a West-Tellem legend. Raymond Ridder was a youngster working for the Lakers then, and he witnessed the workout. "Kobe just destroyed Cooper," he says.

West doesn't remember how long he watched, but Tellem says it was only about fifteen minutes. "Jerry said something like, 'I've seen enough,'" says Tellem. "Later he told me privately, 'This kid is going to be a superstar, and we're going to figure out how to get him.'"

West's son Ryan was also there that day. He is about the same age as Bryant and was amazed at Kobe's ability. But he was even more impressed months later when he ran into Kobe after a Summer League game in which Bryant had just scored about thirty against pro competition.

"How did it go?" Ryan asked.

"That was easier than I thought," answered Bryant.

Rod Thorn, who followed West to West Virginia and also wore the storied number 44, told West that he was not going to be able to pull off the Bryant pick. But all the orchestration and warning other teams off of Bryant worked. Kobe was drafted at number thirteen by the Charlotte Hornets and then traded to the Lakers for Vlade Divac, whom West loved as a player. Among the immortals drafted above Bryant were Todd Fuller (Warriors) and Vitaly Potapenko (Cleveland).

While it's true that Bryant's refusal to work out was the main reason he didn't get drafted higher—in those days who wanted to take a chance on a high school kid who refused to audition?—it's also true that several teams picking above the Lakers simply didn't believe that strongly in Bryant's potential. "After all, we didn't *find* Kobe," says Mitch Kupchak, who worked under West in the front office for two decades and who was fired as L.A.'s general manager in 2017. "There he was, playing in the McDonald's All-Star Games and all that. But Jerry is the one who really saw his potential."

The strain of seducing Shaq—which took hours of telephone calls—and scheming to get Kobe left West exhausted, he says today. Never a great sleeper, his doctor ordered him to the hospital for three days. But the work paid off. With Shaq and Kobe together, and with deals that West made to bring in complementary players such as Rick Fox, Derek Fisher, and Robert Horry, the Lakers produced a three-peat at the beginning of the century. West, however, was around for only one of the titles, having left the Lakers after a number of disagreements with owner Jerry Buss and an unfriendly relationship with Phil Jackson.

(Kobe first spoke reverentially, then respectfully, of the man who singled him out for greatness at such an early age. That's why both West and co-author Coleman were surprised that Bryant would not agree to be interviewed for *West by West*. Kobe is not predictable, and he and West aren't nearly as close as they used to be. West is much closer to O'Neal, at whose Staples Center statue dedication he spoke.)

"It's not just the ability to see a great player, it's the ability to see how much better that player is going to be," says Geoff Petrie. "That's what Jerry did. Even at its most scientific, evaluating players is still an educated guess.

"Look, Jerry wasn't the only one who thought Kobe was going to be great. We [Sacramento] were picking after Charlotte, and I *guarantee* you I would've taken Kobe. There are some things that are obvious. It was obvious that LeBron was going to be great. Jordan. Kobe. Shaq. What Jerry should get credit for is some of the pieces he put around those great players."

Kupchak struggles to put his finger on exactly what separated West as a talent evaluator.

"It was his gift, and remember it extended to both college scouting and looking at players already in the NBA," says Kupchak. "It was understanding how the pieces fit, what the big picture was supposed to look like. I know that sounds vague, but it's the best I can explain it. Maybe it got down to the fact that he had a way with players, not just after they got here and had problems but while he was recruiting them. He saw things that others didn't see because of the kind of player he was.

"There aren't too many secrets in the scouting world anymore. The great talents everyone recognizes, but a lot of times it comes down to the other ones. I might see a really good player and say, 'Let's take him at twenty-two,' and Jerry says, 'No, we're taking him at fifteen.' With utter confidence.

"Take the example of Vlade." (Divac was somewhat of a mystery, an obviously talented Serbian player but one who hadn't been seen much even on the international stage.) "We saw film, talked to a lot of people who saw him in Europe, and compared him to other American players. When the votes were all in from our scouts, it looked like Vlade was too big a risk. But Jerry just said, matter-of-factly, 'No, guys, we're taking Divac.' And that was that. Some of our scouts used to say, 'Why are we here if we're just going with Jerry anyway?'"

West later said that his scouts didn't talk to him for a week after that. But Divac turned into a really good player for seven seasons, not to mention the eventual bargaining chip for Bryant.

To be clear, factors beyond a genius for evaluation have helped West. In L.A., he had an attractive franchise. Although West had success in his five years running the Memphis Grizzlies and won Executive of the Year in 2004 (despite his success with the Lakers, he had previously received the award only once, in 1995), he never got the franchise beyond the first round of the playoffs. West also had a built-in advantage because of his primacy as a player. He always got return calls. Who wouldn't talk to the Logo? When Magic became president of the Lakers in 2017, some questioned his ability to judge personnel, but no one questioned the fact that players, agents, and other GMs would respond to him.

"We didn't talk very much because, frankly, I was scared to death of Jerry," says Popovich, now the NBA's reigning coaching genius but in 1994 merely the unknown newly minted general manager of the San Antonio Spurs. "R.C. [Buford, with whom Popovich has shared personnel decisions over the past twenty-five years] and I used to sit there and say, 'You call Jerry West. No, *you* call Jerry West.'"

So West wooed players from what amounted to a bully pulpit, never having to prove himself, bona fides in order from the jump. But he worked like he had none of these advantages. He didn't cut corners. He did leave much of the general-manager business-type duties (arena matters, travel issues, etc.) to Kupchak, but he came religiously to the office to examine trade possibilities, study personnel charts, and negotiate contracts. And when it was time to take to the road, West went to all the college games and tournaments, as well as other NBA games, to eyeball potential draft picks and free-agent pickups. "His energy never flagged," says Kupchak. So, as with many upon whom the term *genius* has been bestowed, it's easier to see the sweat rings than the brain waves. Just as important, he did the same thing in Memphis when his hopes of putting together a championship team were slim.

The best way to put it is that West was *in the game*. He was a schmoozer, a gossip (remember that Baylor called him "Louella Parsons"), one of the guys, even if some of the other guys placed him on a pedestal. West's immersion was total. He wasn't above trying to get an advantage for the Lakers, of course, but he was also concerned with rules, salary-cap restrictions, referees, anything that affected the game.

"Whenever he called me, Jerry was *always* unhappy," says David Stern, who became the NBA commissioner in 1984. "But from that dark place where he lived he also always had an interesting perspective on our game and the rules, and he would fill me up with those views. We talked a lot." (That practice continues today with Adam Silver.)

"I don't remember any short phone calls with Jerry," says Petrie. "Once you got done with what you're talking about, he can go on a rant for *hours*. He was a guy you could just call and shoot the shit with. Jerry always knew what was going on. Was he honest? Well, he always protected his own self-interest, that's for sure. But he'd be honest about other things. Call it guardedly honest. That's how you should be. You have to protect your own team's interests.

"What I appreciated the most about Jerry was that he would call and talk about your team, with no ulterior motive. 'Hey, you guys are going to be really good this year. I like that move you made.' It was genuine. It meant something."

Popovich agrees. "As time went on what I found out most about Jerry was his kindness," says Popovich. "He knew that R.C. and I were neophytes, and he went out of his way to make us feel comfortable. I'm not blowing smoke, because, hell, I don't even know Jerry all that well after all these years. I just know that's what he did for us."

That's what everyone else says about West as an executive. What does he say?

I could get players when no one else could get players. It was the same challenge as earlier, as a player, when people would say you can't do this or you can't do that. People told me, "You cannot get Shaquille O'Neal." I said, "Oh yeah? Watch."

You can't be afraid. I was never afraid to go against our scouts and take a player I thought was better than they did. There's also a commonsense element. If you go interview a kid and look into his eyes and it looks like muddy water in there, well, you don't take him.

Intuition is important, but information is more important. I have relationships with many college coaches who will tell me things. And sometimes the best information is trainers. Sure, I call them up. Still do. If a young player can't think the game and play hard for a thirty-game schedule, he won't make it in the NBA.

I would look at the conferences and strength of schedule, but I always believed there would be players at smaller schools. I saw so many games, so many nights out watching kids play. And, look, we had some incredible good fortune in the draft because, lots of times, we were picking low. We never really took a huge backward step to go from say, fifty-nine wins down to forty to get better picks. You need luck, too.

And one other thing: You need to accept change, that the game has changed and the kids have changed. I'm very modern in that sense. But one thing I'm not modern about is this: competition. If a kid does not play hard for thirty games in college, he will not play hard for eighty-two games in the NBA.

What might have been most unusual about West as a GM was his ability to escape his own violent fits of temper, his choice of a hammer rather than a stiletto when he evaluated players, yet talk himself down to earth and back off the ledge.

"Yes, he vented plenty," says Kupchak, "but he didn't make not-thought-out decisions. There were many times I thought he was about to do something rash, but he would stop and talk and think and suddenly get very calm and make a rational decision. I never saw him jump the gun."

Jeanie Buss came into West's circle in the nineties as a teenager.

"I don't know what Jerry really thought of me, but he was totally respectful," Buss said. "He always took the time to explain everything to me. I had all kinds of questions. 'Why did you draft that player?' 'Why did you ignore him?' He never talked down and was very generous with his time.

"He never complained about being the face of the franchise either. I remember once we had to take a trip to Sacramento to talk to politicians and accept some kind of proclamation. They wanted Jerry to come, and I thought, *Oh no, he's not going to want to do this.* But we flew up there and he was very gracious. I'll never forget him for the way he treated me."

That should not give the impression that Buss and West are particularly close these days. Only Buss knows whether she contemplated bringing back West either as a consultant or in any kind of capacity in 2017, but she never dialed his number. She reached out to Magic instead. West, for his part, says that he wouldn't have returned to Laker Land in any case. Too much history, too strange, even though son Ryan is the respected assistant GM there. But maybe that would've made it stranger.

Jeanie and Jerry do share a special connection, though, both having been robbed in the parking lot of the Forum, Buss in 1989, West in 1992. From Jeanie they got $25,000 in jewels, and from West they got about $100 and, worst of all, his 1985 championship ring. When he told the Lakers what happened, they said they would replace it if West paid half. "I never forgot that," he says today.

In 1999 Jerry Buss hired Phil Jackson with the stated goal of turning the Shaq-Kobe team into champions. They had had three seasons together under Del Harris and fallen short in the postseason each time, twice to the John Stockton–Karl Malone Jazz, once to the Tim Duncan–David Robinson Spurs. One might've looked at West and Jackson, two Masters of Different Universes, and said, "Uh-uh, this is not going to work." West was indeed wary of the hire. But O'Neal and Bryant had tuned out Harris, and West gave his blessing because he honestly thought that Jackson had the chops to meld the two superstars. Which turned out to be the case.

West had dealt with coaching ego before. By the time Riley left in 1990—he wasn't technically fired but he would've been—he and West were on the outs. Riley says today that the major part of it was his own fault.

"I made the mistake in 1987 and 1988 of taking too much credit after our championships," Riley told me in 2017. "All of a sudden everybody was talking to me, and I was getting all the attention and all the speaking engagements and all the book offers. I fell into the trap. These days I always tell coaches that before you put yourself out in front of the players you have to be thinking how it impacts the team, what *they* think of what you're doing. I didn't always do that. Coaches are part of this great circle, but they should be on the perimeter, not the inside.

"Jerry knows these things. He always sees the other side of the coin. He sees everything about a franchise. He sees what needs to be right to build a team. How owners should act. How coaches should coach. How practices should be run. How public relations staffs should run. And when he sees something he doesn't like it drives him nuts."

But even when things got bad between West and Riley, there was history between them. There were the workouts on the Santa Monica stairs, the burgers and shakes at Hollis Johnson's joint, the streak, the championship. They even shared an awkward moment in 1976 shortly after West got the Lakers coaching job, which he kept for three years. Riley had finished up an injury-plagued season with the Phoenix Suns, who didn't want him back. Riley thought he could still play. So he made a call to an old friend.

"I know you can't sign me sight unseen, Jerry," Riley said, "but I'd like a tryout."

"Hmm," said West.

"I had patellar tendinitis, but I had surgery, and I'm good to go," said Riley.

There was a moment of hesitation. And then.

"Sorry, Pat, can't do it."

"Why?" persisted Riley.

"Because you know too much about me," answered West.

At first Riley figured that a coach couldn't afford to have someone under him who knew his secrets from the road. But speaking in a 2017 interview Riley told this reporter: "I think Jerry was just trying to protect me from what he was probably going to have to do, which is cut me. I didn't know I was done, but *he* knew I was done."

West had no history with Phil. He was a *Knick*. Relations between them were never smooth. West could never forget how Jackson wore sandals to his introductory Lakers press conference. It's a small thing, but it illustrated one of the differences between them. West was, still is, a straight-up loafers guy, a button-down traditionalist. Sandals Jackson, who for his first interview to be an assistant coach with the Bulls in 1985 famously wore an Ecuadorean straw hat adorned with a macaw feather (it freaked out head coach Stan Albeck and Jackson didn't get the job), was anything but that.

But the trouble went much deeper than style. West saw Jackson as aggressively noncommunicative. He and Coleman wrote about it in *West by West,* and he brought it up again in 2017. "I can't tell you how many times Phil walked right by me," says West. "I mean, you have to be *trying* not to talk to somebody." West is unusual in that he's shy but very attuned to social graces. You say hello, you say goodbye, you shake hands, you look people in the eye, you make sure they're comfortable when they're in your house.

"If there's one organization that shrieks of family," says co-author Coleman, "it's the Lakers. And this cold-shoulderness hurt him deeply. Jerry is a complex person. He can say to you, 'Oh, I don't give a shit about that,' but he cares deeply."

Sometime during the postseason of 2000 another incident occurred that drove a wedge between West and Jackson—the time when he and Kupchak were ordered out of the locker room by Jackson, who wanted to have a players-only discussion. It stung West because he believed that he had always showed restraint with Riley and Jackson, rarely interloping, never second-guessing publicly. Jackson gave his take on the incident: "I know Jerry was hurt by me asking him to leave the room. It has always been what I've done anytime it got intimate or personal, to ask people that were outside, trainers and ball boys in particular."

Trainers? Ball boys? Those are categories for Jerry West?

West says that he was ready to leave even earlier than that. As he sees it, Buss and Kupchak "betrayed" him during a meeting in a Santa Barbara hotel room with free agent Glen Rice. "We had agreed on one thing, and right in front of me they said something else," West told me in 2017. Coleman, his co-author, says, "Jerry considered that the most important sign that it was time for him to leave."

Maybe it was. But more likely it was simply inevitable that a schism would develop between the Lakers and Mr. Laker. Too many years, too many battles, too many slights, real and perceived, too many other GMs getting paid more—West was making about

$3.5 million, less than a couple of other GMs, which was not, according to West, supposed to happen—too much of everything. Too many Busses, certainly. Though Jerry W. never completely lost his respect for Jerry B., he did not appreciate the appearance in 1998 of Jim Buss, Jeanie's older brother, as apprentice general manager, and being tasked with showing him the executive ropes. Not long after he appeared in the Lakers' office, Jim Buss expressed the following opinion in an interview with *Sports Illustrated:* "Evaluating basketball talent is not too difficult. If you grabbed ten fans out of a bar and asked them to rate prospects, their opinions would be pretty much identical to those of the pro scouts." Just what a man who has spent a lifetime around the game, and whose eyes were seemingly made for separating the wheat from the chaff, wants to hear. (Over in Clipper Land, meanwhile, Baylor was hearing from the abhorrent Sterling that he should just go out and find some pro talent on the playgrounds around Los Angeles. It shouldn't be too hard, said Sterling.)

In August 2000, West announced his resignation from the Lakers. Aside from the two years he had spent away from the game after retiring as a player, West had been with the franchise as player, coach, scout, and general manager for forty years. A few years after his three-year stint as head coach, West had even served as "sort-of coach." At the 1981 press conference to announce the hiring of Riley as head coach, Jerry Buss casually announced that West would be Riley's "offensive coach," as if this were a football team and he was doling out coordinator assignments. That came as a surprise both to West and to Riley, neither of whom hid their shock. (West soon left the bench and went into the front office.)

If that was a strange press conference, well, so was the one announcing West's departure from the Lakers. He didn't show up. He was an emotional mess, in much worse shape than he had been back in 1974 when his playing career was over and his first marriage had disintegrated. Karen West had even written a letter to Jerry Buss telling him the extent of her husband's disillusionment with the Lakers and some of the decisions that had been made. "He is a man that if he were suicidal he would be gone," Karen wrote in the letter, which West and Coleman included in the autobiography.

After West resigned, Buss hired him as a consultant for two years for a total of about $2.5 million. So he was technically on the payroll when the Lakers completed their beginning-of-the-century three-peat in 2002. But perplexingly to West, he was never consulted on anything. He was like the character in Jimmy Buffett's "A Pirate Looks at Forty": "My occupational hazard being/My occupation's just not around."

West lives in the present, as much as any near-octogenarian can. But when he looks back, he realizes how lucky he has been. His immortal streak team was one touched by greatness but also tragedy.

- Jim McMillian died in May 2016 due to complications from heart failure. He had been in failing health for years. He lived quietly with his wife in North Carolina, not exactly a forgotten player but one who should've been more widely celebrated. Riley compares him to Draymond Green. McMillian was sixty-eight.
- Flynn Robinson died in May 2013 from multiple myeloma, a cancer of the plasma cells. Electric Eye worked in recreational programs in and around Los Angeles and, as broadcaster Jim Barnett remembers it, finally played some D in masters-age-group competition. "I always told Flynn, 'Why didn't you play like that when you were in the league?'" says Barnett. Robinson was seventy-two.
- Bill Sharman passed five months after Robinson. He was eighty-seven and had suffered a stroke a week before his death. His voice never came back, but, when called upon, he gamely tried to talk. As far as this researcher can gather, no one ever adequately explained exactly what happened to his voice. "Bill Sharman was a great coach," says Phil Jackson, "and an even better man." Mr. Shootaround drove around with a license plate that read "33 STR8." And until the day he died, he always called the Lakers, not the Celtics, the greatest NBA franchise.

- LeRoy Ellis, described by many as one of the nicest people you could ever meet, died in June 2012, ending a battle with cancer that had been ravaging his body for three years. He was seventy-two. One of his sons, LeRon, had an unspectacular three-year NBA career, during which he never lived up to his reputation as a schoolboy prodigy; another son, Lee, was shot and killed in Los Angeles County at the age of nineteen. Lee was last seen playing basketball on a playground.

- John Q. Trapp is probably dead. Everyone seems pretty sure of it, though no one can find an obituary. There was some confusion in 2002 when an NBA player named Trapp died in a knife fight in Detroit, but that turned out to be John Q.'s brother George, who played in the league for five years. After the streak season, legend continued to follow Trapp, who managed in successive years to play on one of the best teams in history and one of the worst, that Philadelphia 76ers team that went 9-73. The story goes that hapless Philly coach Roy Rubin wanted to take John Q. out of the game during a time-out in Detroit, but changed his mind when Q. gestured that Rubin should look into the stands, upon which one of Q.'s friends opened his coat to reveal a pistol.

- Chick Hearn died in August 2002 from complications from a fall in his backyard. The most public of men, he rarely spoke about his own tragedies, the death of his son Gary, soon after the 1972 championship and, eighteen years later, the death of his daughter Samantha, from pneumonia resulting from her battles with anorexia. Before every Lakers home game at the Staples Center, thousands of fans take a photo at the Chick statue. He's wearing a headset. The man was in his broadcast seat for 3,338 consecutive games, from November 21, 1965, to December 16, 2001. That is hard to comprehend.

- Keith Erickson, despite some orthopedic aches and pains from his basketball and volleyball days (Erickson was on the 1964 U.S. Olympic volleyball team that finished out of the medal race in Tokyo), lives a contented and quiet life in Los Angeles. He is often described in the same way as Ellis—one of the nicest people you could ever meet. He was Chamberlain's connection to beach volleyball, and he willingly went along with the myth, spread by the Dipper, that Wilt was a great volleyball player. For a long time Erickson struggled with the drug-overdose death of his daughter Angelica, at age twenty-two in 1996. In the last Father's Day card he got from her, Angelica wrote, "Dear Pop: You're the absolute best. Thanks for making such an effort to understand or sympathize with my crazy ways."

- Happy Hairston died in May 2001 of complications from prostate cancer. His listing on IMDb, the Internet Movie Database, is quite impressive, as was his rebounding and unselfish play on a team that won thirty-three straight games.

In his Introduction to *Wilt, 1962*, Gary M. Pomerantz wrote this:

Wilt Chamberlain died on a mountaintop, alone, in bed, beneath a retractable ceiling that allowed him to see the stars. The gardener found his body, which is how it often works in Hollywood. The Dipper lived alone, a life he chose.

The date was October 12, 1999. "The whole world kind of stopped on that day," West remembers. "Wilt dead? It didn't seem right. It seemed like he was invincible."

From the time he retired from the game in 1974, after one season spent as the mostly uninterested coach of the San Diego Conquistadors, Wilt never really stopped being Wilt. "He was everywhere," remembers Bill Walton. "He owned whatever he wanted to own, went wherever he wanted to go, bigger than anybody, bigger than life."

Roy Firestone would have him on his show every once in a while, and he never disappointed. "Wilt was notorious for using incorrect words," Firestone remembers. "One night he said, 'I can't *phantom* what these players are thinking.' And Wilt liked to be gifted. He'd show up in the studio and say, 'Roy, I'm not doing the show.' And

I'd say, 'You gotta do the show. We told everybody you'd be on.' And Wilt would say, 'Okay, but only under one condition. I gotta come out of here with a VCR.'

"So Wilt would do the show and walk out with a VCR under his arm. Jesus, we would've given him five grand to come on."

Wilt didn't need the money. Whenever he was asked what sign he was born under, he would answer, "The dollar sign." He just needed to be Wilt. Firestone had a good take on him. "I don't think Kareem and a few other big men loved being that tall," says Firestone. "But everything about Wilt was based on the fact that he loved being Wilt, he loved being that size, he loved being that noticed."

On a trip to Florence recounted in Cherry's *Wilt: Larger Than Life*, Wilt's traveling companion, a physician with whom he was close named Stan Lorber, said that Wilt visited the statue of David on three straight mornings in Florence.

> Wilt looked at the statue, and he was transfixed. . . . He said he had never seen anything so magnificent. I wouldn't be surprised if he was also saying to himself, "There's a guy who was built as well as I am."

West has two favorite memories of Wilt. The first is sitting in Wilt's hotel room on the road, talking and watching Wilt put away tons of barbecue. The second is the night Wilt walked into the locker room with sand on the bottom of his feet, fresh from the beach. If you want a capsule shot of the difference between Wilt and Russell, that would suffice. Bill Russell never showed up with sand on his feet.

On the occasion of Chamberlain's death, Tom Meschery, a former Warriors teammate of Wilt's, a man who still rues the fact that he did not grab the game ball on the night that Wilt scored one hundred points, wrote this elegy:

> *This morning, I wake up thinking big:*
> *Time to crack a dozen eggs, fry all the bacon.*
> *I think I'll never shave. Let my beard grow*

as long as an epic . . .
Spend the afternoon with Aquinas' five proofs
of God's existence: the Uncaused Cause,
or was it the Divine Plan that toppled Wilt?
Let the day end as it began with a red sun,
and let there be a blonde soprano
with big bosoms belting out her last aria.

In 2012, the NBA released a documentary about Wilt's one-hundred-point night in Hershey, Pennsylvania, in 1962. None other than his ancient rival Russell did the narration. "He's been gone now for more than a decade," intones Russ at the end of the film, "and I still miss him."

When pressed, West will say that what his streak team did in 1971–72 was more impressive than any of the Warriors' streaks.

"The travel alone and the frequency of games made it harder," says West. "But here is the big thing—the care that you get from the training staff today. Not that we didn't have good trainers, it's just that the technology, the knowledge, the medicine was not there.

"I played less than a thousand games in the NBA. Most people don't remember that. I tore ligaments in my knee and I was in a cast for twelve weeks. Today? That would've been minor."

But West stops there. The main reason he has remained relevant, and why teams even today still seek his services, is that he respects today's game and today's players. He doesn't dwell in the past. Nobody remembers him ever bringing up the thirty-three-game winning streak. West loves the Warriors, the idea that there are a half dozen players on the team willing to share the ball. And as the Finals approach, his half-in, half-out status is taking away some of the joy of expectation.

"But, look, if this is the end for me up here, it's okay," West is saying. "I've had a great run. I've been associated with so many great people, did so many things in my life that I never dreamed possible."

West starts to tear up just a little.

"You know, it took me a long time to grow up, to figure out how to be an adult. That goes back to the way I was raised. And if I hadn't gotten a scholarship to West Virginia University all those years ago? I'd be dead by now. I'm sure of it. So I'd just like to be able to stay around for a while and give a little more."

West is among the largest WVU donors, but wanting to give more money to his alma mater is not his main reason for staying around the game. It's about the competition, about the idea that the team you helped build is better than the team they helped build. It's about trying to solve the grand, beautiful puzzle.

So if West was not all-in with Warriors management, he was certainly all-in with the Warriors team.

"LeBron is the best player in the league," says West. "We didn't talk about him in the MVP race, but he was absolutely the MVP. But we have the best *team*. I'm sure of that. We have six, seven guys who play unselfishly. We have a number of difference-makers, maybe four or five. You know how hard it is to have even two? So if we play at our best we should win. If we play at our best, we *will* win."

One gets the feeling that, even as he says that, he remembers back to so many times when he was better and he didn't win.

*"You did what you came here to do.
You're a complete ballplayer."*
—JERRY WEST TO KEVIN DURANT

CHAPTER 20

A Championship and
a Sad Goodbye

As the NBA Finals were ready to begin for the third straight year at Oracle Arena, the Oakland City Council faced a decision about whether to sell its twenty-seat luxury box back to the Warriors. The deal was scheduled to begin the following season and would've been worth $200,000 for a cash-strapped city. Warriors president Rick Welts offered to buy back the box immediately—heaven knows the Warriors could sell the suite for a king's ransom.

But as it turned out, it was no decision at all.

"Nobody wanted to give up the tickets for the playoffs," council president Larry Reid told the *Chronicle*. So, no sale. If any council member demurred and said, "You know, the Dubs are leaving us in two years so screw 'em," it was not made public.

By the time the third straight Warriors-Cavs championship series began, the Warriors had become the It Franchise with a kind of ineffable It Vibe, not just in the NBA but also in all of sport.

There was really no runner-up. The Patriots and the Spurs are too dour, the Cowboys are too divisive, and, as far as the Yankees and Red Sox go, there isn't much It in Major League Baseball these days. The Warriors had two It Players in Curry and Durant (and Draymond is kind of an It), the It Coach, the It General Manager, the It Ownership, and the It Consultant (fans did not yet know that Jerry West was on his way out).

Also the It Cash Flow. There is a certain disconnect between a franchise that strove to be popular with fans and media, a franchise that always seemed to want to do the right thing, and the franchise that just keeps charging more and more for everything, the leader of a ticket-price arms race.

"The Warriors have set up what is potentially the greatest, and most successful, money machine North American sports has ever seen," wrote plugged-in columnist Tim Kawakami. And he wrote that about the 2015–16 season after the Warriors generated what was estimated to be a $30 million profit just for the postseason.

The figures for the 2017 playoffs were not available at this writing and may, in fact, be down, but only because the Warriors had thirteen home playoff games in 2016 as compared with nine this season. But if Golden State does make less money it was not for want of trying. Postseason ticket prices beggared belief. One season-ticket holder, fourth row near center court, paid $1,050 per game for his seat during the regular season. In succeeding playoff rounds, that ticket went to $1,200, $1,500, $1,800, and—wait for it—$3,300 for the Finals. And it's not just the postseason. The Lakers under Jerry Buss were the first team to get heavily into what is euphemistically called "secondary ticketing marketing," meaning charging more when the opponent warrants it. The Warriors are now all over that.

In keeping with their trendsetting ways, the Warriors will be instituting an innovative season-ticket plan when they move into the Chase Center in 2019. They will require season-ticket buyers to pay a one-time fee that enables them to hold their tickets for thirty years. At the end of that period, long though it may be, the Warriors will pay back that fee. The Warriors say it's a good deal, better than the odious personal seat license program.

But seats will be more expensive and there will be about 1,600 fewer of them (18,000 capacity as compared with about 19,600 for the ancient Oracle). So those leather-lunged loyalists who cheered for players like Vonteego Cummings, Ike Diogu, and Bubba Wilson and helped turn Oracle Arena into *Roaracle*? Gee, we'd like to have you at Chase to watch Steph and K.D. and the boys, but, sorry, you probably can't afford it.

Now, the Warriors are only part of a new wave of venture-capital/hedge-fund/Silicon Valley ownership groups that now operate NBA franchises in Atlanta, Detroit, Memphis, Milwaukee, Philadelphia, and Sacramento. The NBA, a league that was putting out significant financial fires just thirty years ago, is, to put it mildly, glad to have them. But the Warriors ride along on the crest of that wave. With a value estimated by *Forbes* in early 2017 at $2.6 billion, the Warriors trail only the New York Knicks ($3.3 billion) and the Lakers ($3 billion) in the magazine's list of NBA franchise valuations. Those are already ancient valuations. The Chase Center is expected to increase the franchise value by as much as $1 billion, and it's almost a sure thing that the Warriors will surpass both of the currently dysfunctional franchises ahead of them.

Perhaps this is the best metric of Golden State's financial success: Another well-known Silicon Valley venture-capital guy, Mark Stevens, bought into the Warriors in 2013. Because the franchise had increased so much in value even by that point, it cost Stevens $50 million to get in, $20 million more than Guber originally paid to be second-in-command.

The Warriors are playing a game of Monopoly unlike the sports world has ever seen. And while the sports world should be grateful that the Warriors think about things like core values and giving back and all of that, they're not running a charity. They are a thoroughly modern team of Croesusian wealth, the new model, and one wonders if the more traditionally run franchises can continue to flourish, specifically the one in Texas that keeps coming up in conversation, the one that has won five championships over the past twenty years, the one that Pat Riley admiringly refers to as "the last Ponderosa."

Adam Silver says yes. "By no means do I think what the Warriors have accomplished is the sole paradigm going forward," says the commissioner. "There are and always have been multiple paths to success in this league. The San Antonio model has been based on longevity, smart drafting, smart trading, and there's no reason that will go away. The league is so expansive in its use of digital media that players and their agents find that players can have commercial and economic success anywhere. When Kevin Durant, for example, was in Oklahoma City, he single-handedly had more endorsements than all the Warriors combined."

Spurs coach Popovich is also guardedly optimistic that the Warriors model has not taken over. "Because of the draft it's not necessary for every team to have the gazillionaire owners," says Popovich, who works for an organization that has more than once been called the best-run franchise in all of sports. "Teams can lose and still go into the draft and find a Shaq or a Kobe or a Duncan.

"To make it work you have to have owners, a GM, a coach, and players that have synergy, that have an organization strategy and philosophy. Everybody loses for a while and has to come back. We haven't suffered as much yet as guys fade away, but eventually it will happen to us, too. All the stars have to align, no matter how much money your franchise is worth, and right now the stars are aligning in Golden State."

The final word on the subject belongs to David Lee, who was with the Warriors when they turned it around and is now a Spur.

"The number one thing about a franchise being successful is not how big it is or how much money ownership has. It's that the max players, the best players, have to be good-culture guys, great players on the court, obviously, but they also accept that challenge off the court. So guys like Steph Curry there, and what Tim Duncan did here, are more important than owners, more important than anybody."

GAME 1

The Warriors had nine days off between their sweep of San Antonio and the beginning of the series against Cleveland. With twelve straight wins in the first three playoff series, they were poised to make history. No team had ever gone through the postseason undefeated.

So to prepare, Steph Curry hid out like a Trappist monk.

Okay, no he didn't. Among other things, he and Ayesha made a starring appearance onstage at the BottleRock festival in Napa Valley, she preparing food and dropping beats with rapper E-40, he cheering her on and swaying to the music. Meanwhile, a Sherpa from Nepal displayed on social media a photo of himself bringing a "Curry 30" jersey to the top of Mount Everest. His fifteen-year-old son, the Sherpa explained, is a huge Steph fan and asked his dad to take the jersey "to the top of the world."

That's just how things roll for the Currys. It's Steph and Ayesha's world; we're just living in it. And a Bay Area restaurateur named Asif Aslam is glad Steph's on a roll. On playoff nights Aslam finds that orders of curry in his two Indian restaurants increase exponentially. "It's strange, but it really happens," Aslam told the website *SFGate*. "I've heard conversations at tables between the guests bringing up Steph Curry and saying they want to order curry because of him."

As Curry bottle-rocked, Durant stayed quiet, preparing to see if he could, at last, ascend to the Everest of the basketball world. He continued to maintain that, win or lose, he made the right decision by coming to Golden State, and, while he no doubt believed that on a personal basis, he is smart enough to know that that would not be the basketball judgment. The Finals would essentially litigate Durant's decision. The moment he joined on was the moment that the Warriors were *supposed* to win the championship, and thousands and thousands of Oklahomans were waiting for him to fail.

And it could happen. The Warriors were still without Kerr, whose continued neck and back pain had forced him out of post-season coaching on April 22, the third game of the playoffs, against Portland. It was a mystery about whether he could come back because, frankly, Kerr didn't know himself. The Cavs were still the defending champions and they still had LeBron, whose house in Los Angeles, he revealed before Game 1, had been vandalized with racist graffiti. Would that be fuel enough?

It wouldn't. And so emerged a pattern. LeBron was splendidly all over the place, and his Sundance Kid teammate, Kyrie Irving, made indescribable contortionist finishing shots, time after time.

But the Warriors won 113–91. Durant had thirty-eight points and nine rebounds. And with time running out in the third period, Curry pulled up for his sixth three-pointer of the game, which, after it went through, gave the Warriors an 87–68 lead. He might've been onstage at BottleRock as he did his strange high-stepping strut, and the Oracle crowd went crazy. "The third quarter," said James afterward, "was the whole game."

GAME 2

"Any questions?"

Suddenly, Kerr was there, on the podium, ready to address the media before the game. He was wearing that mischievous smile as he asked the question. Over the previous six weeks, Kerr had been a kind of shadowy presence, walking slowly through practice, occasionally talking to the team at halftime, occasionally stopping to talk to the media, tidbits of revelation here and there, short on details. He had received medical treatment at Duke during his absence, and, while he felt better, he obviously was not *cured,* if that was even possible anymore. No one knew. Kerr was always worried that he was a distraction, that the focus would turn to him instead of the team. For almost two years Kerr's recurring back problems have been a major preoccupation for the franchise, not to mention, more obviously, Kerr, wife Margot, daughter Maddy, and sons Nick and Matthew.

Yet he wanted to come back and felt he *needed* to come back for the good of the team.

It was an odd situation. Going back to the 2015–16 season, the Warriors had always played well without him, witness the twenty-seven-game winning streak with Luke Walton in charge. And the Warriors were 11-0 in the postseason under Mike Brown, counting the Game 1 win. In typical fashion Kerr addressed the reality that the Warriors had played just as well without him.

"The team was falling apart at the seams, and so I just had to get back to make sure we righted the ship," he said, smile on his face.

"What's the record without me? Like 812-6 or something?"

Heading into Game 2, it was actually 51-4.

But the foundation for all those wins had been built by Kerr. Plus, there were always doubts about Brown in the head seat, not necessarily because he had been fired three times as a head coach (twice in Cleveland and once with the L.A. Lakers; everybody gets fired), but because he seems eminently tune-outable. LeBron tuned him out in Cleveland. Kobe never tuned him in in L.A. Brown seems like the perfect complement as an assistant, a "bubble machine," as Popovich referred to him, meaning someone who is always up, always positive, a contrast to Kerr, who can turn dark. But sometimes dark is exactly what's needed. Brown himself described Kerr during the Finals as "a fiery, blond-haired, blue-eyed, all-American dude. But he is fiery."

When Kerr was not around, the Warriors missed his needle, that ability to cut through the noise, his knack for defending his guys without sounding defensive. When a steady chorus of retired players started to weigh in about how they would beat today's Warriors, Kerr had the perfect response: "They're all right," Kerr said. "They would all kill us. The game gets worse as time goes on. Players are less talented than they used to be. The guys in the fifties would've destroyed everybody. It's weird how human evolution goes in reverse in sports. Players get weaker, smaller, less skilled. I don't know. I can't explain it."

The 2016–17 season had been a strange one for Kerr. No coach in the NBA was going to send him a sympathy card, not with Curry, Durant, Thompson, and Green on the floor. But with his physical pain and the psychic pain of the Trump election . . .

"Yes, I should be having the time of my life," Kerr said to me during the season, "but between not feeling great physically and the political climate, it doesn't feel as happy and carefree as it did two years ago when I first took the job. My back was healthy, it was all new, Obama was president, and the world seemed kind of normal. This has been a weird year for sure."

If you track the movements of any coach in any sport, the absorption of time is what comes across most vividly. There is virtually no time to take an easy breath. Four, five hours of sleep perhaps, but even in their dreams they see LeBron driving through their defense or Harden drawing four-point plays on long-distance shots.

Now add the burdens of physical misery and what Kerr calls "the constant search for whatever is going to heal me." Indeed, searching for relief became for Kerr and his family like another full-time job. He tried acupuncture, yoga, meditation, and, famously, medical marijuana, none of which helped him.

Nor did Trump's election. If you think that coaches and athletes should shut up about everything besides sports, well, that's your opinion, but it is not Kerr's. He sees coaching as a mission for which grown-ups are called upon to practice leadership skills, and he couldn't get over the fact that the United States of America had elected a man who, as Kerr saw it, exhibited none of those skills. Kerr also looked upon the political landscape as a father and a husband. "I am fearful where this toxic political environment is heading," he said one day.

But it isn't so much *what* Kerr says as the fact that he is willing to talk, and that he can converse about so many things. He had touch as a shooter; he has touch as a speaker. Several drop-in interview sessions with Kerr during the season revealed the essential value in having a well-rounded leader at the top, no matter what his politics. What comes across most clearly is Kerr's passion, the sense that he cares so deeply about the world around him, the fact that he tries to make sense of it.

For their willingness to talk about politics, Kerr and Popovich, who were together as player and coach for four seasons in San Antonio, had become somewhat the matched set during the season. A website called "Popovich Kerr 2020" had sprung up—T-shirts and mugs still available at this writing—suggesting that the citizenry could find no better duo "to revive the concept of American exceptionalism" than "two men with a combined 11 championship rings and 4 Coach of the Year awards." (It's now twelve rings.) Luke Walton is down with the idea—he wore the blue T-shirt at a volleyball tournament that took place during the Finals. They became even more united after Kerr, protesting a ridiculous scheduling stretch, sat out his starters in a nationally televised game against the Spurs, a stratagem made famous in the past by Popovich. It was a clear f-you to the league, another case of the choirboy going rogue. It's interesting, by the way, that Pop would be given the top spot on that ticket. Kerr, though younger by sixteen years, would seem to be the more presidential, leaving Popovich free to fire away with heavier artillery.

One of the most interesting things about Kerr is the degree to which he thinks about the entire team. You can get into a ten-minute conversation with Kerr about the beauty of coaching JaVale McGee, upon whom he depends so much that the backup center would draw a DNP in the climactic Game 5. It seems obvious that a coach coaches everybody, but it isn't necessarily so. Gather your one or two main guys around you, some coaches believe, and the others will jump into the corral with them. And if they don't, so what? Give the ball to the superstars. The Warriors, in keeping with the Lacob-Guber leadership model, are an organic whole from the top to the bottom of the roster. Kerr even messes up his rotation from time to time—West used to complain that Kerr doesn't have any logical rotation at all—just to get a bench player into the game. He learned that from Phil Jackson, who didn't want anyone on the roster going more than two weeks without playing during an important part of the game.

"I'm always thinking about the whole group, and how leadership changes and evolves," Kerr said during the season. "It's very important for the way we do things to have everyone on the same page. His name is almost never mentioned, but Leandro Barbosa [who signed a free-agent contract with the Suns after the 2015–16 season] was one of our most important leaders. He had control of the bench and a great way of holding guys accountable and making them laugh at the same time.

"You think of our team being different this year only because of Kevin Durant. But there are all sorts of different dynamics to think about. Zaza Pachulia and David West, for example, bring seriousness to the group that is really powerful. As a coach you have to cultivate that, encourage it. Veteran leadership, toughness. That all counts. David has been huge for Draymond, as far as counseling him behind the scenes, keeping him in the right place. We didn't have that last year."

Translation of Kerrspeak: With a veteran talking to him all the time, perhaps Green would not have lost his composure in Game 4 of the 2016 Finals, when he entered LeBron's personal space, and would not have been suspended for Game 5, when the Cavs comeback started, and the Warriors would've won the series.

David West is asked if he was indeed called upon to be the Draymond Whisperer. "I talk to Steve about it," he says. "It's become clear that one of my jobs is to keep Draymond in the 'safe zone,' where he is aggressive but still productive on the floor. I've figured out a few communication styles with him that I feel are effective."

Such as?

"One of them is physical," says West. "If I see him building emotionally, I reach out and touch him, shove him, even."

"That sounds dangerous," West is told.

"Not really," he answers, "because he knows I'm coming from a good place."

Ultimately, though, it is the head coach's main job to figure out what is important for his team between the lines, what to stress for a game plan, what to leave in and what to leave out, as Bob Seger put it in "Against the Wind." You decide those things on the basis of a collective knowledge, battles won and lost, and Kerr had three seasons to figure those out; Mike Brown had only one and spent the first couple of months just learning the Warriors' style, learning that set plays didn't have to be called on every dead-ball situation.

Kerr seems particularly important for Curry. If Kerr has a mantra it's this: *We have to take care of the ball and stop the careless passes. And we have to stop falling asleep on the weak side,* and he often directs that message at Curry. Weeks after a February 28 loss in Washington, the game in which Durant was injured, Kerr was still bringing up a Curry defensive mistake that might've cost them the game. With about twenty seconds left, John Wall missed a nineteen-foot jumper, but Curry looked up instead of boxing out, and Washington forward Otto Porter raced by him to get the rebound. Curry had to foul, Porter made both free throws, and the Wizards ended up winning 112–108. Curry is not the only culprit. Defensive coach Adams praises Thompson's on-the-ball defense but says that he, too, is prone to falling asleep when his man doesn't have the ball.

The play also drove Kerr nuts because on multiple occasions he had shown the team a similar play, one from Game 6 of the 2013 Miami–San Antonio Finals. San Antonio's Danny Green fails to box out on a missed shot, Chris Bosh grabs the rebound, gets it to Ray Allen in the corner, he hits a three to send it into overtime, the Heat win, then capture Game 7. "I told the team: 'If Danny Green boxes out, they win the championship,'" Kerr says. "'This is *not* going to be us.'" That is a strong message sent by a strong coach, a coach who knows his team and its tendencies, and how far he can push certain players.

In Game 2, with the Warriors clinging to a 67–64 lead at halftime, Kerr went to Curry and told him that his body language was bad, and that he had to get back to playing with joy. There's that Warriors word. *Joy.* Kerr also had one other message for Curry: Stop turning the damn ball over. Curry had six turnovers in the first half.

Golden State won going away, 132–113. Curry had thirty-two points, ten rebounds, and eleven assists (the first postseason triple-double of his career), and only two second-half turnovers. Durant had thirty-three points and eleven rebounds. The Warriors looked unbeatable. Would they have played like that with Mike Brown coaching? Possibly.

Possibly not.

GAME 3

After Game 1, Jerry West had a talk with Klay Thompson, who had been ice-cold, hitting only three of sixteen shots and missing all five from three-point range. In fact, Thompson hadn't really been in form throughout the postseason. Everyone kept waiting for one of those Klay explosions, such as what happened against the Pacers in December when he scored sixty points. But through Game 1 of the Cleveland series, Thompson had made only 66 of 183 shots. And, since Green is always so active, so versatile, so *Draymond-ingly* obvious in other ways, Thompson had seemingly gone from third wheel to fourth or fifth.

Being a secondary wheel never happened to Jerry West as a player, of course, but remember that during his championship sea-

son he lost his shooting touch, particularly in the Western Conference finals against Milwaukee, and despaired about it.

"It can happen," West said. "But Klay is a shooter, so he has to
keep shooting. The thing you have to remember about him, though,
is that that team counts on Klay to defend."

That was West's message to Thompson. Keep shooting because
they're going to start going in, and keep defending because that is
more important than the points.

"I love Jerry because he always cuts to the chase," Thompson
told NBA-TV after the game. "He doesn't sugarcoat anything; he's
going to tell you what he thinks. He told me how good I am, and
just to get it back."

Thompson also talked to Rick Barry, who gave him similar advice. "There's something about those old-school dudes," Thompson said. "To hear those two have that kind of confidence in you, it
helped me a lot. When those guys talk, you listen."

Because he so rarely speaks for himself, Thompson emerges as
the odd man out in so many rumor scenarios. *Klay wants out. Klay
feels he's being overlooked. Klay doesn't get enough touches.* During Game 1, Portland guard C. J. McCollum sent out a tweet that
read: "Klay gonna get another ring and find his own squad. They
better enjoy him while he there."

The thing is, there was never any evidence to indicate that
Thompson was or is unhappy. And there is no indication that the
Warriors think they can live without him. On the night he scored
his sixty, he took only eleven dribbles. Kobe usually took eleven
dribbles to free himself on one play. The point is, the Warriors look
for Thompson. They want him to score. They *need* him to score.

It's just that talking is not Thompson's thing. It's his father's
thing, and when Mychal is asked about it, he always insists that
Klay is happy in Golden State. The most attention Klay got all year
was on March 13 when a fan asked him to sign his toaster, and
some fans began positing a link between the toaster and the Warriors' end-of-the-season hot streak. The photo of a perplexed
Thompson turning the toaster over before signing it is a classic.

If there is a single tableau that defines the public postures of
Curry and Thompson it would be this:

During his pregame shooting routine, Curry loves to mix in other games. Shooting guru Bruce Fraser will "pitch" to him and Curry will slap at the ball, run around imaginary bases, and finish up with a long jumper. Or he'll go through an elaborate "place-kicking" pantomime before kicking the ball, getting it back, and shooting a jumper. He's even curled. The fans love it and wait for it, and, while it undoubtedly does help Curry relax, it also has quite a bit of look-at-me showmanship attached to it.

But Thompson doesn't seem to notice the Curry show. He's like the circus maintenance man sweeping up Center Ring while the star juggles chainsaws. At least three times during the season, this observer noticed Thompson blithely dribbling into the middle of a Curry game, interrupting his teammate's batting stance or his field-goal prep, and blithely dribbling out again. Curry just shakes his head and sets up again. That's Klay being Klay. It would be delicious to think that Thompson knew what he was doing, but he probably didn't. GM Myers told a story about being at Thompson's house a couple of years ago and hearing, as he prepared to leave, "Hey, when do we play again?" Myers answered: "Tomorrow." And Thompson added: "Who we got?"

But Thompson sure as hell knew what he had in Game 3— a desperate Cleveland team playing before an anti-Warriors crowd. He scored thirty points and continued to play hard-nosed defense on the impossible-to-cover Irving, making him take twenty-nine shots to earn his thirty-eight points. "I knew Klay would come out of it," said West, who watched the game from a fishing camp in Alaska. "He's got too perfect of a stroke."

Still, the Warriors needed Durant's pull-up dagger three-pointer with forty-five seconds left to earn a 118–113 win. In truth, it was an astonishing victory. The Cavs led 113–109 with 1:24 left, but Durant hit a nineteen-foot jumper and the killer trey, after which Curry seemed to pantomime someone either mooning the crowd or squatting as if over a toilet. It conjured up the moment from a 2005 NFL playoff game at Green Bay's Lambeau Field when Minnesota wide receiver Randy Moss fake-mooned the crowd, which led to this immortal line by Joe Buck: "That is a disgusting act by Randy Moss."

Curry laughed it off after the game, and in the succeeding days got peeved when asked about it. But let's be honest: What the hell else was he doing? If you're going to be the little kid sticking your hand into the cookie jar, then at least admit it.

GAME 4

The perfect ending to the season (and for this book) would've been for the Warriors to close out the series in Cleveland and complete the perfect postseason, something no other team had ever done, not even those kingly Russell Celtics, not even those West-and-Wilt Lakers from 1972, not even those Showtime Lakers or Moses Malone's "fo-fo-fo" Sixers from 1983, who finished at fo-five-fo.

But perfection and perfect endings happen rarely, particularly for Jerry West, as he sees it, and the Warriors go down to a Cleveland team bubbling over with desperation, a record number of threes raining down upon the heads of the Golden State players, the weight of history too much to handle.

And so we return to the home of Jerry and Karen as the Logo continues his critique well into the fourth quarter.

"If we get beat, I hope we get beat by about forty. You know why? Because for Game 5 there will be some juice. Not like this."

"Ian Clark. I have no idea how Ian Clark gets on Kevin Love, okay? I have no clue. And why is he in instead of Patrick McCaw? I have no earthly idea. I love McCaw. He'll defend the hell out of you."

(A thousand personnel men scribble in their notebook: *Per JW, check on McCaw availability.*)

"Omigod, LeBron can't miss," says Karen West after another long James three, one of a Finals record twenty-four converted by the Cavs.

"But, Karen, they're all in rhythm shots. That means we're not playing defense."

"Andre's going to miss both of these free throws. You can tell when it's going to happen. He's really good when he gets going right away, but that didn't happen tonight." (Iguodala misses two free throws.)

But then Iguodala makes a dunk. *"He's quick off his feet. That's one of the things I like in a player."*

(A thousand personnel men scribble in their notebook: *Per JW, look for p's who are quick off feet.*)

"Klay, dammit, you're late on the switch!"

"Omigod! There's Jonnie!" says Karen suddenly. She has spotted their youngest son in the stands when the camera follows a fan who has been ejected.

"Where? I don't see him," Jerry says. "Run it back."

"There!" says Karen as she runs to the giant screen.

"I still don't see him, dammit."

"THERE!"

"Okay, I see him now."

It's a delightful scene, two parents seeking out their son, who has been on TV dozens of times. West feels blessed that he is close to his two youngest, that he has somehow come out on the other end with kids who love him when he was not the easiest father to deal with, when he was a man haunted by the coldness he felt from his own father. There is precious little around the West household to suggest that a basketball immortal lives there, but there is much to show that he is a family man, framed photos scattered all over.

"I love Zaza. But Zaza has been awful."

The most obvious basketball memento in plain sight is a West Virginia University magazine with a young West on the cover, going for a tip-in sixty years ago when he was a Mountaineer. "I was quite a leaper," he says. There are no words to describe how proud West is about being a West Virginian. Many of his personal items were donated for a Jerry West Collection at WVU; there is more of West's career in Morgantown than in his home. One of the few things he bothers to point out during the evening is a photo of his home in the tony West Virginia resort of Greenbrier, where at the Prime 44 West restaurant one can order the "Jerry West Salad" or grab a friend and hunker down on the "Nothing but Net" Jerry West 44-ounce prime porterhouse.

"The only way to describe what Jerry is in West Virginia is that he's a god," says West Virginia native D'Antoni, a West neighbor at Greenbrier, echoing George Raveling. "We West Virginians kind of have a chip on our shoulder about people looking down on us and making jokes, and we look out for each other a little bit. It's genuine. And you know what makes us feel good? We have Jerry West. Nobody else does."

The game goes on and on like a rainy day. But that's okay. West is never without something interesting to say. During one time-out, he shows off his wine cellar and smiles when told it appears to be "Popovichian." West doesn't drink that much, but that's not what wine cellars are about.

Eventually, late in the fourth quarter, even West gives up as the Warriors can't mount a rally in what turns out to be the streak-stopping shellacking. But West is calm, just a normal guy watching a game with his wife in the living room when the outcome didn't turn out the way he wanted it to. Perhaps the game had been too one-sided to get really exercised about it, and the Warriors' series lead seems safe at any rate.

Elton John's "Rocket Man" plays during an ad.

"I love that song," says West. "He might be my favorite. Seen him a bunch of times. A big basketball fan, too. You know he only writes the music, right? Bernie Taupin writes the lyrics and sends them to Elton to write the music."

Jerry West knows about tandems. Words and music. Music and words. Baylor and West. Shaq and Kobe. Steph and K.D. Elton and Bernie.

"You know the only guy I might like better? Stevie Wonder. A genius."

"Do you know him?" West is asked.

"I do know him. Hell, I know everybody, and half the time I don't know why or how."

The subject of J. R. Smith and the struggle he and his wife had with the birth of a premature child comes up.

"Let me tell you something: J.R. has come a long way since he got to Cleveland. He deserves a lot of credit. But you know who else does? LeBron. You cannot overestimate what LeBron James's presence has meant to Cleveland."

(This is not a setup line for West's future pursuit of James when he gets to the Clippers. Or even if it is, this is at least the dozenth time over a one-year period that this observer has heard West go out of his way to praise James.)

With about three minutes left, West officially throws in the towel.

"Well, you come over to watch a game with somebody, and the team gets their ass kicked," he says. "Not much fun."

"Tell you the truth," his visitor says, "it was the most fun I've had watching a game in a long time. Sorry about the result, though."

"Shame because we had a big bottle of champagne in there ready to celebrate," West says.

Karen rolls her eyes.

"Really?"

"Oh, hell no," West says. "We're not really celebratory people. Even if we had won, it would be upstairs, read for a while, go to sleep."

A State Farm commercial comes on, one of the endlessly looping ones featuring Chris Paul and DeAndre Jordan of the Los Angeles Clippers.

"Hey, Jerry, there's your new guys," West's visitor says.

West looks at the screen, trying to figure out what to say.

"Could be," he says, shaking his head soberly. "Could be."

From her chair, Karen West smiles and shakes her head approvingly.

Up in Golden State, watching a game with West was known as "Jerry Duty." But, thinks this visitor as he leaves, it was something much more fascinating than that, the opportunity to go spelunking into the mind of a basketball genius.

GAME 5

Word arrives that someone paid $90,000 for two floor tickets to what most observers believe will be the closeout game at the Oracle. Someone else got a bargain—two ducats for only $41,000 each.

Kerr was loose before the game. He wore a shirt that read "Supervillains." He was asked if he felt pressure to win Game 5.

"Probably not as much as them," he answered. "I'm just doing the math."

That is the kind of leader you want to go into battle with.

The essence of the game, the essence of the Warriors, came down to one four-minute stretch. It happened to occur in the second period, but it could've been in the third or fourth. Probably not the first, because the Warriors, for reasons that drove West (and Kerr) to distraction, often started slowly.

From 7:39 to 3:06 of the second period, the Warriors outscored the Cavs 22–2, turning a 43–39 deficit into a 61–45 lead. Here's how it went. Durant three-pointer. Durant three-pointer. Curry three-pointer. Durant two free throws. Green basket off a slick pass from Iguodala. Curry twelve-foot jumper off a Durant pass off a 1-3 pick-and-roll. Green three-pointer. Durant three-pointer off a pass from Curry on another 1-3 pick-and-roll. (In last year's Finals, Curry had 26 assists and 30 turnovers. He would finish with 47 assists and 19 turnovers in this one.) Curry technical foul conversion.

A careful Warriors historian might contrast that with an almost identical span of time in last year's Game 7, specifically the final four minutes and thirty-eight seconds. From that point on, the Warriors didn't score, Curry, Thompson, Iguodala, and Green all missing shots.

The 22–2 surge effectively ended this Game 5. And when it was officially over, Iguodala climbed onto the scorer's table to lead cheers, Durant received his rightful Finals MVP trophy (so he and Westbrook each got one this season), Kerr wept openly (a few weeks earlier he wasn't even sure he would be *at* the Finals, far less coaching in them), everybody thanked everybody else, everybody hugged everybody else, and, as the on-court mayhem continued, it was time for a quick assessment of this team. Which is:

It has to be considered among the best single-season teams of all time. It won sixty-seven regular-season games and won sixteen postseason games by the following margins: 12, 29, 6, 25, 12, 11, 11, 26, 2, 36, 12, 14, 22, 19, 5, and 9.

Here's what I found to be the most interesting thing about them. When Durant signed on, Kerr found himself with two of the five best scorers in the game, both of them unselfish players who can set screens, read screens, and find the open man. So the temptation would be to run a pick-and-roll offense with Curry and Durant about a hundred times a game. What could go wrong? If the defense somehow scrambles to cover both, there are Thompson or Iguodala spotting up or there is Green going to his little pocket spot at the foul line. Or when you get tired of doing that, simply isolate Durant, spot Curry and Thompson on the perimeter, and have Green or somebody else diving for the basket.

But Kerr didn't do that. The Warriors continued to play unselfishly, cutting, moving, running after misses and sometimes after makes, working the ball around, endlessly screening away, finding daylight, looking for anyone who was open, and in general playing like, as Kerr puts it, "our hair is on fire." Their three-year run has been unprecedented. Under Kerr—and, to be fair, Walton and Brown and a big help from defensive guru Adams—the Warriors were 254-54, for an .825 winning percentage. That is the best three-year record in NBA history.

As the 2017–18 season begins, the principals are poised to Hamptons-ize the NBA for several more years—Curry and Durant are only twenty-nine and Thompson and Green are twenty-seven. They have the potential to become that rare generational team, to be talked about with the Celtics of the fifties and sixties, the Lakers of the eighties, and the Bulls of the nineties. The NBA might be a kleptocracy, but the Warriors' formula will be difficult to duplicate because no other team has all the ingredients. Which are: an unselfish scorer, Durant, who both posts up and thrives in transition; a deadeye, Curry, who hits from long distance, creates his own magic, and moves without the ball; a classic jump shooter in traffic, Thompson, who can defend and doesn't bitch about touches; a power forward, Green, who can also shoot threes, makes plays with the ball, and, by the way, was the 2017 defensive player of the year; and a super sub, Iguodala, who thrives on the big stage, having finished this closeout game with twenty points, four rebounds, and three assists.

Before sending off Golden State in pursuit of the gods, though, we should give them a more modest goal: winning two championships in a row. But it's a cold, hard fact that we haven't seen this kind of team before, and many (most?) of the off-season NBA moves were made to weaponize against Golden State. It will be a hard task to beat them, but down on Thunder Road they're still spoiling for a fight. A few days after the Warriors' title win, Oklahoma City's official Instagram account sent out a photo reminder to citizens about recycling. Inside one of the blue bins was a magazine, specifically a copy of the *Sports Illustrated* that followed the Warriors' championship.

Kevin Durant was on the cover.

A moment frozen in time after the final game. The jubilant Warriors gambol down the tunnel en route to the champagne-soaked locker room and God only knows what else after that—Draymond will end up spending the night on Klay's couch for reasons he won't be able to quite recall. Jerry West waits off to the side, peering in at the line of players. Green, in full gallop, spies him, screeches to a halt, and hugs West. They talk for a solid minute. "I'm not going to let you go," he tells West. West tells him that he's already gone. Then Durant comes by and shares a hug with West. "You did what you came here to do," West tells him. "You're a complete ballplayer."

Joe Lacob and Peter Guber come by, but West turns icily away. He meets Karen, takes her hand, and starts out a rear exit.

A visitor stops him. "So, this is the end, I guess?"

West shakes his head. "It is." He looks downcast. Later he will say it was one of the saddest moments of his professional life. Some part of him must want to share in the locker-room celebration, but he doesn't go in. Too many mixed feelings, and, anyway, Jerry West has a lot of practice staying away.

He turns to leave, then turns back. "You know what I'll miss the most?" the Logo says to me. "Watching these guys play."

*"I'm the last leaf on the tree / The autumn took the rest /
But they won't take me / I'm the last leaf on the tree"*

—TOM WAITS

EPILOGUE

On a Monday morning in June, only one week after Golden State
won the NBA championship and Jerry West walked sadly out of
Oracle Arena as an ex-Warrior, the Los Angeles Clippers' new
high-level, high-priced consultant met the press. His gray mane was
neatly parted, ol' Cement Head battened down on top as usual.
The late, great Chuck Daly used to say, "No man looks bad in a
blue suit," and West had one on, along with a white shirt and blue
tie. He looked like a million bucks, maybe four million bucks,
which is what an educated guess puts his annual salary at. Yes,
Steve Ballmer wanted West badly.

Still, this will not be an easy union. The Clippers are in a different place than the Warriors were back when West signed on in
2011. Though best known for postseason nosedives, the Clippers
are a nominally elite team with a newly signed (albeit flawed) max
player in Blake Griffin, a coach who has already won a championship (Doc Rivers with Boston in 2008), and a record of winning 60
percent of their games over the past six seasons. West will need to
find his place. But that's what he does. That's who he is.

Sitting on the dais with him were Rivers (looking casual in golf shirt) and veep of basketball operations Lawrence Frank (looking schoolboy in shirt and khakis). It could've been a TED Talk, with West in charge as the CEO of something or other.

The Clippers had already traded away Chris Paul, a player West liked a lot, and didn't have a pick in the upcoming draft. Yet West was energized and upbeat, and it didn't seem like an act. He skillfully deflected questions he didn't want to answer by simply answering a different question—somewhat of a West specialty—or infusing his replies with smiley-face optimism.

> Q: You had said publicly in the past that you wanted to end
> your career with the Lakers. Could you address that?
> A: You know, none of us have control over our destiny. None of
> us. Obviously it's a different time and place. I've always said
> that I'm proud of my time with the Lakers. But I wish them
> well. When they're playing the Clippers, no, I don't wish
> them well.

Though he didn't go into detail about the circumstances under which he left the Warriors, West made it clear that he hasn't forgotten them. "Nobody's going to beat these guys for a couple of years if they stay healthy," said the cold realist West, a line that Rivers probably *won't* be using for motivation during the season.

In the days that followed the championship, there is no doubt that the NBA clock continued to turn under Warriors Standard Time. The trades involving Paul (to Houston), Paul George (to Oklahoma City), and Jimmy Butler (to Minnesota) were big news, but the Warriors, who didn't even have a draft pick, always had a trump card.

There was Curry signing an insane five-year deal worth about $201 million, playing passably well in a Web.com golf tournament, and watching as the jersey he wore in Game 3 of the Finals drew a record $135,000 at auction. There was Durant accepting—nay, *mandating*—a contract of about $9 million less per year so the Warriors could keep their core pieces intact. (Wonder if Westbrook found that "cute.")

There was GM Myers lowering his long, lean frame into a seat at his sewing table where he skillfully stitched together retention deals for Andre Iguodala, David West, Shaun Livingston, and Zaza Pachulia and cagily added rotation pieces Nick Young and Omri Casspi (who in true Warriors fashion was welcomed by texts from Kerr and Durant). And there, marching as always to his own drummer, was Klay Thompson on an international promotional tour, blowing dunk shots, air-balling threes, arm wrestling a teenager, drunkenly dancing onstage and shouting "We the champions, *mothafukkah*," and just in general yukking it up in a kind of Klay Over China tour.

There are two leagues right now—the Warriors and Everybody Else.

As I look back on a year of being around West, what comes across clearest is the fact that he is a man of both endless self-examination and endless action. Is that a dichotomy? Or does one result from the other? With West it's hard to tell. When he stops to think about his life, which is often, he can't believe how far he's traveled. Yet that realization is accompanied by the absolute necessity of proving himself again and again, staying relevant, outlasting the pack.

"We all have a shelf life, and maybe I've had a little more than most," West told me during one interview. "But you have to have the desire to stay on top, to win, and I think I had *that* more than most, too. I have thoughts about when is the time for me to stop working. Sometimes I think it should be now. But then I think, *No, not now.* I like action. I like to stir it up. I'm not afraid to make decisions. Do the legwork and trust your instincts. And I am *highly* opinionated about players. That will never go away. That is the competitive part of me."

Put in Guber's terms, West has a lot of *aliveness*.

"I've been fortunate to have worked for great organizations, and I hope in some way I've helped turn them that way. But even when I was with the Lakers, I used to look at other teams and think, *Why aren't they better? What could they be doing differently?*"

(It was one of the joys, and frustrations, of interviewing West. You could be asking him for his opinion on, say, Curry or Durant, and, before he circles back, he's liable to give you a ten-minute deconstruction on the roster of the Sacramento Kings.)

"My perspective on life has changed over the years because, at this point, I truly realize how lucky I've been," West continued. "I've had a guiding star that has led me through a minefield. You know, self-worth, self-esteem, is a big thing in people's lives, and growing up I had none. *Zero.* So, I think, *How did I ever, ever, get to the point where so many people respect me?*"

And what's your answer?

"Well, maybe it's because I was fortunate to have this intestinal fortitude to keep going. *No* meant *yes* to me. I was very, very stubborn. And basketball gave me something I loved. I was a loner. I could've fished or hunted alone, but there was basketball. Always basketball. And so you find that and you find some success in it, and what does that do for a loner? It makes you feel *protected.* Every kid needs that. What would I have done without this game? I just don't know." (And the game could ask: What would we have done without West?)

When he and Jon Coleman were collaborating on *West by West,* they became immersed in a book by Joseph Campbell called *The Hero with a Thousand Faces,* a work of comparative mythology first released in 1949 that has influenced, among others, Bob Dylan, the Grateful Dead, and George Lucas. Coleman says that he and West tossed it around for three nights, West fascinated by Campbell's exploration of hero myths in different cultures. One of Campbell's theories is that myths that tend to endure share a basic formula:

> A hero ventures forth from the world of common day into a region of supernatural wonder: fabulous forces are there encountered and a decisive victory is won: the hero comes back from this mysterious adventure with the power to bestow boons [blessings] on his fellow man.

West goes out of his way to insist that he's not a hero, but as his life has unfolded, he does tend to see it in mythopoeic terms. A boy, innocent and lonely, picks up a round ball, twirls it, shoots it, finds magic. He sets off on a journey, achieves excellence, glory even, bestowing boons on his legions of fans. But he is also tortured by endless trials. His quest continues because redemption is never realized. Redemption is for others, not for Jerry West.

So perhaps, as he enters the eightieth year of his life, West is precisely where he should be, back in L.A., where his pro journey started and his GM career flourished. We see West as he gazes at that imperfect Clippers tableau, frowning at all the question-mark pieces, a Montrezl Harrell here, a Miloš Teodosić there, an injury-prone Griffin all around, nothing quite in sync, but secretly happy because there is a puzzle that needs study and assembly, thriving on conflict from without and especially within, finding something resembling a curious peace in his eternal dissatisfaction.

ACKNOWLEDGMENTS

In 2010 Jerry West and Jonathan Coleman collaborated on an autobiography, *West by West: My Charmed, Tormented Life*. I didn't want to rewrite that book and *couldn't* have rewritten it anyway since it was such an honest deconstruction of West's life, particularly his boyhood. Any material I used from the book is attributed, gleaned from interviews with West himself or checked with Coleman. I'd also like to thank Jon for his time and assistance; we became faithful correspondents during my fact-gathering and writing process.

I don't like footnotes—dealt with too many of them during my English-lit days—so material drawn from other books is also attributed within *Golden Days*. Besides *West by West*, here is a list of books that were important for my research: *Jerry West* and *The Show*, by Roland Lazenby; *Wilt, 1962*, by Gary M. Pomerantz; *Wilt: Just Like Any Other 7-Foot Black Millionaire Who Lives Next Door*, by Wilt Chamberlain and David Shaw; *Wilt: Larger Than Life*, by Robert Allen Cherry; *Elgin Baylor: The Man Who Changed Basketball*, by Bijan Bayne; *The Rivalry: Bill Russell, Wilt Chamberlain, and the Golden Age of Basketball*, by John Taylor;

Tall Tales and *Loose Balls,* by Terry Pluto; *The Pivotal Season,* by Charley Rosen; and *The Last Innocents,* by Michael Leahy.

I also consulted: *Golden,* by Marcus Thompson II; *The Book of Basketball* by Bill Simmons; *Giant Steps,* by Kareem Abdul-Jabbar and Peter Knobler; *Pistol: The Life of Pete Maravich,* by Mark Kriegel; and *The Art of a Beautiful Game,* by Chris Ballard. Speaking of Ballard, I kind of dreaded when he or fellow *Sports Illustrated* writer Lee Jenkins did stories about the Warriors because I knew they would be so damn good and original. But I always learned something from them, and I was glad when they showed up and we could hang out.

My research began at the LA84 Foundation Sports Library in Los Angeles. Many thanks to Michael Salmon for opening those doors. It was fun for an old newspaperman to get lost in old newspapers.

First, to cover the modern-day Warriors part of these acknowledgments . . .

Thanks to the various Bay Area–based journalists with whom I shared the season, especially old friends Scott Ostler and Bruce Jenkins of the *San Francisco Chronicle* and Ray Ratto, who's been various places but is now with NBC Sports Bay Area. Ray and former Warrior/current radio personality Tom Tolbert steered me to the best beer in Alameda. Tim Kawakami, then of the *San Jose Mercury News* and now with *The Athletic,* is quoted several times in the book because of his extensive knowledge of Bay Area sports. Thanks also to Connor Letourneau and Ann Killion of the *San Francisco Chronicle,* Anthony Slater of the *San Jose Mercury News* (also departed for *The Athletic*), Tim Bontemps of the *Washington Post,* Scott Cacciola of the *New York Times,* Monte Poole from NBC Sports Bay Area, and Erik Malinowski from *Bleacher Report.* Erik's *Beta Ball,* a book about the Warriors, came out too late for me to delve into it.

I also had some great conversations with Ethan Sherwood Strauss, late of ESPN.com.

Speaking of the former World Wide Leader, I miss Marc Stein! Ran into him several times during the season, and it was always worthwhile. I trust we'll be hearing from him before this comes out. Meanwhile, I'll be reading Zach Lowe.

Obvious debt of gratitude to the entire Golden State Warriors organization, in particular Raymond Ridder, the peerless PR pro, and his worthy staff, which includes Dan Martinez (who has since gone to the Atlanta Hawks), Brett Winkler, and Matt de Nesnera. Among the players, a particular shout-out to Steph Curry for sharing his time and perspective, and his father, Dell, for doing the same. Also, special thanks to Warriors players Kevin Durant, Shaun Livingston, and David West.

There were many times that Steve Kerr just wanted to go home and lie down after practice, but he spent time talking to me, as he did with others. Sometimes Steve and I even got off politics and talked about hoops. On my trips to the Bay Area I never failed to connect with assistant coach Ron Adams, who always had something interesting to say (not necessarily about basketball), and I also thank Mike Brown, whom I had interviewed before when he was with a different team, the one that plays in Cleveland.

I did long interviews with co-owners Joe Lacob and Peter Guber, and promise to the latter that I pilfered nothing from his exquisite home office. Thanks to GM Bob Myers for his time and for fact-checking. Rick Welts was generous with his time and insight; we go back to what we like to think of as the Pioneer Days of the NBA, which are the early eighties. Larry Riley, still listed as the Warriors director of player personnel, isn't as active with the team as he once was, but he'll always be remembered as the one who drafted Curry; in Phoenix one morning he shared his memories of Draft Day 2009. I thank Steve Nash for a great talk in Manhattan Beach; it's still hard thinking of him as a Warrior because we go back to the *Seven Seconds or Less* days with the Suns. Dan German, a minority owner of the Warriors and transplanted East Coaster, was a helpful sounding board.

Interviews with the following members of the Warriors organization were extremely helpful: Kirk Lacob, Travis Schlenk (now the GM in Atlanta), Jonnie West (for obvious reasons), Nick U'Ren, Ken Lauer, Eric Housen, and stat whiz Sammy Gelfand.

As for Warriors legends, Tom Meschery (from a restaurant in Sacramento), Rick Barry (from an Italian deli in St. Petersburg), and Chris Mullin (from his coaching office at St. John's) were enormously helpful. My meeting with Tom inspired a Where Are They Now? story in *SI,* and lines from his poetry appear in this book. A special shout-out to Jim Barnett, a former Warrior and current broadcaster who is still going strong.

Interviews and follow-ups with Jeff Austin, Curry's agent, were a great help, as were the restorative jogs past his home in Manhattan Beach. Okay, restorative walks.

As for ex-Warriors, thanks to Luke Walton for a great interview from his current home in Laker Land, and to David Lee from his current home in Spurs Land.

Four interviews with coaching legends, two of whom are still on the bench, were extremely important. They are: Miami Heat president Pat Riley, Phil Jackson, San Antonio's Gregg Popovich, and Houston's Mike D'Antoni. Their insight over the years has never failed to help me understand this game. Speaking with David Stern has always been a delightful challenge ("I'll try to make this simple, McCallum, because I doubt you can grasp it"), and, on the day that I interviewed him in his New York office, he seemed as busy as ever. One of Stern's best hires, Ed Desser, once the league's director of programming, gave me the benefit of his impeccable memory. Thanks also to Stern's successor, Adam Silver, for his thoughts on Jerry West and the league.

Hubie Brown, predictably, was indispensable. Who besides Hubie remembers everything about the early seventies and can still speak knowledgeably about the game as it's played in 2017?

I spoke a long time with Steve Lavin, whose father, Cap Lavin, was such an important part of the Bay Area basketball story. I couldn't use much of that info in the book, but I have a lot of it in a Lavin interview on my website, jackmccallum.net.

As for the Lakers part of this story, the first person I went to (besides Jerry West) was the incomparable Bill Bertka. One of the joys of being on the beat over the years was running into Bill. Next on the list was Elgin Baylor. I'm not sure he wanted to talk about a subject that is not entirely pleasant for him, but he was, as usual,

Elegant Elgin. He should be better remembered, but I've been saying that for decades.

I thank Ryan West, who knows a lot about the Lakers, a lot about basketball, and a lot about Jerry. So does his mother, Karen, whom I also thank for her hospitality. So does Kim West, Jerry's nephew and lawyer. So does Mitch Kupchak, the Lakers' former general manager who helped me with an interview. Current team president Jeanie Buss also offered a window into the past and the present, as did Jerry Colangelo, an NBA fixture for six decades.

Thanks to two other ex-Lakers: Kareem Abdul-Jabbar for sharing his thoughts on a long-ago streak-busting game in Milwaukee, and Mychal Thompson for sharing his memories of West and for a couple of perceptive comments about a certain current Warriors player named Thompson.

I always enjoyed speaking with Geoff Petrie when he was an executive in the league, and his memory is as sharp as ever. Also, he didn't have to prepare lunch but he did. And Bill Walton didn't have to build a fire in his San Diego home to talk to me, but he did. As with Hubie, Bill remembers all.

Arn Tellem, a close friend of Jerry West's and an astute observer of all things NBA, was also very helpful.

Besides West and Riley, the other surviving members of the streak Lakers are Jim Cleamons, Keith Erickson, and Gail Goodrich. I got valuable material from interviews with all of them; Cleamons, always the coach, even moved around a couple of saltshakers to explain how the Lakers set screens.

A special shout-out to Lynn Shackelford, who was Chick Hearn's broadcasting partner during the 1971–72 season. He remembers everything.

Thanks to one of my former editors at SI and longtime Celtics expert Dick Friedman for editorial guidance. There was no way to get Roy Firestone's impersonations of West and Wilt Chamberlain into the book, but they're rolling around in my head. (Also, he does a great Sinatra.) Shout-outs to Jillian Lashmett for indexing and Jen Reynolds for extensive website work.

This book could've taken a couple of different directions, and my editor at Ballantine, Brendan Vaughan, helped keep it on the correct course. Thanks as always to my agent, Scott Waxman, and my wife, Donna, who now knows more about the 1971–72 Lakers than one woman should.

As for non-humans, a tip of the wallet to BART, Bay Area Regional Transport, which saved me, oh, ten grand or so as I metroed between San Francisco and Oakland.

Finally and most obviously, I took up a great deal of Jerry West's time over the twelve months I was working on the book. He was unfailingly generous and accommodating and, more important, insightful and interesting. I only wish my father were alive so I could've called him and said, "Hey, I watched a Finals game with Jerry West. What have you been up to?"

—Jack McCallum
Stone Harbor, NJ
August 2017

PHOTOGRAPH CREDITS

INSERT 1

West dribbling (Hulton Archive/Getty Images Sports Classic/Getty Images)

West, Baylor, and Coach Schaus (Bettman/Getty Images)

Chamberlain and Russell (Bettman/Getty Images)

West and Robertson posed (Bettman/Getty Images)

West and Robertson (NBA Photo Library/National Basketball Association/Getty Images)

Lakers and owner Jack Kent Cooke (George Long/Sports Illustrated Classic/Getty Images)

Coach Sharman (Bettman/Getty Images)

Hairston and Jackson (Focus On Sport/Getty Images)

Bill Russell (Focus On Sport/Getty Images)

Radio announcer Chick Hearn (Andrew D. Bernstein/National Basketball Association/Getty Images)

West and Stallworth (James Drake/Sports Illustrated Classic/Getty Images)

McMillian and Dandridge (Walter Iooss Jr./Sports Illustrated/Getty Images)

West and McMillian (Heinz Kluetmeier/Sports Illustrated/Getty Images)

Gail Goodrich (Focus On Sport/Getty Images Sport/Getty Images)

Riley and Jackson (Walter Iooss Jr./Sports Illustrated/Getty Images)

Chamberlain on the bench (Walter Iooss Jr./Sports Illustrated Classic/Getty Images)

1971–72 Lakers (NBA Photos/National Basketball Association/Getty Images)

West and Riley coaching (Manny Millan/Sports Illustrated/Getty Images)

Kobe Bryant (Steve Grayson/WireImage/Getty Images)

Buss congratulates West (Garrett Ellwood/National Basketball Association/Getty Images)

INSERT 2

Rick Barry (Walter Iooss Jr./NBA Classic/Getty Images)

Chris Mullin (Andrew D. Bernstein/National Basketball Association/Getty Images)

Curry in college (Kevin C. Cox/Getty Images Sport/Getty Images)

Curry on draft day (Don Smith/National Basketball Association/Getty Images)

Lacob and Guber (Rocky Widner/National Basketball Association/Getty Images)

Curry and Ellis (Rocky Widner/National Basketball Association/Getty Images)

Bob Myers (Jack Arent/National Basketball Association/Getty Images)

Rick Welts (Alex Trautwig/Major League Baseball/Getty Images)

Kerr on the Bulls (Manny Millan/Sports Illustrated/Getty Images)

Westbrook and Durant at OKC (Christian Petersen/Getty Images Sport/Getty Images)

Steph Curry shooting (Joe Murphy/National Basketball Association/Getty Images)

LeBron James (Ezra Shaw/Getty Images Sport/Getty Images)

West and Thompson (Juan Ocampo/National Basketball Association/Getty Images)

Durant and Curry heads together (Gregory Shamus/Getty Images Sport/Getty Images)

West and Green (Noah Graham/National Basketball Association/Getty Images)

Durant and Westbrook on different teams (Ezra Shaw/Getty Images Sport/Getty Images)

Steve Kerr and coaches (Ronald Martinez/Getty Images Sport/Getty Images)

Durant and Curry shake hands (Andrew D. Bernstein/National Basketball Association/Getty Images)

James and Durant hug (Ronald Martinez/Getty Images Sport/Getty Images)

Curry family (Ezra Shaw/Getty Images Sport/Getty Images)

Logo and Durant (Andrew D. Bernstein/National Basketball Association/Getty Images)

INDEX

ABOUT THE AUTHOR

JACK MCCALLUM is the *New York Times* best-selling author of *Dream Team* and *Seven Seconds or Less* and a longtime member of the staff of *Sports Illustrated*. While concentrating mostly on basketball—in 2005 he won the Curt Gowdy Media Award from the Naismith Memorial Basketball Hall of Fame—he has also edited the weekly Scorecard section of the magazine, covered five Olympic Games, and written about virtually every sport, including bowling, bicycle racing, squash, and wrestling. McCallum teaches journalism at Muhlenberg College and lives with his wife in Bethlehem, Pennsylvania.

jackmccallum.net
Twitter: @McCallum12